Bicycling Around New York City

A Gentle Touring Guide

Trudy E. Bell's

Bicycling Around New York City

A Gentle Touring Guide

MENASHA RIDGE PRESS
BIRMINGHAM, ALABAMA

Library of Congress Cataloging-in-Publication Data

Bell, Trudy E.
   Bicycling around New York City: a gentle touring guide/Trudy E. Bell.
      p.   cm.
   Includes index.
   ISBN 0-89732-125-1
   1. Bicycle touring—New York Metropolitan Area—Guidebooks.
   2. New York Metropolitan Area—Guidebooks.   I. Title
   GV1045.5.N72N492   1994
   796.6′4′097472—dc20   94-22356
                                                                        CIP

Map design and type composition
by Carolina Graphics Group, Inc.

Menasha Ridge Press
3169 Cahaba Heights Road
Birmingham, Alabama 35243

To Roxana Katharine Bell,
a wonderful companion on life's road,
in the hope that she will come to
love bicycling and travel even more than her mom

ACKNOWLEDGMENTS

This book could never have existed, much less been so rich, without the contributions of many people. Some I've mentioned in specific rides; others played crucial behind-the-scenes roles.

First, major thanks go to Arlene Plevin, who gave me my first opportunities to write about bicycling when she was editor of the League of American Wheelmen's (now League of American Bicyclists) magazine *Bicycle USA*; she also first give me the telephone number of Dennis Coello, freelance editor for Menasha Ridge Press.

To Dennis I owe a tremendous debt: first, for his faith in signing me up for this book without having read any of my other clips, and then for his encouragement, understanding, and skillful suggestions during the writing. To Menasha Ridge Press publisher Bob Sehlinger, associate publisher Mike Jones, managing editor Leslie Cummins, and especially Frank Logue of Carolina Graphics, I thank for their dedication in executing this book.

Next, I must thank the various friends, colleagues, and even strangers who suggested local places of interest or, in some cases, mapped out basic routes.

To Sandra Coffey, a former student in my "Bicycle Touring: an Introduction" class at the South Orange Maplewood Adult School, and to her husband Jim, many thanks for the excellent route from their bed-and-breakfast inn Coffey House to Montclair, New Jersey.

To Rick Ofstie, a former *IEEE Spectrum* colleague, his wife Kate and their two children, I owe thanks for hospitality during my mapping of several rides in Connecticut. To Rick I am also indebted for the suggestion for an off-season expedition to Greenwich Point Park—and a couple of other wonderful ideas for my next book!

For the special permit to visit Greenwich Point Park during the regular season as well as the leaflet with its bicycle tour of Greenwich that forms the basis of my "Off Season Ride to Old Greenwich," I thank Francis H. Keegan, director of the Department of Parks and Recreation, Greenwich, Connecticut.

To Alan Wolf, long-time cycling companion in Morristown, New Jersey, I am grateful for several excellent suggestions. It was Alan who discovered the wonderful toy store that I incorporated into "From New Jersey to Florida." Alan also helped map an alternate route in "From Dover Plains to Kent." Most notable, he revealed his discovery of the superb homemade ice cream shop Confectionately Yours, inspiring the ice cream detour in "Delaware & Raritan Canal."

To Glenn Zorpette, a fellow editor at *IEEE Spectrum*, his friend Wayne Lovington, and Glenn's girlfriend Jeanne Burke, I am indebted for their designing the entire "Land, Sea, and Air" ride around Stratford, Connecticut. Glenn and Jeanne also devoted an entire day giving me a personal tour of the historical haunts, while Wayne spent an afternoon on his bike verifying the route for "Cruising the Milford Beaches" and adding a few embellishments of his own.

To Alice Pitcher and Kemper Peacock, the proprietors of Old Drovers Inn, I owe thanks for the map on which they drew the basic route "From Dover Plains to Kent."

For hospitality and local tips (including for rides that, alas, did not make it into this book), I am grateful to Sandra and Jim Coffey at Coffey House, Janet Druckenmiller of Druckenmiller's B&B, John and Mitzi Durham at Apple Valley Inn, Glen and Carla Hester on Staten Island, Barbara Lebkuecher of the Custer Institute Observatory, Barbara Notarius at Alexander Hamilton House in Croton-on-Hudson, New York, and Dick Thompkins of Bed & Breakfast Reservations Inc. in Chatham, New Jersey. Moreover, to the many cyclists and other strangers along the way who incidentally suggested places to see, I wish to express my gratitude. Thanks also go to all the people who carefully read the draft chapters and made excellent suggestions and corrections.

For patient companionship during the sometimes frustrating exercise of scouting and verifying routes, I thank Connie Baumann, Mark Edelman, Karen Fitzgerald, Loyd Searle, Eileen Serow, and Alan Wolf. In this category, special thanks go to Jim Arth, a cyclist whom I met while researching the ride on Roosevelt Island. Jim was a cheerful partner on more than a third of the rides in this book—including during one soggy week mapping out some of the Long Island rides—and was a steady supporter during the writing of this book.

For inspiring me to take up cycling again in adulthood and helping me buy my first second-hand bike in 1983, I thank John F. King; John also showed me some of the charms of Holmdel Park, included in "Sandy Hook: A Day at the Beach." For early guidance and companionship in my entry to bicycle touring, I thank Karen Fitzgerald and Richard Shuldiner. For keeping me in touch with the needs of novices, I thank all the students of my bicycle touring classes held through the Learning Annex and the South Orange-Maplewood Adult School as well as the heads of those schools for giving me the opportunity to teach: Wendy Kramer and Don Hamingson.

Above all, I wish to thank my late father, R. Kenneth Bell, and my mother, Arabella J. Bell, for their faith in me—and for their hours of caring for their granddaughter Roxana Katharine on many mornings so I could finish this manuscript.

And to my dearest Roxana, I thank you for help in child-testing certain rides ("Rahway River Ramble," "Of Convents and Bike Paths," and "Exploring the Great Swamp"), and for being such a great traveling companion through life.

To you, dear reader, thanks for buying this book. I hope you will enjoy reading and following it as much as I did researching and writing it. If you have any corrections or suggestions for a future edition, please send them directly to me: Trudy E. Bell, 18 Cherry Place, Maplewood, NJ 07040; fax: (201) 378-3602.

Trudy E. Bell

TABLE OF CONTENTS

Index Map

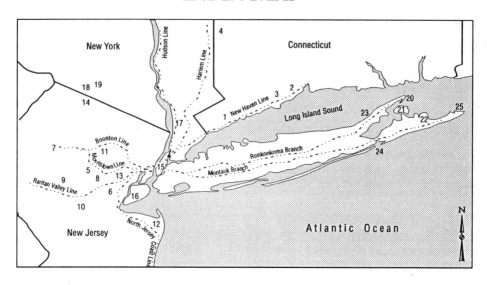

The railroad lines shown are the Long Island Rail Road (out to the tips of Long Island); Metro-North Commuter Railroad (to Connecticut and upstate New York); and the New Jersey Transit trains (to New Jersey).

INTRODUCTION

Bicycle touring in and around New York City? On your own or with the whole family?

You bet! Less than an hour from the clamorous steel-and-glass canyons of Manhattan, you can be riding along surprisingly rural country lanes, smelling the sweet fragrance of corn fields and listening to the varied calls of a mockingbird. There you will find woodchucks, deer, frogs, raccoons, opossums, sheep, Canada geese—in short, far more than the limited city wildlife of squirrels, roaches, and pigeons (Woody Allen's "flying rats").

Timing your ride for the right season can increase your enjoyment both on and off the bike.

- In late April or early May, enjoy the blossoming cherry and apple trees in Stratford, Connecticut, while you tour the birthplace of the helicopter (see "Land, Sea and Air").
- In mid-May to early June, plan a weekend to Montclair, New Jersey, to admire the colors in a world-renowned garden of 6000 varieties of irises and visit the laboratory and home of inventor Thomas Edison (see "Food for the Mind and Body Ride").
- In mid-June, pick fresh strawberries and taste world-renowned merlot as part of your outing to Mattituck, Long Island (see "Wine Country Wanderer").
- In July, rent a boogie board and splash into the bathwater-warm Atlantic on the popular Jersey Shore (see "Sandy Hook: A Day at the Beach").
- In the second week of August, head to Connecticut for the annual oyster festival (see "Cruising the Milford Beaches"). Or plan an overnight trip on any of the rides with a campground option, and lie out under the stars away from trees and lights to watch the spectacular annual Perseid meteor shower. After midnight on a moonless night, you may see 50 to 60 shooting stars per hour streak across the summer constellations (try this on the "Netcong Getaway," "Cedar Point Park Pilgrimage," or "From New Jersey to Florida").
- In September, slip away for a long weekend at a romantic bed-and-breakfast inn at the end of Long Island; with most of the summer beach people gone but the Atlantic still as warm as bathwater, the cycling is blessedly free from traffic (see "Shelter Island Vacation").
- In October, head to upstate New York to pick your own apples or drink fresh-pressed cider, gasp at the brilliant golds and vermilions of the autumn maples, and ride through the oldest covered bridge still standing in Connecticut (see "Of Apples and Animals" and "Dover Plains to Kent").

In the New York City area, the weather for riding is best from early April through late October. But don't put your bike into storage after the last leaf falls. Instead, be ready to take advantage of those isolated 60-degree days that somehow find their way into December or January: take the "Off-Season Ride to Old Greenwich" to tour a Connecticut park unavailable to Greenwich non-residents the rest of the year.

This book assumes you have no knowledge of bicycling beyond the physical ability to balance and ride. Its purpose is to introduce you to the world of cycling beyond the limits of New York City's comparatively small parks, and give you practical and tested directions to take full advantage of a bike in the tri-state area.

All the rides in this book are completely original; they are not based on preexisting routes of bicycle clubs or other sources. Each one I personally designed and cycled to ensure that it would indeed be satisfactory for a book subtitled *A Gentle Touring Guide*. To be sure, some of the areas (such as the Great Swamp Wildlife Refuge, the Delaware & Raritan Canal, and the end of Long Island) are long-time favorites with cyclists—for lovely reasons that will be evident when you get there. But others have been virtually undiscovered although they are ideal for cycling, and appear in print here for the first time (including the "Rahway River Ramble," "Dover Plains to Kent," and the "Old Croton Aqueduct Trail").

Where noted, some of these rides—even some of the overnighters—can be enjoyed by children as well as adults. Bicycle touring is one of the best ways for the whole family to enjoy an outing. Kids are natural adventurers. Even at 18 months, my own daughter Roxana loved the breeze in her face, and my ability to stop at any time to watch pairs of butterflies fluttering a dance in the air, or to gaze at convoluted orange fungi, or to be surprised by a woodchuck waddling out of the underbrush with its young in its mouth. When kept bribed by graham crackers and songs, she was good for an hour and a half in the bike seat before needing a break to run around (and giving me a break to rest!). A few of the rides are even suitable for children riding their own bikes (for example, "Of Convents and Bike Paths" and the shortest version of the "Old Croton Aqueduct Trail").

This book is also intended to grow with your abilities—or to be shared with a more experienced partner. Many of the basic rides offer longer options that you can take as you get stronger and more adventurous, or that a stronger rider can take while others enjoy some local sights.

Throughout, this book is permeated not only with my love of cycling, but also my basic and deeply held philosophy: if you want to get someplace fast, take the car. To me, the main purpose of bicycle touring is to enjoy the journey itself, and only incidentally to reach its end. And that is the essence of a vacation: truly living and savoring each moment instead of being fixed on a goal. So on these rides, you will have plenty of chances to pick wild blackberries, browse in a local craft shop, explore a lighthouse or astronomical observatory, hike along a nature trail, cast a fishing line into the surf, or nuzzle with your love.

Bicycle touring is really very simple: all you need to do is get out on the road and enjoy!

Distances: you will surprise yourself
This book features basic rides from 8 to 45 miles, with all kinds of options to

make the distances shorter, longer, or in between. As an aid to novices, the rides within each state are listed in order from the most gentle to the most challenging, taking into account terrain and traffic as well as distance. For stronger riders, where possible I've suggested ways of linking two or more rides, either to create a very long one-day ride or a weekend's minivacation.

Don't be scared off mileages of 10, 20, 30 miles or more. Many people, who may still think of a bicycle as a kid's toy, have no idea how efficient a machine it is, and how much ground it lets just plain folks cover.

Given a whole day, most teenagers or adults in half-way decent condition can ride 20 or 25 miles on relatively flat terrain and feel only pleasantly exercised. Even a person really out of shape can usually manage 5 to 10 miles without much travail. People who love to ride every chance they can will often surprise themselves by the end of a summer by regularly enjoying rides of 30 to 50 miles. Small children naturally take to bikes because of the independence and thrill. And cycling is such a healthful, aerobic, low-impact sport that it can be enjoyed well into one's 70s.

Topography of the rides

Most of the rides in this book are flat to gently rolling, in areas with light to moderate traffic and plenty of greenery. That triple combination of flat, little traffic, and scenery is no mean feat to come by in the tri-state area, whose flat areas tend to be congested and whose beautiful areas tend to be hilly. In fact, because some of Western New Jersey and northern Westchester County is so idyllic and pastoral, I have included several rides in those areas despite a few challenging climbs. But never fear: any challenge is so noted in the introduction to each ride, so you won't be caught unawares.

But don't make the mistake of passing up the best rural charms because of a hill. Even if you don't like your lowest gear, simply get off and walk the bike, enjoying the change of pace of a hike and searching for berries or other natural wonders.

Secret to long rides: low gears make it easy

The key to lasting for a long or rolling ride is conserving your energy: make pedaling as *little* work as possible.

Most novices simply work too hard, pushing hard on the pedals so their feet turn slowly. Instead, take advantage of your bicycle's marvelous lower gears. If you have a 10-speed, adjust the bicycle's left gear lever so the chain is on the smaller of the two front chainwheels. Then keep it there. Don't use the bigger chainwheel except maybe on the fastest of downhills. (If you have a 15-speed or higher, with three chainwheels—a configuration known in bicycling jargon as a triple crank—put the chain on the middle chainwheel.)

Then use the right gear lever to adjust the chain on the rear cogs so that for most terrain, your feet are always circling at least once a second—even up inclines, as much as possible. In cycling jargon, you want to maintain a high cadence—at least 60 to 80 revolutions per minute.

Yes, it will feel as though you're hardly working: that's precisely the idea. At high cadence, bicycling is exercising your heart and lungs, not straining your knees and thigh muscles. High cadence takes advantage of the fact that your heart can recover from aerobic demands in a few minutes, while your thigh muscles take 48 hours to recover from anaerobic strain. High cadence is the secret to enjoying a long ride, not dying on hills, and smiling—and having the power to ride—when you see the bicycle the next day.

If you are lucky enough indeed to have a 15- or 18-speed bicycle with a triple crank (three front chainwheels), you're set for nearly painless climbing of even considerable hills. Right when you start heading up a real hill, adjust the left gear lever to drop the chain onto the smallest of the chainwheels. Officially called an alpine gear, this powerful little cog is more widely known as a "granny gear," presumably because with its leverage even your granny could climb hills. Your feet will spin and you will travel only as fast as you can walk—but you will ride up that hill with greater ease than you could push the bike on foot. You'll also get a wonderful aerobic workout; pace yourself so you're breathing moderately, and you'll last until the crest. And toast with your water bottle to your triumph at the top.

Relax for group happiness
Here are a few hints to help cyclists of differing abilities to enjoy each other's company on the road.

Never, *never* make the difference in strengths an issue of competition in self-worth. That is the quickest way to create unhappiness and lose friends. Let weaker pedalers set the pace from the front, with stronger and more experienced ones keeping an eye on them from the rear, riding what's known as "sweep." The slower pace will conserve the energy and maximize the endurance—and enjoyment—of the weaker riders, and will encourage the normally faster riders to relax and take in the scenery.

At lunch breaks, the stronger riders can go off for a fast-paced solo circuit. Or they can ride later in the day after the main ride is over or at dawn before the ride begins (see "A Pre-Breakfast Warm-up"). Or, if a ride in this book shows a longer and a shorter option, the group can split accordingly and later meet by prearrangement to finish the ride together. A very antsy strong rider can double his or her mileage by repeatedly riding a bit ahead and then back to his or her companion(s). But in so doing, don't lose sight of the whole point: just being together and enjoying a day of exercise out in the sun and fresh air.

A note for families: For infants and toddlers, there are a number of sturdy seats that can be bolted to the back of a bike, complete with safety belts passing over a child's shoulders and feet. There are also trailers in which one or two kids can be towed behind a parent's bike. For seats and trailers with the best construction and safety, stick with ones sold by reputable bike shops or mail-order bicycle-supply catalogues—not ones you may see at toy shops or discount stores.

For somewhat older children—or for a couple of widely differing physical strengths—consider a tandem (a bicycle built for two), with the less experienced rider as the "stoker" in back. For tandems, there are setups for adjusting the height of the pedals in back so even a kindergartner can pedal—or coast—behind a larger "captain" at the front set of handle bars. Children on their own bikes should ride between their parents, or at least in front of an adult. But don't underestimate the strength and endurance of 12- and 14-year-olds, who can outlast many adults.

Geography of the rides

Some of these rides start from within the five boroughs of New York City. Thus, if you feel like doing a day ride close to home, you're only a short bike ride or subway ride away from some of the starting places (see "Manhattan's Other Island" and "Clay Pit Ponds Meander").

Many of the rides, though, fall into the greater tri-state area, encompassing upstate New York (which some self-centered city-dwellers define as north of 96th Street in Manhattan), Long Island, Connecticut, and New Jersey. In these cases, all the rides fall within three hours' traveling distance from the city: from as far south as Princeton, New Jersey, as far west as Netcong, New Jersey (half an hour this side of the Pennsylvania border), as far north as Dover Plains, New York (near the Connecticut-Massachusetts border), and as far east as the tips of Long Island.

Roughly, those destinations mark the ends of the various commuter rail lines. Three-quarters of the rides are designed to be reached by public transportation, with specific instructions given in the introductory section to each ride. Driving instructions are also given.

Getting out of the city

Since few New Yorkers own cars, and some don't even know how to drive, a fair number of city-dwelling cyclists must rely on public transportation.

Not to worry. Amtrak, the Long Island and Metro-North commuter railroads, New Jersey Transit trains, the PATH (Port Authority Trans-Hudson tube lines between Manhattan and New Jersey), the Staten Island ferry, and some private bus lines will take bicycles during specified off-peak hours under certain conditions.

The Long Island Rail Road, the Metro-North Commuter Railroad, one New Jersey Transit train, and the PATH require *bike passes*. The passes are no big deal to get, but are necessary because the conductors really do ask for them. The quickest way to obtain them is in person (although if you apply in the winter, you may as well do it by phone and mail). As requirements (schedules, the times bikes are not allowed, how the bike must be packaged, additional fare, and other factors) can change, the safest course is to call the line in question before you commit to your travel plans.

Here's the scoop for carrying bikes on public transportation from New York City. Please note that these policies do change over time, as do the telephone numbers. My suggestion would be to call before each trip—or at least call each spring—for updated information.

Subway Bicycles come under rules prohibiting items that interfere with passenger movement or pose a hazard to passengers or transit operations—especially during the commuter rush hour. This policy has been erratically enforced over the years, and (according to an MTA official) is up to the discretion of the transit officer on duty at the time. On lightly traveled weekends, some subway personnel and ticket booth people are even kind enough to open the exit gates for you to enter (after paying your fare) so you don't have to hoist your steed over the turnstiles. Put your bike on the very first or very last car of the train to avoid blocking traffic, and don't use more than one seat. The policy has changed several times, so for an update call the New York City Metropolitan Transit Authority during business hours at (718) 979-0600.

PATH (Port Authority Trans-Hudson) line to Newark, Hoboken, or Jersey City, New Jersey A permit is required; it is free, and good for life. Two bikes are allowed per car. Bikes are not allowed during specific weekday morning and evening commuter rush hours. For an application, you have to call one of those annoying voice mail lines activated by the buttons of a Touch Tone telephone. Dial 1-800-234-PATH, press 1 for information, press 8 for literature, press 2 to order literature, and then record your name and address and ask to be sent the bicycle permit application.

Metro-North Commuter Railroad to upstate New York and Connecticut A permit is required; it costs $5 and is good for life. Bikes are not allowed during certain critical hours and on holiday eves. That can make it a trick planning for a holiday weekend if you can't leave work early, so familiarize yourself with the railroad's rules. Also, only four cyclists are allowed per train, two in the very first car and two in the very last. Some conductors are strict, while others are lenient. Wear a big smile and throw yourself at their mercy. Groups of more than four cyclists traveling together must make advance arrangements with Metro-North.

Also, try to avoid a route that calls for switching trains. Once another cyclist and I were headed up to northern Westchester County, which called for changing trains at Croton Harmon. Since the first train was full, and the second train was a small diesel instead of a large electric, sorry Charlie. We had to change our itinerary and pedal along more southern Westchester County roads.

For an application, go to Grand Central Terminal's ticket window #27 between 6 A.M. and 11 P.M. (ring the bell for service), and you can be issued a pass while you wait. Or you can apply by mail by writing to Metro-North Commuter Railroad, Station Service Department, 347 Madison Avenue, 3rd floor, New York, NY 10017, or call (212) 340-2176.

Long Island Rail Road to all points out on Long Island A Cyc-n-Ride permit is required; it costs $5 and is good for life. There are weekend and holiday restrictions, so read the permit carefully. Applications can be picked up at any LIRR station or the LIRR ticket office in New York Penn Station at 34th Street and Seventh Avenue in Manhattan and mailed in. Or write Cyc-n-Ride, LIRR, Jamaica Station, Jamaica, NY 11435, or call LIRR public affairs at (718) 990-8228 or (718) 217-5477.

There are weekend and holiday restrictions, so read the permit carefully. And once again, be watchful when changing LIRR trains at Jamaica, which you must do for many journeys from Penn Station in Manhattan. Once another cyclist and I, headed out to Fire Island, misunderstood which car we were to board. We didn't move quickly enough and were left hanging around the platform with our bikes for two hours until the next train. Not fun.

Amtrak This I have included for completeness, although no ride in this book requires using an Amtrak train. No permit is required, but bikes are allowed only on trains that have baggage cars. These trains run only about once a day on any given line, generally after midnight. Therefore, Amtrak is viable only if you're planning a weekend trip, not a day ride. The advantage, though, is that Amtrak goes farther north than Metro-North (up to Boston and Montreal) and farther south than New Jersey Transit (down to Washington, D.C. and beyond), should you wish to explore farther afield than this book takes you.

The procedure is that you take your bike to Penn Station in either New York City or Newark, New Jersey, buy your ticket, take it to the baggage room where you pay $5 and get a box. Then you take off the handlebars and the pedals, put everything in the box, and wait at the other end for your wheels to show up. You can send your boxed bike on ahead, and it will be held in the baggage room at your destination for up to 48 hours.

For details, call (212) 582-6875. To make sure that the baggage room has a box waiting for you, call ahead to the train station baggage room. The number for the baggage room at New York Penn Station is (212) 630-7635; for the baggage room at Newark Penn Station, call (201) 596-2326.

New Jersey Transit Bicycles are not permitted on NJT buses. They are, however, allowed on NJT trains under certain conditions.

On all NJT rail lines, collapsible bicycles may be carried. No permit is required. Taking the front wheel off a standard bike is *not* considered collapsing the thing; it must have a frame that disassembles or folds such as the Bike Friday by Green Gear Cycling. It also includes the Montague BiFrame, the wonderful full-sized mountain bike that folds in half at the seat tube. I have a Montague (I love its lively handling), and have successfully tested this regulation. (Since a standard bicycle with both wheels, the seat, and the handlebar removed and stored in a flexible bike bag is about the same size as the folded Montague, such a compact package may fit the requirements; it may be worth checking. *Note:* the package would still weigh about 30 pounds.)

In August 1992, the NJT started an open-ended experiment of carrying standard bicycles from New York Penn Station on the New Jersey Coast line to Bay Head and on the Raritan Valley line to High Bridge. Two standard bicycles are allowed per train, where they will be stowed in the car where wheelchairs are normally put. (If a wheelchair user is riding the same train, however, by law that person is given priority over a cyclist.) You must also carry two bungee cords at least 24 inches long for securing the bike.

During this experimental period, you may obtain a schedule and permit application by calling NJT's Office of Customer Services at (201) 491-9400 Monday through Friday, 8 A.M.-6 P.M. (from New Jersey, call toll free 1-800-772-3606). After NJT has assessed ridership, safety, and other issues to its satisfaction, the hope is to open the other lines to standard bicycles as well as to charge $5 for a lifelong pass.

Staten Island ferry Bicycles are allowed on the lower deck with the cars for the same fare as pedestrians. Arrive a few minutes early, for you must get a ticket. For information, call (718) 390-5253.

Staten Island Rapid Transit Operating Authority (SIRTOA) train that runs from the ferry to the southern, wooded part of the island does not allow you to simply walk on with your bike. However, bicycles are allowed for prearranged group events. Even half a dozen friends with an itinerary qualify as a group, I was told. Call (718) 876-8304 at least a week ahead of your trip with the information about your starting time and group size. Ask to speak with a Deputy Superintendant, who will inform the ticket agent on duty of your plans. When you reach the SIRTOA station at the ferry terminal on Staten Island, show some identification to be admitted onto the train for the normal fare. For a SIRTOA schedule, call (718) 447-8601.

Private bus lines There are scores of private bus lines radiating outward from the Port Authority Bus Terminal in Manhattan. Call the specific line to find out its policy on bikes. While some forbid bicycles, others with luggage compartments will take a bike for a nominal surcharge. There's no uniform policy.

Bicycle There's one other way to get out of Manhattan that should not be overlooked—and that's by the bicycle itself. The Brooklyn Bridge between Manhattan and Brooklyn has a special lane in the middle (much of it on wood planking) rising above the traffic that is exclusively for pedestrians and cyclists. The George Washington Bridge between West 178th Street in Manhattan and Fort Lee, New Jersey has a sidewalk on which bicycles may be walked across. And good old Broadway, if followed north, will literally take you all the way to Albany. (Since this last route takes you through Spanish Harlem, I do not recommend it to lone females, although I rode it solo once with no incident.) Those are the most popular with cyclists, although others exist.

What to wear

Many cyclists in New York City strike some people as piebald clowns, with their skin-tight black Lycra shorts and multicolored jerseys. You don't have to dress up like a court jester in order to ride a bike, if you're more the low-key type, but the specialized clothing does have practicality that is worth duplicating in mufti.

Cycling shorts have *padding*. There are two pelvic bones called the ischial tuberosity (try that in a cocktail party) that rest on the bicycle saddle. Even if you are careful to rise off the seat when you ride over bumps, after 15 or 20 miles, these "sit bones" could be feeling a bit bruised. This problem is especially acute for the wider pelvic structure of women, especially if they are riding a bike with a man's narrow saddle. It's nothing serious, but why suffer?

If you don't feel like wearing Lycra, you could get some touring cycling shorts, which are made of a fabric similar to khaki. But be forewarned: get ones where the padded insert is either genuine chamois or an artificial equivalent such as Ultrasuede. An insert of polypropylene—found in most so-called touring shorts—may keep you dry but is pretty useless as padding.

Alternatively, some of the bike shops and mail-order bicycle merchandise companies sell padded cycling underwear, which solves the problem for any outfit. Just make sure whatever shorts you wear come down nearly to the top of your knee—not for modesty, but to prevent chafing from your inner thighs rubbing up and down against the seat for hours.

For extra padding, get your bike a seat cover, either of the gel type (such as those by Spenco or Vetta) or of fleecy wool. Either works fine. I both wear padded shorts and have a Spenco gel seat cover; with the two I have ridden a century (100 miles in a day) without any saddle-soreness whatsoever.

A *light-colored shirt* reflects sunlight and keeps you cool in the summer; bright colors increase your visibility on the road. Yellow is the best of both worlds.

Cycling jerseys are made of polypropylene, which wicks moisture away from your body. If you can take wool next to your skin, light wool is also excellent. Cycling jerseys also have their pockets in the back instead of the front or side, so your thighs don't keep hitting your keys or wallet with every pedal stroke.

A cotton T-shirt is not a good choice. Cotton becomes abrasive when wet, rubbing the skin raw at friction points; it also becomes clammy with sweat, and can chill you on a cool day when you stop. If you insist on wearing cotton, minimize both effects by changing your shirt as soon as you stop for lunch and again when you board the train to return home. If your T-shirt has no pocket, a runner's fanny pack worn to the rear is an excellent substitute.

Some cyclists swear by hard-soled cycling shoes, saying they deliver full power to each pedal stroke. Personally, I dislike cycling shoes because they make my feet feel as if they've stood on a hard floor all day. Besides, we're touring, not racing, so who cares about the last percent of efficiency? Comfortable, stiff-soled *walking shoes* are just fine, and will leave you prepared for a spontaneous hike along a nearby trail. Sneakers may be adequate, although if they're worn you may find the feel of the pedal uncomfortable on the ball of your foot. Avoid sandals: they won't give you the support you need and they are very uncomfortable if your pedals have toe clips; also, I once read about one cyclist who ripped off her toenail when riding in sandals. Try whatever you have—you can always change your choice next ride.

Bring a *nylon or GoreTex windbreaker* on every ride, even if the day is scorching hot. A day that feels hot in Manhattan is going to be noticeably cooler outside the city, particularly on Long Island next to the ocean, or in the mornings or evenings in the spring or fall. It will also keep you from a chill in the night air if you've lingered later outdoors than you expect, or if the air conditioning in a restaurant or on the train home is blowing full blast.

A nylon windbreaker stuffs up small and can be crammed into a pocket, tied around a seatpost, or wedged into a tool kit—and you'll use it so often you might even consider keeping it with the bike. Untreated nylon is not waterproof—but coated nylon is worse, as it won't breathe at all and will drench you with your own sweat even when you're sitting still. GoreTex is slightly heavier than nylon, but it will keep you relatively dry if you should get caught in a light rain.

As with your shirt, opt for light or bright colors—again, yellow is ideal. The windbreakers intended for cyclists often are longer in the back to cover your lower back when you're bent forward, and may be trimmed with reflective tape.

What to bring

In bicycling, your body is the engine as well as the passenger. So you must keep it well hydrated and nourished. For these reasons, the introduction to each ride describes what you are likely to find (or not find) in the way of food and drink along the way.

Rule number one: *Always carry water*, and drink before you feel thirsty. Try to drink at least half a bottle per hour, even on cool days; double or triple that when it's hot and you're dripping sweat. Don't wait until you're thirsty; thirst is an early sign that you're already partially dehydrated.

A standard bicycling water bottle holds a pint; the large ones hold a fifth (really!), or 26 ounces. My main touring bike is fitted with two cages, and can carry one of each size. On long trips through areas with few services, or on very hot days, I've been known to carry a third bottle. Both bottles and cages come in a wonderful rainbow of standard and neon colors, to suit the most demure or outrageous spirit. For function, sniff the bottle to make sure it is completely odor-free; a new bottle that smells like plastic will *always* smell like plastic and will make the water taste like plastic, too. Color makes no difference, except avoid black: it will absorb the sun's rays and heat the water more than light colors.

Rule number two: *Always carry a snack, no matter how short the ride.* More than once, when I've completely run out of food, I have wondered if I could possibly make it to the next McDonald's, and whether my handlebar bag was edible. Even if you ate just an hour before, your body has a strange tendency to hit bottom unpredictably—and all at once.

Even for a one-hour quickie of 5 to 10 miles, I now carry a couple of small boxes of raisins for a quick energy boost. For a full-day or multiday tour, I also carry a stick of jerky or a packet of pretzels, to replenish salt lost through sweating. (Two key symptoms of needing salt: even drinking endless amounts of water doesn't slake thirst, and your muscles feel weak with an internal quivering. Confirmation: straight salt doesn't taste at all salty at first—and then suddenly is overwhelmingly salty.) For an independent bike-camping tour, I carry a full emergency meal that can be reconstituted with just water: a little box of good old Kraft dried macaroni and cheese, a tiny can of tuna, and some dried milk. More than once I have had occasion to bless this habit of always carrying food.

Rule number three: *carry a heavy-duty lock*. The New York City area is famed for grand larceny—a reputation that, I hate to say, is deserved. Outside the city itself, you can be a bit more casual and make do with a cable lock of some sort, but within the five boroughs *never* leave your bike unattended without the protection of a serious lock.

Even locked, it's best to keep one hand on the bike. In midtown Manhattan, cycling companion Jim Arth and I once foiled an attempted theft outside the Vanderbilt YMCA on East 47th Street about 7 P.M. one weekday evening. The would-be thieves were on bikes themselves; from the top tube of one of their bikes dangled a 4x4 about three feet long, which they were about to wedge inside an innocent U-lock and twist to break. (Jim just lounged against the side of the building next to the bikes while I went inside and alerted the management.) In Central Park one early morning, Jim had a bike stolen when it was actually leaning against his hip, when he bent over to pick up his helmet off the ground. I had one ripped off one weekday evening outside the busy West Side YMCA when it was locked for only 90 minutes.

Carry a small first-aid kit, especially on a multiday tour. Many camping and sporting goods stores sell a light nylon pouch with samples of all the basics. While no one plans to be injured, it's nice to know you could clean and soothe the road rash right when it happens. Or, you might be able to help a fellow traveler.

At the least, carry one of those portable boxes of the baby wipes brand-named Wet Ones. Not only are they meant for cleansing, but they are a bike-grease cutter par excellence—far better than many of the products advertised just for that purpose. And you never know when you'll have to fiddle with your grease-covered bike chain.

Carry a tool kit, and know how to use it. Bicycles are mechanically reliable, but East Coast roads have a fair amount of broken glass and numerous potholes. I minimize the chance of flats by using Kevlar-belted tires, and highly recommend them: even when I was commuting and touring at a peak annual rate of 2000 to 3000 miles, I averaged only one flat tire a year.

The problem is, you never know when a flat will occur. Murphy's Law guarantees it'll always be a nuisance. You'll be back on the road in less than half an hour if you know what to do and you're prepared with a patch kit, tire levers, and a pump. A spare tube is even better than a patch kit, in case you get a blow-out that cannot be patched.

If you don't always cycle in the company of a mechanical genius, the best favor you can do yourself is to take a basic bike maintenance and repair course, often offered by a local bike club, YMCA, American Youth Hostels chapter, or adult education center.

Carry bungee cords and a few safety pins. Bungees are essential for lashing purchases onto the bike; once I even used a bungee's hardened-metal hook to hold two parts of the bike together when I lost a screw en route. Safety pins can attach maps to your brake cables, as well as fix miscellaneous rips and tears.

Get familiar with the route
As I have seen with my bicycle touring students, when you're out enjoying the scenery, it can be very easy to bypass your next turn. Here are a few hints for minimizing the chance of missing a turn or a sight you wish to visit.

Before heading out onto the road, compare the route map in this book with the narrative description. Underline or highlight directions in the narrative and any sight that appeals to you.

Also, annotate the route map. Note landmarks (parks, churches, etc.) marking turns, and which ones you'd like to visit. Write which intersections are "T" (where the road you are on dead-ends at another where you must go either right or left) or "Y" (where the road you are on splits into two at a fork).

Note very long or very short mileages. Even if you don't have an odometer, you can use your watch. As most sight-seeing novice cyclists seem to ride about 6 or 8 miles per hour, each mile takes 7 to 10 minutes to ride. Calibrate your own comfortable riding speed; then if you have a three-mile stretch without turns in front of you, you know you can relax for 20 minutes or so.

With such an annotated description or map, you may spend less time on the road wondering where you are, and you'll be sure to stop at sights that appeal to you rather than accidentally passing them by.

In an ideal world, this book would be all that you need for any outing. But the world is not ideal. **The maps in this book do *not* show every small street.** You may want the comfort of a larger map that does. Moreover, if you should get off the main route, or you decide that time is running short and you'd like to devise a shortcut, you should have options.

Probably the best backup advice I can offer is *take a county map* along with you. In the descriptions, I have noted the county or counties relevant to the ride. Hagstrom makes the county maps I prefer, as they seem to show the most detail; Geographia county maps are also widely distributed. You can buy either type in many book stores, stationery shops, and corner news stands, in addition to specialty map and travel stores. Hagstrom has its own store in midtown Manhattan on 43rd Street just east of Sixth Avenue.

Just be aware: maps have errors. I have corrected them where I ran across them in plotting these routes, and so you may well find certain differences between the routes I show and the map you've bought. Moreover, new construction can suddenly start in unbuilt scenic areas, and thus may not appear on either the map or in this book. In such cases, be prepared to ask a local resident about your chosen alternate route or any changes you find.

Safety on the road: an ounce of prevention
Safety is something that, after logging some 6000 miles as a bicycle commuter on the streets of Manhattan, plus countless more thousands of miles touring places ranging from Vermont to the length of Baja California, I really take to heart.

While the tips below may sound like a prescription of all the horrors out there that a protective mother may recite to her teenaged daughter venturing out on her first date, I neither mean it to scare you away nor for you to chalk me up to being too much of a fussbudget. With enough riding, any cyclist will eventually have need of them. So just keep the tips in the back of your mind and rest easy that you'll know what to do, just in case...

First, *wear an industry-approved helmet.* Do it. I don't even want to recount the time I fell, cracking my head on the pavement and gouging the high-impact plastic of the helmet; but my skull was unhurt, and I really got religion about head protection. I still show that gouged helmet to the students of my bicycle touring classes.

If you're riding with children, absolutely make sure even the smallest has a helmet as well. (Effective July 1, 1992, New Jersey enacted a state law requiring bicycle helmets for all children under 14. And they're serious: parents or legal guardians can be fined up to $25 for a first offense and up to $100 for subsequent offenses.) Any bike shop worth its salt will carry one or more models of helmets for children.

Virtually all helmets on the market have passed the ANSI impact test. Only a few of those have passed the more stringent Snell tests. Since there's no difference in price, look for the Snell stickers inside the helmet. Personally, for maximum protection I go for hard-shell models. For riders who insist on having the feeling of the wind through their hair, try one of the ultralight helmets with super ventilation. White or yellow are best for visibility; even if you like the Darth Vader look, avoid black, which absorbs the sun's rays and can become very hot.

Second, those *fingerless bicycling gloves* are also a good idea. Not only will they protect your palms if you should fall, but every moment you're riding they will lessen road shock of the bumpy East Coast roads on your hands and arms. I also like super-padded grips for my handlebars.

Another "bennie" of wearing bicycling gloves is that if you tan (which as a redhead I, alas, do not), the gloves will give you the characteristic bicyclist's suntan: the little oval on the back of the hand and perhaps little dots on the knuckles where the sun penetrates the open weave. (I've often thought of marketing a template to produce that pattern in a tanning studio, for vain cyclists in the winter. But that's another story.)

Third, try a *rear-view mirror*. A rear-view mirror prevents a car from sneaking up behind you and startling you, as some are wont to do. They also allow you to keep an eye on heavy traffic without turning your head. I prefer the models that clip onto my helmet because (to me) the models that clip onto my eyeglasses have too small a field of vision. But either is better than the ones that mount on the bike itself, because on a bumpy road the latter can vibrate so much you have trouble distinguishing the image.

Fourth, *be visible*. Wear light and bright colors. My strategy is to look absolutely ridiculous. I'd rather have people stare and think "what a weirdo biker" than miss seeing me altogether. My helmet is covered with bright fluorescent yellow tape, as is the frame of my bike. I wear a reflective vest, which is particularly visible on overcast days—and in the winter on the streets of Manhattan, I was known to sport an international orange hunting jacket.

Some cyclists also like to attach a 6-foot-high orange flag that waves over the tops of cars. I have a little spring-mounted international orange flag that sticks out horizontally to the left (which can be clipped down onto the seatstay when not in use). This bobbing orange flag creates a fascinating psychology in the minds of drivers, which I've observed over and over again in my rear-view mirror. The average New York area driver, when passing, gives the knees or shoulders of a bicyclist about three feet of clearance (somewhat more in the suburbs). But the horizontal flag must make me seem about a foot wider, because drivers try to give their normal clearance to the tip of the flag instead of my body, buying me four feet of clearance instead of three. Give it a try yourself.

Last, speaking of psychology, *act like a vehicle*. In the automobile codes of Connecticut, New Jersey, and New York, the bicycle is considered a vehicle, just like a car, with the same rights and responsibilities on the road. Bicycles are allowed on most roads, excepting certain major highways, bridges, and tunnels. Many automobile drivers are not aware of all this.

The laws in most states require cyclists to ride "as far to the right as practicable." How far right is practicable is a point that has sparked great debates in the bicycling magazines on how a rider should share the road with cars. The preponderance of experienced riders in the tri-state area—and I share this view myself after about a decade of commuting and touring—believe that, on a road without a paved shoulder, there may be times when you should *not* ride all the way on the right edge of the lane. Instead, you might feel safer riding about a quarter of the way into the lane, roughly where the passenger in a car would be. If so, keep alert and watching in your rear-view mirror, and be *prepared* to move right instantly if necessary.

Why is hugging the right edge sometimes a bad idea? First, the far right edge of the road is likely to be broken up by potholes, gravel, glass, slippery wet leaves, or drains with tire-eating slots—all of which you'll miss if you're a few feet to the left. Second, if a driver comes up behind you, he'll see you and *know* he'll have to slow down and move around you to the left. Since this may involve him encroaching into the lane for oncoming traffic, he is likely to pass you with more care than if he felt you were so far to the right he could whiz by without swerving. And he'll be somewhat less likely to crowd you off the edge of the pavement when he makes a right turn. Just like the horizontal flag, much of sharing the road with cars is a matter of pure psychology: visually you want to take up a greater volume, so they'll treat you more like a car.

Now, acting like a car means a cyclist must also obey automobile laws: riding with traffic, stopping for stop signs and red lights, signalling, moving into left turn lanes instead of turning from the far right (with some exceptions). Ride a straight line—don't wander several feet back and forth across the lane. Avoid riding two abreast excepting on the most quiet of roads. All this is part of being predictable to cars so they think of you as a vehicle. For more detailed tips, read John Forester's reference bible *Effective Cycling* (MIT Press). As a super-defensive rule of thumb: Obey all the traffic laws yourself, while not trusting drivers to do the same.

Here are some other tips to file away in the back of your mind. Most are from my own experience.

Most of the rides in this book take you on roads with very little traffic. But if it's not your lucky day, or if you're venturing on a route of your own, you could be beset by automobiles. *In traffic, never be in a hurry, even if you're in a hurry.* This calls for a kind of Zen suspension of your spirit if you're late for something. Being in a hurry increases the risk of missing a driver parked at the right curb opening the car door in your path, not seeing a pothole or slick oil spot, or not hearing a car approaching from behind to pull abruptly ahead of you to make a right turn.

If you get caught in the rain, ride extra slowly, avoiding painted lines, puddles, and piles of leaves. The biggest problem with rain is that it wets the metal rims of your wheels and seriously reduces your braking, thereby increasing your stopping distance. The only way to compensate for that is reducing your speed.

The painted lines that separate road surface from shoulder often get dangerously slick in the rain. Puddles can disguise potholes; in addition, the water may be mixed with engine oil from the pavement and make your rims even slicker. Piles of leaves in the fall often congregate over tire-eating drainage grates, and can be extraordinarily slippery when wet. If you're riding in a group, the first rider noting the hazard can point to it to alert the riders behind.

Whatever you do, please *do not plug your ears with portable headphones* and listen to music while riding. Not only is that practice outright illegal, but more than you may know, you need your ears to warn you about traffic approaching from behind or the dog barking up ahead. Plus—back to the fun part—your ears will also alert you to waterfalls, birds, frogs, and the conversation of your companions, which, of course, is what touring is all about!

Speaking of animals, here's another tip to help you cope with various encounters: *If a dog starts running after you, get off the bike and command: "Go home!"* Yes, your instinct is to pedal like hell, but few cyclists can outrun a big dog. Take advantage instead of the doggy psyche: dogs are territorial, setting up a ruckus because you entered their turf.

At the first warning bark of a dog bounding toward you, shout: "Go home!"

in an authoritative tone. Get off the bike, put the bike between you and the dog, and walk along the road, continuing to command: "Go home!" A familiar walking figure is one the dog is used to obeying, and normally the dog will prance barking alongside you until he comes to the edge of his territory. When you've walked past that, he'll just stand and bark, allowing you to safely remount and ride off. As scary as this sounds, it is the practice followed by organized tour groups, and in more than a decade of riding, I've never had it fail.

If you get separated from your companions, go back to the place you were last together. That way you can even undo a wrong turn. Some people like riding alone but meeting for snacks and lunch. If that is your style, before the ride, set up several prearranged "compression stops" during the day where everyone will wait for the others to make sure there's still perfect attendance. And make sure *everyone* has a map and complete route instructions. To cover all bets, you might even arrange one phone number as a central message center for emergencies.

If night is overtaking you, hatch an alternate plan. Riding in the dark can be dangerous; changing plans is only inconvenient. If you have a tent, you can set up camp almost anywhere—and, of course, you have extra water and your emergency snacks, right? Or check into a roadside motel. Or have a friend come get you.

Any book on outdoor activities would be remiss without one last warning: If you stop to spend some time hiking, *stick to well-marked trails.* Don't go crashing off through the underbrush. In addition to poison ivy and other unpleasantness, you could put yourself at risk of being bitten by certain ticks infected with a bacterium causing Lyme disease. The first symptoms are often a large, red swelling around the bite and flu-like symptoms. If treated with antibiotics, recovery may be assured. But if unrecognized and left untreated, Lyme disease is a life-long debilitating illness. Lyme disease has been found in just about every state of the union, including the tri-state area: in fact, it is named after the town of Lyme, Connecticut. Just about every county and state park you enter is likely to have information leaflets on Lyme disease, rabies, and other health hazards; ask for one and follow its suggestions.

Having listed all these contingencies, don't let any of the warnings discourage you from riding. If you're prepared to prevent the worst, you can calmly enjoy the best—with confidence.

CONNECTICUT

OFF-SEASON RIDE TO OLD GREENWICH

Fairfield County, Connecticut

This ride will allow you to go where few people are admitted—if you go in the winter. That special place is the 147-acre Old Greenwich Park, strictly reserved for Greenwich, Connecticut residents and their guests eight months out of the year. But from December 1 through March 31, its spacious beaches, hiking trails, and intriguing ruins are open to all, making this short ride perfect for one of those let's-play-hookey, 60-degree days that somehow get stirred in between January snows, or for the year's first warm-up in mid-March. Also, for a delicious contradiction in sports, take your ice skates for some turns on the skating pond in the forested Bruce Park. If through good old American know-who you're lucky enough to have a Greenwich friend and can visit in the summer, take your swimsuit and sailboard instead.

In the more preferable and warmer riding months, even without a visit to the park, there are the craft shops and historical buildings of Old Greenwich, Riverside, Cos Cob, and downtown Greenwich to enjoy—not to mention some excellent seafood. Bird-watchers might want to tuck small binoculars into their handlebar bags for spotting migratory fowl in Bruce Park during spring and fall. Or try your hand at lawn bowling, provided you're dressed in white. And should you like to spend some time and money doing some serious antiquing or simply sharing some quality time with your love, the ride is a good

Ride Ratings

Length: 12 or 15 miles
Configuration: line—same route each way
Difficulty: flat to gently rolling; traffic is light to moderate
Surface: good pavement throughout

—Highlights: This ride invites you to poke around the shops of Old Greenwich, luxuriate in a bed and breakfast inn, picnic on Grass Island, visit museums, listen to live jazz, take a steamboat ride; a special winter treat is the exploration of Greenwich Point Park.

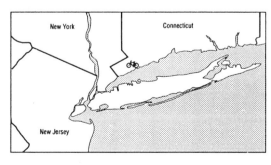

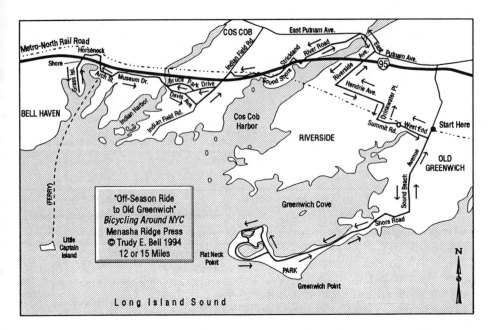

excuse to for sleeping late at one of several rambling bed-and-breakfast inns.

One note: Old Greenwich and surroundings are prime tourist areas. In the warm months that means traffic of all types—pedestrians, Rollerbladers, baby strollers, other cyclists, and, of course, cars. This is not a ride for pulse rate and aerobics; in fact, when I was there in late April, my cycling companion Jim Arth remarked that he'd never before seen such a pretty route that was so well-traveled. So, take your time to enjoy the varied scene; the drivers are by and large considerate, for many of them are taking their vintage automobiles out to see and be seen. But do ride watchfully.

The ride starts from the Old Greenwich, Connecticut station of the Metro-North Commuter Railroad (see the introduction for information about obtaining a pass for your bike on Metro-North). If you're driving, take the Connecticut Turnpike (I-95) and get off at Exit 5 (Old Greenwich). Turn right at the end of the off ramp onto Sound Beach Avenue and follow it to the train station on your left. There you may park for the day for a few dollars (*note:* the yellow-striped spaces in the back of the lot are shady), and you can provision up at the nearby Food Mart, deli, and pizzeria.

Turn left out of the Old Greenwich railroad station onto Sound Beach Avenue, which is the main street through the busy little shops, cafes, and nooks of Old Greenwich. The business section of town ends after a quarter mile, though, and you'll be pedaling between stately houses on both sides of the streets.

Follow the road as it bends right around a triangle and joins Shore Road. In another quarter mile, at the corner of Wahneta Road, is a white clapboard mansion that cries out to be a bed-and-breakfast—and it is. It is the Harbor House Inn at 165 Shore Road, Old Greenwich, Connecticut 06870, phone (203) 637-0145.

Just a tenth of a mile beyond Harbor House, follow Shore Road where it makes a sharp left, and ride out onto the narrow neck of land out to Greenwich Point. Right where the neck is most constricted, perhaps only a few hundred feet across, is a kiosk, where from April Fools Day until after Thanksgiving a guard who may be a college student earning tuition—will check every voyager for Credentials. And don't smugly think that just because you're on a bike, you'll be waved right through. Jim and I watched as a cyclist and a rollerskater were carded; we ourselves were admitted in late April only because of permission granted by the Greenwich Department of Parks and Recreation for the research of this book. In fact, the bulk of this ride was inspired by the Greenwich Bike Route leaflet put out by the parks department; Greenwich Point Park was included at the suggestion of my work colleague and former Greenwich resident Rick Ofstie.

Once in the park, ride carefully around the white shards of seashells on the pavement—debris left by enterprising gulls dropping shellfish onto the hard surface to break them open and scoop out the juicy unfortunate. Those shells are sharp enough to puncture bike tires, and who needs to start the day with a flat?

Greenwich Point Park was build on land purchased in 1640 from the Siwanoy Indians for 25 colored English coats. Now the southeastern edge, to your left, features a clean, sandy beach that is surprisingly wide and flat at low tide. Because Greenwich Point juts out into the Long Island Sound, the lapping waves are tame enough for the gaggle of splashing toddlers and their parents. Shaded shelters with benches allowed the fair to enjoy the seascape out of the sun's burning rays. Even in April, the hotdog, ice cream, and candy concessions were turning a good business.

Just past the Seaside Center of the Bruce Museum on your left (open 10 A.M.-5 P.M. Wednesdays through Saturdays in July and August), you should bear right at the fork to keep the water on your right. A walking path will parallel your ride. After a quarter mile, where the road bears right, stop to get your bearings at the watercolor map of Greenwich Point in the little shelter and to admire the carvings on the two-story-tall totem pole. Continue your wanderings through the stone gate, past the area to your left where signs inform you that a clambake permit is required. I've never been to a clambake, but have always wanted to since seeing the musical *Carousel*. Humming "This Was a Real Nice Clambake," bear right onto the one-way road toward the yacht club and past the dry-docked white-and-blue sailboats on your right. As you pass the yacht club the road bends left, and you'll pass a stone building where chimes play every noon and evening at 6 P.M.; although I missed them, I understand their sweet song over the water is worth timing your visit.

You are now rounding the very tip of Greenwich Point. The road will carry you past a small pond on your left, and a launch area for sailboards on your right; windsurfers may be skimming across the Sound. If you've brought a lunch, you can stop at the picnic tables to your right, grill a hotdog or two on one of the public barbecue grates, or refill your water bottles at the restrooms. In late April, this spot is definitely worth a stop. The maple flower pollen is golden on the road, the dogwoods and cherry trees are dressed in lacy pink and white, and the fuzzy brown goslings toddling after mama and papa geese pose in endearing family portraits. In fact, this whole area is worth exploring on foot, for nearby there are some hanging gardens on the wall of a small cliff you can scale.

Resuming the ride, bear right at the fork to begin circling the large pond on your left. The parking lot you'll pass on your right leads to more picnic tables, these with a view of the Long Island Sound and Little Captain Island—another haven for Greenwich residents and their guests. Soon you'll be entering a narrow lane, where a fence on your left protects a small wildlife sanctuary.

Turn right at the triangle. Here the road rejoins the two-way traffic at the dry-docked sailboat area. You are now retracing the way you rode in, with the bay on your left. Pedal through the stone gate, past the totem pole, and turn right to enter the parking lot, following the one-way signs. Turn left where the road dead-ends into the sandy beach, refreshing yourself if you wish at the concession stand on your right. Pass the Bruce Museum once again, and ride past the guard kiosk to exit the park.

Half a mile out of the park, follow the road as it bends sharply right, and pass Harbor House Inn on your left. Turn left at the triangle onto Sound Beach Avenue, once again entering downtown Old Greenwich.

At the light immediately after the flashing yellow light, turn left onto West End Avenue; this intersection is marked with a Mobil gas station and the fire department. In a quarter mile, ride around the traffic circle and continue straight onto Summit Road, which begins as a brief steep climb and then becomes a gentler uphill—the only notable one of the entire ride. Turn right at the first stop sign onto Drinkwater Place (sounds like a good idea), cross over the railroad tracks, and roll past a wonderful old school with a large lawn on your left. Follow the road as it bends left around the school, turning left at the stop sign onto Hendrie Avenue. You'll know you've done it right when you see the Bike Route sign directing your way.

Coast downhill, past Eastern Middle School. Here, at the stop sign, if you turn right into the school grounds, a sign informs you that you can visit the George F. Markscheffel Memorial Nature Center—but I must admit, I could never find the place! But then, on a weekend the schools are closed, and maybe the nature center is too. Perhaps you'll have better luck than I.

Continue down Hendrie Avenue until it ends at a "T" intersection. Turn right onto the unmarked Riverside Avenue, watching for cars. In about a quarter mile, you'll pass over the very noisy Connecticut Turnpike (I-95), with which your route will braid from here on out—16 crossings in all in the round trip.

At the light, a corner marked by the St. Catherine of Sienna Church, pay close attention. Dismount and walk your bike on the sidewalk at your left, so that you have turned left (west) onto U.S. Route 1 (East Putnam Avenue), but are opposing the heavy traffic. The sidewalk slopes downhill across the Mianus River; in the water down to your left boats are docked and you can hear the thunder of the nice upriver waterfall under the traffic noise.

At the first intersection across the bridge, turn left at the light onto the relatively quiet River Road. Soon your path is going to make a peculiar Z, ducking under I-95 three times in quick succession. Follow River Road past the wharfs and through its left bend, passing under the turnpike the first time; here you will see signs for the Chart House, a restaurant noted for its seafood and prime rib (dinner on the way back?). Follow River Road through its sharp turn back under I-95.

Turn left at the grassy triangle onto Strickland Road. On the hillside just above you, that colonial saltbox house is the Bush-Holley House, built here in Cos Cob around 1685. It houses rare examples of colonial furniture and is open to the public. A separate building features works of local artists working around the turn of the 20th century. On Strickland Road you'll make the third stroke of the Z, carrying you once again under I-95.

Hang your first left, under the railroad tracks, onto Sound Shore Drive, which bends to the right—under I-95 again!—and takes you past the Cos Cob railroad station. Turn left at the next light onto Indian Field Road, and this time ride over I-95.

Make the first right onto Bruce Park Drive—and settle back for a leisurely spin through the lush 59-acre Bruce Park. Magnificent old oaks and maples with their huge boles dot the grassy lawn to your left, which is encircled with a fitness circuit for joggers and racewalkers. There is also a lawn bowling green here, where—if you're dressed in white—you can experiment with rolling the asymmetrically weighted balls to score points. It takes a fair amount of skill, and I've played it only once (in Beverly Hills, California, no less); it's rather like a rolling version of bocci, which old Italian gentlemen often play in Central Park.

Stay on Bruce Park Drive as it winds past tennis courts on your left and then takes you on a bridge over the Bruce Park Skating Pond. In the winter there is supervised ice skating here, while in the spring and fall you can watch for birds stopping on their annual migration.

Once you're over the bridge, bear right onto Davis Avenue. In a quarter mile, go halfway around the traffic circle to continue straight on Museum Drive (don't follow Davis Avenue under I-95!). Bear right at the next triangle to follow Museum Drive, which heads up and left past the Bruce Museum. The Bruce Museum of Arts and Sciences, which until 1909 was the home of Robert Bruce and his sister Sarah, now exhibits displays of history, art, natural history, and science. The building overlooks Greenwich Harbor. On the lawn outdoors are giant sculptures, such as the brushed aluminum curved-ladder creation by Luis Avata titled "Searching for Peace."

Continue past the museum, straight through the light at Steamboat Road. Here the road you're on changes its name to Arch Street. At your left is the Lexington Showboat Hotel, whose Showboat Harbor Grill features live bands and dancing on Thursday through Sunday nights. For reservations and information, call (203) 661-9800 or (800) 243-8511; the address is 500 Steamboat Road, Greenwich, CT 06830. It is also a short walk from the Greenwich train station, should you decide to take the train and stay there. On the waterfront side of the Showboat Hotel is a ferry landing, which between mid-June and mid-September will take Greenwich residents and their guests out to Island Beach and Great Captain Island; both islands are Greenwich town parks with swimming and picnic areas. There is also the six-acre Roger Sherman Baldwin Park right on the waterfront, complete with multicolored geometric bandshell. Another place to keep in mind apres ride!

Arch Street curves right and guess what? passes under I-95 again! At the second light after the underpass turn left onto Horseneck Lane, then make the first left onto Shore Road, and once again under I-95—your last time, at least for now! For you're almost at the end of the ride out.

Take the first left onto the rather unpromising-looking unmarked Grass Island Road; the only landmark is a sign that reads State of Connecticut Pollution Control Project. Pass by two kiosks. At the end of the road is the tiny Grass Island Park, marked with an American flag. There is a small grassy lawn with a solitary picnic table and a white building with restrooms that are open from 9 A.M.-5 P.M. seven days a week from mid-April to mid-November. But best of all, the miniature peninsula is a great place to watch the multitude of white and blue sailboats drifting in and out of Greenwich Harbor—with an occasional steamboat docking at the Showboat Hotel.

The return is essentially the same route you took to get here; unfortunately, this part of Connecticut is so built-up that, although there are nice places to bicycle, it is almost impossible to link them together to form a larger loop.

Return on Grass Island Road past the kiosks; turn right at the "T" intersection onto Shore Road. Turn right at the next "T" intersection onto Horseneck Lane. Turn right at the light at the next "T" intersection onto Arch Street, and pass under I-95. At the Showboat Hotel, go straight through the light onto Museum Drive, and up around the museum. Turn left at the "T" intersection to stay on Museum Drive (Indian Harbor Drive heads to your right). Go halfway around the traffic circle to continue straight on Davis Avenue; in mid-August, summer apples have fallen uneaten from trees lining the road. Cross the bridge over the Bruce Skating Pond, bearing right at the flower gardens to stay on Davis Avenue, through the restful shade of Bruce Park.

Turn left at the "T" intersection onto Indian Field Road. Here you'll be pedaling next to a shady forest separated from you by a shoulder-high wall that's three to four feet thick and made of boulders. According to an 1871 Department of Agriculture report, such stone walls made up a third of Connecticut's fencing—amounting to 20,505 miles of stone walls! Now, that's almost enough stone walls to encircle the earth's equator. In fact, in the late 19th century, the states of New England and New York had more miles of stone walls than the U.S. has miles of coastline or railroad track today. The work that went into them would have built the pyramids of Egypt 100 times over. Moreover, the stone walls changed the face of the colonies and even their politics. Their fascinating history is recounted in the highly readable and well-illustrated book *Sermons in Stone: The Stone Walls of New England and New York* by Susan Allport (W. W. Norton & Co., New York, 1990).

Cross over I-95 and turn right at the light onto Sound Shore Drive. Careful! Note that Sound Shore Drive is actually the second right turn; the first is an I-95 off-ramp! Sound Shore passes under I-95 and bends left under railroad tracks. Turn right at the "T" intersection onto the unmarked Strickland Road, which also takes you under I-95 in the first leg of the Z. Turn right at the stop sign onto River Road, marked by the triangle of flowers. Pass under I-95 twice more as the road hairpins, then go straight pass the boats in the Mianus River to your right.

Turn right at the "T" intersection and dismount your bike, lifting it up onto the sidewalk and heading right to parallel the very busy U.S. Route 1 (East

Putnam Avenue). After crossing the river and climbing the hill, turn right at the first light onto Riverside Avenue, past the Catholic church and senior citizens' home. Cross over I-95.

In half a mile or so, after the stop sign, make the first left onto Hendrie Avenue; after the recent heavy traffic, its quiet is welcome. Climb the gentle hill, at the school turning right at the stop sign onto Drinkwater Place. Cross over the railroad tracks and turn left at the "T" intersection onto Summit Road, coasting down the slope.

Now, play close attention. Go three-quarters of the way around the traffic circle at the bottom of the hill, so that you head left through the one-lane stone tunnel. You are now on the one-way Arch Street. The road will take you past Binney Park on your right, which in mid-August may be filled with migrating Canada geese heading south. At the stop sign continue straight, but take a look to the right. There is an amazing weeping willow with its trunk bending at a 45-degree angle over the pond, as if dipping its long tresses into the water to wash.

Turn right at the "T" intersection onto the unmarked Sound Beach Avenue. Turn right at the next "T" intersection to stay on Sound Beach Avenue. In a third of a mile, turn left into the Old Greenwich railroad station.

CRUISING THE MILFORD BEACHES

New Haven County, Connecticut

Ride Ratings

Length: 20 or 23 miles
Configuration: loop
Difficulty: first half is flat, the return is rolling; traffic is light in spring and fall, but moderate to heavy in summer.
Surface: good pavement throughout

—Highlights: This route can be combined with "Land, Sea and Air" for a total of 55 miles; the main attraction is the beach, though seafood lovers should make a point of going in mid-August for the annual Oyster Festival.

Milford, founded in 1639, made its fortune in shipbuilding and oystering. In fact, to this day, sometime around the third weekend each August is the annual oyster festival, where the main route through town is blocked off for a mile-long block party. You can listen to live bands, picnic on the grass, buy T-shirts, balloons, local crafts, and knickknacks, and, of course, enjoy your fill of fresh oysters.

Aside from the oyster festival, which snarls all automobile traffic for a weekend (leave the four-wheeler home), Milford is not a tourist attraction like Old Greenwich or Mystic Seaport or other more well-known Connecticut meccas of the rich or wannabes. It's a normal town with normal people, many of them blue collar workers—itself kind of a treat for those who live in the fast-paced overpriced hothouse of New York City. Bring your swimsuit and beach towel and a fat novel: the modest length of the ride will give you plenty of hours to lie on the sand, catch some rays, and maybe flirt with some locals intrigued by the speckled suntan left on the back of your hands by your cycling gloves.

By the way, if you feel like making a weekend of your time on Connecticut's shoreline, this ride can be combined with the "Land, Sea, and Air" ride through Stratford, Connecticut. The Stratford ride, just west of Milford on the other side of the Housatonic River, includes the

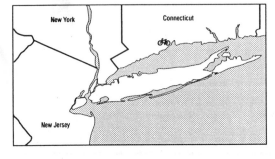

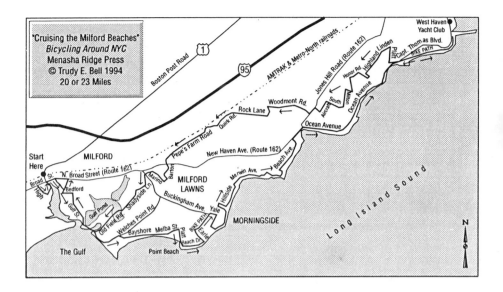

possibility of a night's stay at Marnick's, a motel right on the water of the Long Island Sound. The distance of the combined rides, including the link, is about 55 miles. (For directions linking the two, see the end of the Stratford ride.)

This wander around Milford has a lot of little twists and turns along little one-block-long residential streets, but have patience: the aim is not to get you from Point A to Point B as fast as possible but to stay along the beaches on the way out, and to avoid congested main highways on the way back. Its directions have been confirmed by Milford resident Wayne Lovington, an amateur historian and cyclist who followed my initial description and added some neat suggestions of his own including the directions for linking this ride with the one in Stratford. By the way, the maps for this area seem to be abysmal; if a map conflicts with these written directions, follow the directions—not the map.

You can get yourself and your bike to Milford by taking the Metro-North Commuter Railroad's New Haven line to the Milford train station (see the preface for details about obtaining a pass for your bike on Metro-North). Alternatively, you can drive up Interstate 95 to Exit 38 or take the Merritt Parkway to Exit 54. In either case, head south briefly on the Milford Parkway, following the exit signs to U.S. Route 1 South. At the stop sign at the end of the offramp, turn right. At the first light, turn left onto High Street. Drive two-thirds of a mile on High Street. Immediately after passing under the railroad overpass, turn right into Metro-North's unrestricted parking lot.

The train station building itself—where you will disembark if you took the train—is across High Street from the unrestricted parking lot. The original brick station house on the south side of the tracks is closed, but north of the tracks is a modern gray wooden station house where you can refresh yourself at the restrooms and concession stand. This modern station house is open 4:30 A.M.-11 P.M. weekdays and 8 A.M.-11:30 P.M. on weekends (but is closed on holidays). The ride begins at the High Street entrance to the train station parking lot.

Head south on High Street toward Milford Center. If you've done it right, one block south you'll encounter divided Broad Street (Connecticut State Route

162), which is the main road through town, with all kinds of delis and other stores for picking up lunch. Cross Broad Street (at this intersection of Broad and High there's a bicycle shop), continuing straight in spite of the dead end sign. At the end on your right are the Milford Historical Society's historic homes, which are open to the public.

Turn left onto unmarked Helwig Street, go past dry-docked boats and abandoned greenhouses; on your right is the Chandlery, a store for boaters, plus the Milford Boat Works and Marina in the small Milford Harbor. Breathe deeply of the salty sea air from the Long Island Sound. A little farther on, the small shopping complex to your left has a couple of fish restaurants and a deli where you can buy lunch.

After this short nautical tour, Helwig rejoins Broad Street (Route 162). Turn right at the light onto the busy highway, crossing a stone bridge over the Indian River. This is Memorial Bridge, built to salute the Milford residents who perished in wars and to immortalize the town's earliest settlers.

Immediately after crossing the bridge, turn right onto the narrow, unmarked Shipyard Lane, passing between the Indian River and the library. This lane takes you along the banks of the harbor and the public boat launch ramp. The ramp is a nice spot to stop and view the harbor; you'll often see children fishing and may be able to buy a hotdog or snow cone from a vendor. Eventually, after riding a short distance through a nicely wooded drive, you will join Harborside Drive. Keep going.

At the end, turn left onto Bedford Avenue. (Actually, if you continue straight instead, you'll come to the head of the Milford Independent Disabled Persons' Handicapped Trail.) Turn right at the "T" intersection onto the moderately busy Gulf Street; here, despite the traffic on the August day I was riding, a flock of 8- to 12-year-old boys on BMX bikes cavorted up and down curbs.

Gulf Street carries you across a narrow bridge between Gulf Pond (to your left) and The Gulf (to your right), along the swimming beach with a view of Charles Island off in the sound. The beach is open to the public with no fee, unless you're a nonresident wanting to park your car there. Shortly, you'll pass Poor Girls of Gulf Beach, a hotdog and seafood stand that is clearly a local hangout, where patrons sit on tree stumps while savoring their mustard-drenched fingers and looking out at the beach.

A short ways after Poor Girls, the road becomes particularly narrow and begins its first modest rise and bends left. Half a mile after Poor Girls, just after a liquor store, turn right onto Westland Avenue. At the end, turn left onto Bayshore Drive. Continue along the beach; Bayshore Drive turns into Melba Street. Stay on Melba Street now, passing beach bungalows and year-round houses—one of which belongs to Wayne. After passing Buckingham Avenue, the road becomes a bit busier, but there's plenty of room on the wide painted shoulder.

Here come a few quick turns. Turn right at the light onto Platt Street, left where it bends left onto Moorhouse Lane, and take the immediate right onto Virginia Street. At the "T" intersection, turn left onto Point Beach Drive through a pleasant, quiet beach community. Turn left at the dead end sign onto Earle Street, right at the "T" intersection onto the unmarked Atwater Street. Then turn right onto the paved bike path just before the busy Melba Street (which becomes Edgefield Drive). Whew! Did it! The only problem with this bike path, you'll discover, is that it is not well-maintained, so watch out for the potholes and sand. Eventually the bike path becomes a sidewalk.

Now for a lovely interlude, turn right at the light onto the unmarked Yale Avenue, which is distinctive for the stone kiosk or bus shelter. At the flag pole, turn right onto Ridgefield Drive past country manors, turning left at the "T" intersection onto Little Pond Road. At the end, turn left again onto Morningside Drive.

Here, pedal slowly, for this is the most beautiful section of the entire ride. Savor your view of the Long Island Sound stretching almost to the horizon. The road descends sharply to a quiet drive right above the shoreline. Stairs to your right lead down to the rocks below as well as to a retaining wall made of even pink slabs, looking like nothing so much as a wide pink plaza inviting you to sunbathe. At the second staircase you pass stop and pick some summer apples, sweet in late July. Then sit on one of the stone benches to be soothed by the rhythmic breaking surf and the smell of salty seaweed on the humid breeze.

When you're ready—and only when!—remount your bike to continue along Morningside Drive. Follow it where it bends left onto Norwood Avenue, heading away from the ocean. Turn right at the "T" intersection onto Ridgewood Drive, then make an immediate right at the stop sign onto Edgefield Drive.

Whoa, not so fast! Make an immediate right onto the one-way South Street, then left at the end onto the one-way Hillside Avenue. Once again, you're paralleling the beach, whose sand is to your right. Follow the road as it bends left at the end, turning right at the stop sign onto the moderately busy Merwin Avenue.

A quarter of a mile later, take the right fork at the "Y" intersection onto the unmarked Abigail Street; this intersection is hard to miss because it welcomes you with the Memories Lounge and a sign informing you that you are entering the town of Woodmont. Keep bearing right, past the street with the wrong way— do not enter sign, until the road bends left. At this point you will pass a surprising Spanish-style mansion behind 10-foot iron gates, an apparition straight from California.

Turn right at the "T" intersection onto Mark Street and hang an immediate left at the next "T" onto the unmarked King's Highway. Turn right onto Beach Avenue and follow it as it winds around past volleyball games on the sand and impressive rocks looming out the water. You are now pedaling next to the Long Island Sound again, along a miniature swimming beach. You just might be tempted to go wading into the lapping salt water. Well, the only way to be rid of temptation is to give into it, so spread out your towel, relax, soak up some rays, and find out what happens next in your novel.

Beach Avenue bends to the left, then right, then right and left again around a little park. When I was there, the park was the center of a block party with whole families eating hotdogs from under a striped tent and children batting balloons around and adults tapping their feet to the band. Even without the festivities, you might want to check out the park's playground equipment and horseshoes.

Continue around the park on Beach Avenue. At the stop sign, turn right onto Hawley Avenue, which bends left and becomes Anderson Avenue. At the light, turn right onto New Haven Avenue, our old "friend" Route 162. This road can be very busy, so ride with care. Fortunately, you have less than a quarter mile on it. Bear right at the "Y" intersection onto Ocean Avenue.

After picking up a snack at the Bay Brook Shopping Center on your right, continue straight, eventually catching glimpses of the Sound. Although Ocean Avenue is also busy, the sidewalk is wide enough for riding if you prefer. The beach itself has pinkish sand and was clean, with remarkably few sunbathers, even on a sunny Saturday afternoon in late July. Well, even if Connecticut is not famous for its beaches, you know a good thing when you see it—time for another stop to wiggle your toes in the sand! This is also the last time you'll have the chance, so if you've delayed gratification until now, indulge yourself.

Just beyond the beach is Bradley Point Park, and lo and behold! there's a paved bike path. Yes, take it: you can pedal out to the rocks of Bradley Point itself to see people fishing in the shallows. Plus there are benches for napping and trees casting shade over the grass inviting you to picnic and breezes tempting you to fly a kite. Bradley Point also has some Revolutionary War significance, as it is where British invasion forces under the command of Brigadier General Garth landed on July 5, 1779.

If you're in the mood for some serious seafood and a tour along a bike path, continue reading for an option of a little detour that will add another three or four miles. If you prefer to continue on with the main route, drop down to the double asterisks (**) below.

Follow the bike path east through the park and its parking lot. Eventually the path widens to a concrete beachside promenade and passes on the beach side of a long, low apartment complex (where, by the way, bicycle riding is not allowed from 4:30 P.M. to sunrise; walk your bike if you are passing through during these hours). After leaving the complex, the path begins paralleling the busy Captain Thomas Boulevard, past a building with public restrooms. In fact, eventually the bike path divides into separate lanes for cyclists and joggers.

You'll also be passing some serious seafood restaurants here: Chick's, Jimmie's of Savin Rock ("very famous amongst locals," observes Wayne), the Captain's Galley, and others. In fact, at the public parking lot you'll pass, there is a bike rack where you can lock your steed before heading to a restaurant, to the beach again, or into nearby Morse Park. After the parking lot, the bike path narrows and comes to an unceremonious end. At this point, turn around and retrace the entire route two miles or so, through the apartment complex and (**) into Bradley Point Park again, and back out onto Ocean Avenue heading west.

Now watch carefully. At the light, turn right onto Hazel Street, then make an immediate right at the "T" intersection onto Platt Avenue, noting the three-story Victorian home on your left immediately after your turn. Just before the fenced-in tennis courts on your right, turn left onto Linden Street.

A quarter mile later, bear left at the "Y" intersection onto the unmarked Highland Avenue (it will be your second left; the first is Bluff Avenue). Highland Avenue, true to its name, is a climb—the only significant climb of the ride. But the quiet residential streets and the view of the Sound to your left make it worth it. After passing Walter Brennan Memorial Park (was it named after the actor?? no clue) on your right, follow the road as it turns left and becomes Arlington Street. Make the first right onto Sharon Avenue, then the next first right onto Dawson Avenue. Now, say good-bye to the last view of the ocean on this ride and enjoy the downhill reward.

Turn left at the end onto Roosevelt Avenue, crossing the divided Colonial Boulevard and turning slightly right to continue onto Honor Road. Follow Honor Road as it curves left. At the "T" intersection, turn right onto Lake Street; turn left at the end onto Milton Avenue. At the grassy triangle, turn right onto Park Avenue—a short street—and then make an immediate right at the end onto South Street.

After climbing a bit, you'll crest at the Seth G. Haley School, then coast downhill—but not too fast. Take the first left onto Aircraft Road, At the end, turn right onto Contact Drive, and then left at the "T" intersection onto the busy Jones Hill Road—our Route 162 with its many names.

You won't be on this highway long: after all, avoiding traffic is the purpose of all these twists and turns. Take the first right onto the Woodmont Road; although it has moderate traffic, it's better than Route 162. Ride up a rather steep but short hill; the school with the playground marks its crest. Bear left at the stop sign to stay on Woodmont and coast down the other side past another playground. Turn left at the flashing red light onto the busy Merwin Avenue. Immediately take the first right onto Lilac Lane, riding to the end.

Turn right at the "T" intersection onto the unmarked Rock Lane past houses and industries. Follow the main road as it bears left and becomes Quirk Road (Rock Lane becomes just a little spur to the right). Turn right at the "T" intersection onto the busy, unmarked Anderson Road. Take the first left onto Woodmont Road, following the signs To PEPE'S FARM ROAD.

Now you're riding through a light industrial area of miniature low, modern factory buildings, which are pleasantly set in lawns and parking lots. Turn right at the next "T" intersection at Plastic Tool Systems Inc. The road curves left, then right, past other small single-story industry and office buildings, then curves left again and becomes Pepe's Farm Road.

Turn right at the end onto the busy Route 162—now, in its Protean way named New Haven Avenue—and make an immediate left onto Barton Road. When I was there, the corner house actually had statues of pink flamingos in its yard. I was so thrilled: I didn't think people in real life actually did that, at least not outside of Florida and not on the eve of the 21st century.

Climb gently up Barton Road, which bends left. At the end, turn right onto Berner Terrace. Once again, ride to the end, and turn right onto Marino Drive, which bends left. At the stop sign, it changes name to Hoover Street. Continue straight. Where it crosses the unmarked Pond Point Avenue (marked by a Wawa Market and shopping center), it becomes Shadyside Lane. Continue on Shadyside as it meanders hither and yon.

At the end of Shadyside Lane, go straight across the very busy Buckingham Avenue onto Old Field Lane. Pedal along Old Field for about a mile, past Gulf Pond on your right and past an old saltwater farm. At the road's end, Poor Girls is right across the street from you. Turn right at this "T" intersection onto Gulf Street. At this point, as you ride along Gulf Street, you're backtracking the initial part of the ride. Turn left onto Bedford Avenue, right onto Harborside Drive, and left at the end of Harborside onto the busy Route 162 (Broad Street), following all its curves into downtown Milford.

In Milford Center, Broad Street splits so that traffic in each direction goes one way through town past the long and skinny grassy park aptly called Milford Green. In the green is a marker noting that in 1666 a group from Milford led by Connecticut governor Robert Treat migrated south and west and founded Newark, New Jersey. I'm not sure he'd be entirely happy with the way that city turned out . . .

Here next to the green, you might want to treat yourself to the creamy ice cream at What's The Scoop. The August afternoon I was there, the college student serving the ice cream noticed my cycling gear and confided she was also an avid rider who lived for her 30-mile tour each afternoon to work off the ice cream she nibbled all day! After munching the last of the sugar cone, continue just a hundred yards or so father west on Route 162. Turn right onto High Street and into the Milford railroad station.

LAND, SEA AND AIR

Fairfield County, Connecticut

This is truly a ride for the history buffs. Stratford, Connecticut, offers not only a wealth of Americana from the 17th through the early 20th century; it is also a cradle of early aviation, the birthplace of the first practical helicopter, and such well-known companies as Avco-Lycoming, Chance-Vought, and Sikorsky. In more modern technological history, Stratford is also the home town of Kenneth Olson, founder and president of Digital Equipment Corp., a pioneer builder of minicomputers in the 1970s.

It's also a ride for the beach bums—bring your swimsuit, your sunscreen, and your fishing rod for some sunrise casting into the gentle surf of the Long Island Sound.

In addition, it's a ride for hikers and mountain bikers—considerate ones, of course—who can explore the rocky back roads and fire trails of the Roosevelt Forest, a hilly state forest. Or simply bring a blanket and a book and relax away from virtually any other human being.

Feel like doing nothing more complicated than relaxing with a beer? Then bunk up for the weekend at Marnick's, a completely unpretentious two-story motel (yes, a motel, not a bed and breakfast—there's nothing chichi here), with terraced rooms facing the water at rates that, for the tri-state area, are unbelievably cheap. Rooms with an ocean view carry only a $5 premium, and the rates in the summer

Ride Ratings

Length: 23 miles
Configuration: Figure-eight
Difficulty: Half is flat, the other half is rolling with steady climbs; traffic is light to moderate
Surface: good pavement throughout, though there are off-road options

—Highlights: This ride can be combined with "Cruising the Milford Beaches" for a total of 55 miles; it leads you through woods and along beaches for a taste of Americana, aviation, history, and excellent seafood; overnight bikers can enjoy a motel on the water and stargazing through a telescope in an astronomical observatory.

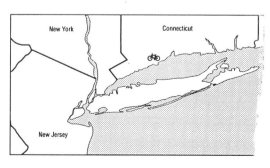

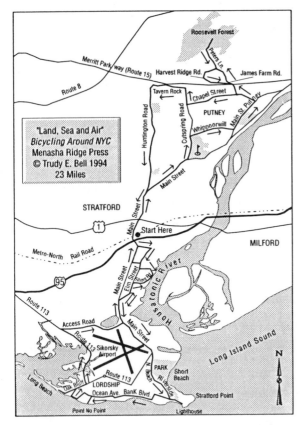

Land, Sea and Air"
Bicycling Around NYC
Menasha Ridge Press
© Trudy E. Bell 1994
23 Miles

are only a smidge higher than those off-season. And there's no required minimum stay—an almost unheard-of option during peak vacation season in the tri-state area!

Don't forget your evening clothes for a night of fine dining. There are two high-toned seafood restaurants across the street from Marnick's. Don't be put off by the Formica and the obvious grandparents-and-the-grandkids-for-a-weekend ambiance in Marnick's own coffee shop; the place has a mean kitchen for seafood.

From the 1950s through 1980, Stratford was a center for Shakespearean drama—in fact, the town was named for Stratford-on-Avon. Katharine Hepburn, James Earl Jones, Christopher Plummer, and other greats graced the stage at Stratford's Shakespeare Theatre (now renamed the American Festival Theatre) before it closed in 1983 and became a cultural park. For information call (203) 375-5000.

This Stratford ride—designed by my editorial colleague Glenn Zorpette, his girlfriend Jeanne Burke, and his history-buff buddy Wayne Lovington—can be combined with "Cruising the Milford Beaches" for a full weekend of cycling. The combined distance of both rides, plus the five-mile stretch in between, is about 55 miles, which can be done by strong cyclists in a single day—but at the penalty of not being able to explore all the nooks and crannies. Your choice. To aid you in plotting which way you might want to go first to make it a two-day overnight: the distance from the Stratford railroad station to Marnick's is under six miles; from the Stratford railroad station to the nearest point on the Milford Beaches ride is about five miles; from Marnick's to the nearest point on the Milford Beaches ride is about 10 miles. The directions for linking the two, mapped out by Wayne, are at the end of this chapter.

Stratford is less than 90 minutes from New York City's Grand Central Station on the Metro-North Commuter Railroad's New Haven line; see the preface for information about bicycle passes and allowed times. The ride starts at the Stratford railroad station. If you drive, you can also park at the station for free on the weekends; if you're staying at Marnick's you may prefer to go directly there, check in, and leave your car so you can tumble right into the steamy shower afterwards without hassling with bike racks and driving back and all.

All you need on this ride is a water bottle, as there is plenty to eat and drink along the way. In fact, you might want to arrive hungry and save your appetite for an early lunch at a bakery featuring powdery Portuguese rolls, a local favorite.

But before you head off, walk around the train station: the south building has been converted to the National Helicopter Museum, open a few hours each summer afternoon. Take a few moments to gaze at the carefully mounted black-and-white stills of Igor Sikorsky in formal jacket and homburg hat flying the erector-set frame of the first helicopter. The volunteer at the museum is generally a retired gentleman who knew Sikorsky personally, and will tell you Sikorsky came to Stratford originally to make flying boats, the first true airliners, and needed placid water on which to test them. So he set up shop on the usually quiet Housatonic River.

When you're ready to begin your ride, turn right out of the train station onto busy Main Street (Route 113), heading north. The gold dome directly ahead of you is Stratford's town hall; the street is lined with flowering cherries and dogwoods that bloom exuberantly in late April. Cross four-lane Connecticut State Route 1, continuing north for another three-quarters of a mile to a triangular grassy park with a bandstand; this is Paradise Green.

Stop and lock your bicycle's frame to the snakelike bike rack to explore the shops on your right. One of them is Altieri's deli and bakery, one of the few places one can obtain Portuguese rolls: round, flat rolls similar to peasant bread, whose opposite sides are pinched to form two little tails, the whole powdery with white flour. Glenn's favorite sandwich is tuna on a Portuguese roll. If you want to take some rolls back to the city, though, I'd advise you to wait until as close to your departure time as possible and to have the bakery put them into a plastic bag, because they dry out fast. At Paradise Green you can also enjoy an above-average slice of pizza, a Baskin-Robbins ice cream cone, and a tune-up of your bike at the local Schwinn dealer.

By the way, when I was there again in August, one house on the right a little south of Paradise Green had a ceramic bust of Elvis Presley on a purple-satin-draped altar in the front yard; only later did I realize that the day of my travel, August 16, was the anniversary of the King's passing (1977)! R.I.P.

After window-shopping and eating, continue north on Main Street, leaving the shops behind. In another three-quarters of a mile, just after the Cutspring Deli, turn left onto Cutspring Road—a road that was dirt until about 1950, said Glenn. On your right is Mill River Country Club, one of Stratford's two golf courses, bordered by a forsythia hedge that in late April is a quarter mile of glowing gold.

Make the first right onto rolling Whippoorwill Lane. A quarter mile down and to the left is a gingerbread-elaborate fantasy house built by a local real estate magnate who also loves old cars (amazing what you can learn from a local native guide).

At the "T" intersection at the end of the lane, turn left onto the unmarked Main Street-Putney, riding under the high-tension power lines and past the gravestones of the Putney Oronoque Cemetery; a few hundred yards later, turn right into the Boothe Memorial Park—the creation of a pair of eclectic, eccentric brothers, David Beach and Stephen Nicholas Boothe.

This is the former homestead of the Boothes, a very old Stratford family. Today there is the oddest assortment of buildings, including a Dutch windmill, an aviary, an organ house, an outdoor church, an old trolley station, a museum of local Indian artifacts, a set of old tollbooths from the Merritt Parkway, and the dome of an astronomical observatory. Picnic tables overlook the Housatonic River, which is visible only in the late fall, winter, and early spring before the trees are in leaf.

Walk through the sunken formal gardens and step into the 19th-century white clapboard Putney Chapel—a popular place for weddings, and formerly located a hundred yards north until the number of trucks colliding with it caused it to be placed in the Boothe Park for safekeeping. During brief hours some days, you can get a tour of the old Boothe home and the farm equipment museum. Large sheltered barbecue pits are available to groups, and seem to be a favorite with sociable retirees sitting in folding chairs and sipping cider while waiting for their chickens to grill.

If you're there on the second or fourth Friday of the month, the Boothe Memorial Astronomical Society offers meetings and views through the telescopes to the public.

When you've had your fill shaking your head at the sheer variety, roll your steed out of the drive and head right to continue north on Main Street. Turn left at the next intersection onto Chapel Street (the now-empty triangle was once the site of the Putney Chapel).

Less than half a mile later, turn right at the "Y" intersection onto James Farm Road. This intersection is impossible to miss, as in front of you is the Chapel Street Elementary School. Behind it are the segmented arched structures of the Harry B. Flood Junior High School, which is built with only one narrow slit of a permanently sealed window in each classroom—"not enough to see out of, but enough to tell if it was snowing," observed Wayne. The school was designed by an architect who believed that windows were not energy efficient and were distracting to students. "So for three years Glenn and I existed in a fluorescent-lit, temperature- and humidity-controlled, nearly subterranean hell," Wayne recalled.

James Farm Road passes over Connecticut's scenic Merritt Parkway. Perched atop each stone wall of the narrow concrete bridge is a majestic stone eagle, guarding the tree-lined rolling parkway below. The Merritt Parkway, stretching 38 miles across Connecticut between Greenwich and New Haven, was designed and built between 1934 and 1940 as Connecticut's first median-divided highway. It was named for Schuyler Merritt, a prominent Stamford, Connecticut resident and a nine-term congressman who envisioned and spearheaded a project for a scenic highway preserving as many trees and shrubs as possible. Each of its 35 overpasses is ornamented with elaborate sculptures in French, Italian, English, and classic Art Deco styles, no two of which are alike. The parkway, built as a Works Project Administration (W.P.A.) project after the Great Depression, was recently put on the National Register of Historic Places.

Continue across the bridge. Now you're climbing a bit. Turn left at the next "Y" intersection onto Peters Lane; it will be your second left after crossing over the Merritt Parkway. Peters Lane heads down for a while, past a log cabin on your left.

In three-quarters of a mile, you'll pass through the gates of the Roosevelt Forest, a state park that offers camping all year round—but only for Stratford residents and their guests. "It's the only way we've kept the place so clean," explained the phlegmatic guard at the kiosk who issued a pass for our car.

Cyclists can ride right through without a pass (go slowly over the wicked speed bumps), although you might want to stop and get a map of the color-coded hiking and biking trails. The old "blue dot" trail goes right through the park, bringing you out near the top of Cutspring Road, but it is passable only on foot or a mountain bike. The park is open from 9 A.M. to 3 P.M. during the week and to 5 P.M. on the weekends. There are no facilities, so bring water and a snack. But if solitude and trees and birds and a retreat with a book away from people is what you have in mind, here is an idyll.

When you're ready to leave, retrace your path out past the guard's kiosk onto Peters Lane. For sheer variety, take the first right onto Harvest Ridge Road, an obviously new road that curves in a gentle downhill past some large new homes, bringing you back out onto James Farm Road just north of the Merritt Parkway. Turn right to cross over the parkway between the two guardian eagles, and turn right at the Chapel Street Elementary School and the Flood Junior High to resume your progress on Chapel Street.

At the end of Chapel, turn right at the "T" intersection onto Cutspring Road, noting the little arrow on the pavement to your right painted by a bike club and directing you the same way. In a quarter mile, turn left onto Tavern Rock Road, still following the little arrows; this is a steep but short climb through sun-dappled forest that makes the effort worthwhile. Turn left at the first stop sign onto Huntington Road for a long and gentle coast through Stratford's northern residential area. The traffic is moderate and moves faster than 30 miles per hour, but the road is wide and the two-mile downhill a pleasure.

Huntington road merges with Main Street (Route 113) at familiar Paradise Green. Cross U.S. Highway 1 and continue past the town hall with its gold dome topped with a weather vane, but be sure to look back at its spectacular colonnaded front overlooking the park. Pass the railroad station and ride under Interstate 95. You are now in the old section of Stratford. At the flagpole in the center of the road, turn left onto East Broadway, and right onto Elm Street—the original main street through old Stratford.

Take your time down Elm Street so as not to miss the spirit and the treasures of time. Elm Street was once part of the old King's Highway that generally followed Indian trails and was the oldest mail route in America. The first post rider made the trip from New York to Boston in January 1673; your imagination can boggle at the snow and other tribulations. Elm Street also was once canopied by majestic, 100-foot-tall elms, until they fell casualties to the devastating Dutch Elm disease earlier in this century. Now you'll see good-sized oaks and maples and magnificent quanzans—the last being my absolutely favorite tree in the world, a variety of flowering cherry that in late April is dressed up for dancing in fluffy, ruffled, tissue-soft pale pink blossoms.

Look at the houses to your right and left. Many are fine middle-aged homes, built during a spurt of growth in the 1940s and 1950s; others are two or three centuries old, with tiny plaques displaying their dates with demure pride. The red Edward Curtis house on the corner of Broad Street, built in 1745, has settled so that it is tilted at an angle reminiscent of the Leaning Tower of Pisa, yet the loving care of its paint and grounds bespeaks its being still very much alive.

Across Elm Street from the Curtis house is Academy Hill, where local soldiers gathered before shipping off to fight in the Civil War. The cemetery there includes the grave of William Samuel Johnson, who was the chairman of the committee on style of the Constitution of the United States. Responsible for the form of the final document, Johnson was in effect the editor of the U.S. Constitution, and many scholars credit him for the poetic nature of the Preamble. His father, the Anglican minister Samuel Johnson, was the first president of New York City's Kings College—better known today as Columbia University.

At the first light, which marks the intersection with Ferry Boulevard, you have a choice. If you wish to link this Stratford ride with the one "Cruising the Milford Beaches," make the first left onto Ferry Boulevard and pick up the directions at the end of this chapter. Otherwise, ride across Ferry Boulevard and make an immediate left just on the other side onto the alley-narrow, unmarked Stratford Avenue.

Turn right at the end onto Lockwood Avenue, keeping one eye to the right for the creek deep in a stone-walled bed only three feet across. At the dock (Bond's Dock), follow the one-way sign to the right as the road becomes Shore Road. But before continuing, stop to gaze at the red-paint-peeling dilapidated cottage on stilts over the water.

This oystering cottage, which is the last of many fishermen's shacks that used to dot the shoreline, was where Katharine Hepburn stayed when she was acting in Stratford's Shakespeare Theatre around 1957. A bit beyond, you'll pass the theatre itself up on a rise to the right, under extensive renovation in the late 1980s by the State of Connecticut.

After Shore Road bends right, you'll be riding along a small cove, now unfortunately overlooked by some modern condos. This little inlet, known as Mac's Harbor, was the landing place traditionally ascribed to Stratford's first settlers, who arrived in 1639. At the inner end of the harbor was Stratford's first meeting house, burial ground, and mill—no traces of which are perceptible now. At that time, Stratford had not yet changed its original Indian name of Cupheag. (The first reference to the name Stratford appeared in 1643.)

Turn left at the stop sign to resume your journey down Elm Street. Half a mile later, turn left at the light onto Main Street (Route 113). After passing a strip mall with its hamburger stand and a deli and a place called the Cricket (a local hangout famous for its foot-long hotdogs), you'll find yourself riding by chain-link fences of hangars, jet engine manufacturers, and the Sikorsky Airport. The airport is small, intended for light aircraft and general aviation, and small commercial planes making scheduled stops. Historically, it is also the site of Sikorsky's maiden flights and subsequent refinements of the world's first practical helicopter. At this point, the wide highway also develops wide painted shoulders that make your cycling comfortable.

About a mile after joining Route 113, bear left onto the lightly traveled Short Beach Road (Route 113 curves right). The nicely developed Short Beach Park used to be a town dump; now sailboards dot the water, and picnic tables and barbecue grills await your pleasure. Windsurfing is safe even for beginners, because the Long Island Sound has no big waves. A resident's sticker or pass is required for entrance by cars, but cyclists can cruise through without stopping.

After exiting the park, turn left to resume your route on Short Beach Road. At the dead end sign, turn right onto Lighthouse Avenue, then hang an immediate left onto Riverdale Drive. Here ordinary middle-class homes mix with understated million-dollar residences in an odd historical hodgepodge; between them all, you get some beautiful glimpses of the Long Island Sound.

Turn left at the "T" intersection onto Prospect Drive, ride past the former gun club of the Remington Arms Company, until the road dead-ends at a lighthouse. This peninsula is that part of Connecticut jutting farthest out into the Sound.

After a little sightseeing around the neatly kept lighthouse grounds, turn around and ride back out Prospect Drive. Make the first left onto Cove Place, heading toward the water. At the end, turn right onto Bank Boulevard. On your right are widely spaced stately mansions with acres of green lawns; on your left another lawn slopes down to the sand of Lordship Beach, which commands a view straight across the lapping Sound to distant Long Island. Linger along this half-mile, for it is among the most beautiful sections of the ride.

At the end of Bank Boulevard, turn right onto Lordship Road, and make an immediate left onto Ocean Avenue. In three blocks you'll reach Washington Parkway, distinguished because it is a wide boulevard with a stretch of lawn separating the two directions of sparse traffic. Turn left here and go to the sea wall at the end; Marnick's Motel—named after its founders Marge and Nick— is waiting for you on the right.

Architecturally and every other way, Marnick's looks like nothing special. It's a two-story high family motel built in the "modern" era several decades back, with basic clean motel facilities. The dress-down atmosphere of the attached diner encourages Sunday brunches with grandparents and the kids, both of whom you'll see aplenty. Definitely middle class, with no fanfare—a business whose success is apparently based on solid repeat customers rather than flashy advertising.

But you know the injunction about the proverbial book and its cover. Order one of Marnick's lobster rolls and you'll think you've died and gone to heaven— sweet, tender morsels of real lobster (not yuppie Sealegs) drenched in butter stuffed into a top-split hotdog bun. A classic.

When I was there in August and wanted nothing so much as to lean back on my terrace with a private dinner alfresco overlooking the lapping Sound, I brought back the *Daily News* and a couple of tall cold ones from the nearby corner Penguin Market (which has a walk-in freezer from which you make your selection) and ordered to take out Marnick's special of the night: steamed mussels over linguini. We're talking serious butter and garlic, and enough food for two, so piping hot I could barely carry the tin to my room. The total tab was about $10. If something a bit more upscale—and more pricey—is what you'd prefer, there are two seafood restaurants across the street, which will be glad to pour you a glass of wine over a linen table cloth.

If Marnick's is not the destination of your day's ride (too bad), retrace your path back one block and turn left to continue on Ocean Avenue. Take the second left onto Third Avenue and turn right at the end to pedal along Beach Drive between real beach bungalows on pilings of wood or cinder block. At the end, turn right onto unmarked Fifth Avenue and cycle past permanent houses; one to the right with a very large lawn mystified me because tomatoes were planted in containers in the back. (Maybe the soil in the containers was better than what nature provided so close to the beach?)

Turn left at the "T" intersection onto the unmarked Ocean Avenue, and make an immediate left onto the unmarked Oak Bluff Avenue. In a few hundred yards, this road will dead-end in the parking lot of Long Beach. Car parking is available only for Stratford residents, but cyclists aren't given a second glance by the bored, novel-reading college student guard under the beach umbrella. So bring your swimsuit and sun lotion. The beach is gravelly (let's face it, the Connecticut shore isn't Malibu—or even the Jersey Shore) but the Long Island Sound is bathwater warm and placid, particularly late in the summer.

When you've enjoyed your fill of gulls and sun and (mini)surf, return the way you've entered, continuing up Oak Bluff Avenue. At the four-way stop at Stratford Avenue, turn left onto the continuation of Route 113, taking care to avoid the occasional patches of sand on the narrow shoulder. You are now riding through a rustling saltwater marsh, one of the largest remaining on the East Coast north of Florida and one that is now protected.

After about three-quarters of a mile, make the first right into Sikorsky Airport to gawk at the Corsair Memorial: a pedestal holding a bent-wing, propeller-driven Chance-Vought Corsair F-4U fighter responsible for winning some of the great air battles in the Pacific theatre during World War II. Nearly 6700 Corsairs were built during the war in the large group of brick buildings then called Chance Vought Aircraft, now visible on the far side of the airport when standing at the memorial. If your wanderlust includes the wild blue yonder, you can also enjoy watching the small planes take off and land.

Exit the airport by the way you rode in, turning right to continue north on Route 113. Turn right at the light onto unmarked Access Road, past a vacant lot dotted with golden dandelions, several plowed fields, and the little lake called Fresh Pond on your left. At the "T" intersection with the hangars of Textron Lycoming directly ahead, turn left onto Main Street, watching for the drainage grates along the shoulder that could grab your wheels and cause a spill. Just after the wide painted shoulder begins, turn right at the "Y" intersection onto Elm Street—this time heading north to take in some sights missed on the way down.

Number 1670 Elm Street—a gray, flat-topped house with a pink door—was the house of Alfred Ely Beach, one of the first publishers of *Scientific American* when it was still a weekly tabloid newspaper in the 1840s. A brilliant writer and inventor, Beach created the famous pneumatic subway beneath New York City, first made public in the 1870s and whose tunnel was featured in the movie *Ghostbusters*. Beach also invented the swinging-arm typewriter, a design that remained in vogue for a good 100 years. He also invented a pneumatic tube system used for mail delivery underneath New York City, and machines he invented made it possible to tunnel under the Hudson and Thames Rivers. But his real monetary success came from *Scientific American*, and the magazine and some patent money supported the next four generations of Beaches in Stratford.

Continuing north, you'll also pass the grounds of the Phelps Mansion, which unfortunately, was razed following fires in the 1970s. The estate was the site of one of the most famous documented occurrences of poltergeists—"the Stratford knockings"—in 1850 and 1851. At the time, the knockings were attributed to the restless spirit of Goody Bassett, a woman who two centuries earlier was convicted as a witch and hung—the first execution in Fairfield County and the second in Connecticut.

Farther north, the two white wooden pillars topped with flagpoles flank the front entrance to the American Festival Theatre. Most remarkable now in the overgrown parking lot is the small gray stucco outbuilding that may have stored costumes, whose windows are blocked by black-and-white posters of actors and actresses in various classic roles—including Katharine Hepburn, unmistakable for her high cheekbones and radiant smile.

One block past the next light, turn left onto unmarked Academy Hill. On your left is the white-shuttered Judson House Museum, home of Ye Olde Stratford Historical Societie (yes, indeed). Its hours are Wednesday, Saturday, and Sunday 11 A.M.-4 P.M.; for information on exhibits, call (203) 378-0630. (I missed its limited hours during both my visits—too bad, for it's an excellent example of a 1750-era Stratford house.)

At the end of Academy Hill, turn right onto the busy Main Street. On your immediate right will be the beige clapboard Christ Church; it is the oldest parish in the Episcopal Diocese of Connecticut. On your left is the house of William Samuel Johnson (you remember, editor of the U.S. Constitution); the spacious white mansion, built in 1799, now gives professional offices to several doctors.

On the left is the white-steepled First Congregational Church; the graveyard in the rear has a lot of 18th-century slate gravestones carved with the angel of death. If you're into rubbings, bring your paper and crayons.

Ride past the flagpole, following Main Street as it bends left and passes under the overpass for Interstate 95. Make an immediate right, and you're back in the Stratford train station parking lot, ready to enjoy a glass of iced tea at the station coffee shop before returning to New York City on Metro-North.

For those wishing to enhance their historical appreciation of the ride by learning more about Stratford's colorful history, there are two major books. The most recent is *In Pursuit of Paradise: history of the town of Stratford, Connecticut* by Lewis G. Knapp, published by the Stratford Historical Society in 1989. An earlier one, with some antiquarian details about Goody Bassett, the Phelps mansion and its poltergeists, is William Howard Wilcoxon's *The History of Stratford, Connecticut, 1639-1939*, Stratford Tercentenary Commission, 1939, kindly lent to me by Glenn.

For roadway buffs, at least two excellent articles describe the architecture and history of the Merritt Parkway. The most comprehensive and accessible is "Fifty Years on the Merritt," by Tim Appenzeller and Marius Muresanu, published on pages 58-67 of the November 1990 (vol. 10, no. 3) issue of *Metropolis*— a New York City-based magazine of urban architecture and design widely available on newsstands. A shorter account is "The Merritt Parkway: More Beautiful with Age," in *Connecticut Automotive Magazine*, vol. 1., no. 1, April 1991, pages 26-28.

* * * *

To connect the Stratford ride to the Milford ride from the intersection of Elm Street and Ferry Boulevard: head east on Ferry Boulevard, crossing the

Washington Bridge over the Housatonic River. You have now entered New Haven County and the western outskirts of Milford. Ride along the busy main U.S. Route 1 (Bridgeport Avenue), past shops and antique stores, until the first major intersection. At the light, turn right onto Naugatuck Avenue.

Now, head straight while counting the right turns. At the fifth right, make the right turn onto Milford Point Road and follow it until it dead-ends at the Smith-Hubbell Wildlife Sanctuary—a good place to stop and prowl around. If you're lucky, perhaps a groundskeeper will be available to identify the various sea birds.

When you're ready to move on, backtrack a little ways along Milford Point Road, bearing right onto Seaview Avenue to pedal alongside the stretch of beaches overlooking the Long Island Sound. On your right are numerous short access roads to the beaches, which are open to the public. These roads also have houses with neighbors and close-knit families; according to Wayne, "bicycle visitors are almost always welcomed for conversation and cold drinks. Really. I'm not kidding."

Seaview Avenue eventually changes its name to East Broadway. At the first large intersection, look to the right at the Soundview Hotel on the beach: another relic reminiscent of Marnick's only, alas, it is now abandoned. Continue straight through the condominiums along East Broadway.

At the "T" intersection, turn left onto Viscount Drive. Take the first right onto Monroe Street, and then take the next right onto Nettleton Road. Follow this bumpy, winding road through the marsh grasses of the Silver Sands State Park. The park, now under construction, is expected to be completed in the late 1990s, featuring ballfields, a boardwalk, concessions, and the like. At present, enjoy its untouched wilderness.

At the end of the park service road, turn left onto East Broadway (the other end of the one you'd been riding on earlier). On both sides of the divided boulevard, you'll be passing closely packed beach homes. After a mile or so, turn left at the major intersection onto Seaside Avenue. A mile later, at the long and skinny park of the Milford Green, you'll intersect with Broad Street (Connecticut State Route 162).

Turn right onto Broad Street into Milford Center, pedaling alongside the green. At the first intersection, turn left onto High Street, and an eighth of a mile later turn right into the Milford train station. Now you're ready to begin the Milford ride.

DOVER PLAINS TO KENT

Fairfield County, Connecticut and Dutchess County, New York

This ride was indirectly inspired by one avid touring-cyclist friend of mine, Richard Shuldiner, who announced one summer that he intended to spend every weekend in two-wheeled exploration of what lay at the end of each Metro-North Commuter Railroad and Long Island Rail Road line.

That thought led to a number of the rides in this book, particularly this one—for how else would someone end up in obscure Dover Plains? Unless you're into drag racing, it's hardly a hot tourist spot (there's a nearby drag strip of some renown). But that makes it perfect for some secluded bicycle touring. This particular route was suggested by Alice Pitcher and Kemper Peacock, the proprietors of Old Drovers Inn in Dover Plains, who also kindly provided my cycling companion Alan Wolf and me with a complete map.

Although we went in late July, this ride is ideal for autumn: in late September through mid-October the golden foliage of the Hudson Valley and the Berkshire Mountains can rival that in Vermont. On this ride you will tour both, starting in the Hudson Valley and eventually climbing into the foothills of the Berkshires. Along the way, roadside stands offer homemade jams and jellies, fresh-pressed cider, and a dozen varieties of crunchy apples.

Two hours north of New York City by either car or Metro-North Commuter Railroad, this area is something you'd want to save for

Ride Ratings

Length: 27 miles
Configuration: loop
Difficulty: First third is flat to rolling; an occational steep climb; little to no traffic
Surface: good pavement throughout; optional mile of hard-pack in the Indian reservation

—Highlights: This almost traffic-free ride features some lovely country scenery including the oldest covered bridge in Connecticut; there's a chance to stay in a bed-and-breakfast and shop for antiques and gourmet items.

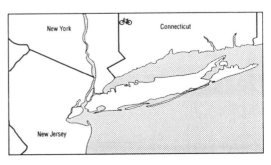

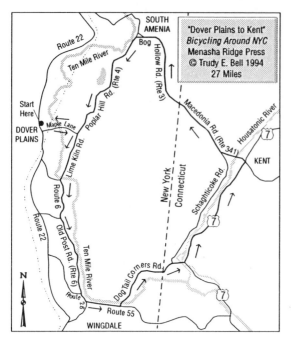

"Dover Plains to Kent"
Bicycling Around NYC
Menasha Ridge Press
© Trudy E. Bell 1994
27 Miles

a weekend minivacation rather than a one-day trip. Even after you've pedaled the relatively short basic ride, there are so many scenic roads—particularly in northwestern Connecticut—that you can't go wrong just heading out to explore with the bike map published by the Connecticut Department of Transportation (see the appendix for information on obtaining this map and the preface for obtaining a pass for taking your bicycle on Metro-North).

The ride starts at the Dover Plains railroad station— the last stop of Metro-North's Harlem line. By the way, if you plan to stay at the Old Drovers Inn and have arrived by train too late on a Friday night to pedal the four miles to the inn, the proprietors would be happy to meet you at the station and drive you and your bikes there.

If you drive from New York City, take the Saw Mill River Parkway to its end north of Katonah, then Interstate 684 and to New York State Route 22 north. Park either at the Dover Plains railroad station, or at Old Drovers Inn (if you're staying there), which is located just off Route 22 on Old Post Road (Dutchess County Route 6) between Wingdale and Dover Plains.

Near the Dover Plains train station, you may want to forage for water and a light snack at Alfie's, the Hometown Luncheonette, or other eateries, but it's not essential. On this ride, you don't have to worry about starving: between the stretches of trees and scenery there are plenty of little oases of restaurants and other services.

Turn left out of the train station parking lot, cross the tracks, and head east on Maple Lane. You're riding through the outskirts of Dover Plains, a rural town that covers a surprisingly large area. After crossing over the Ten Mile River, which is more like a large creek, you'll begin riding along cornfields on your right. Bear right at the yield sign at "Y" intersection onto the quiet Lime Kiln Road. This stretch of the ride is flat. With the rocky palisades rising to your left, it is quite evident that you are riding along a valley between two ranges of hills.

Shortly after crossing an iron bridge, turn left at the stop sign at the "Y" intersection onto Old Post Road (Dutchess County Route 6). At this intersection, a lone bench under a solitary tree turns the traffic triangle into a tiny park. Since Old Post Road has no shoulder but a bit more traffic, ride with care. In late July, the fields of growing corn filled the air with their fresh green sweetness and their golden tassels stretched to the green hills beyond. The sides of the road were practically hopping with wild rabbits. Already I could feel the city's tension easing from my shoulders.

Within a quarter mile of joining Old Post Road you get your first climb, a taste of the rollers later in the ride. Near the crest of your second climb, at the intersection of Old Post Road and East Duncan Hill, is Old Drovers Inn. The three-story white clapboard farmhouse peeps out from under the heavy trees. There the proprietors Alice Pitcher and Kemper Peacock met Alan and me with warm smiles while their tiny white Yorkshire terrier Jed (whom Alan aptly called a "guard puppy") regaled us with energetic barks. All then showed us through the inn. The name refers to the inn's past, where as far back as 1750 it catered to the traveling cattle drovers: a group of East Coast "cowboys" who bought herds of cattle and swine from New England farmers and drove the animals down the post roads to New York City markets. Eventually the drovers got so rich they hired others to do the dirty work, while they themselves galloped ahead to make arrangements at inns and to down more than one glass of rum.

Although the drovers are long gone, their watering place remains. Restored and preserved by Olin Chester Potter in 1937, the inn still serves hot buttered rum and mulled ale in the cold months. A musket still hangs above the great stone fireplace of the Tap Room with its low, heavy-beamed ceiling. An old stone-floored kitchen still has its cauldron and pig-scalder.

Upstairs, on wide pine floors, is a handsome double bed in a bedstead carved to look like a sleigh, fine antiques, and beautiful comforters. Three of the four guest rooms have working wood-burning fireplaces. The walls of the Federal Room—where breakfast is served on polished mahogany tables—are decorated with murals of the Hudson Valley painted in 1941 by Edward Paine, a noted muralist of the period.

Be forewarned, the inn is not cheap; in fact, its rooms and its dinners sport prices typical of midtown Manhattan, in the range of what I consider "expense account" places. On the other hand, when Alan and I were there, it was offering sophisticated Manhattan-type fare, such as cheddar cheese soup and pan-roasted quail. The cost per night also includes a breakfast. For information and reservations, call (914) 832-9311.

Across the street is an antiques shop for browsing, plus the private Catholic shrine, San Silverio. The stations of the cross are in an outdoor garden where you can stroll for peace and contemplation.

From Old Drovers Inn, continue south on Old Post Road, riding along the plateau at the crest and then coasting downhill, under high-tension power lines, alongside the Ten Mile River to your left.

Nearly three miles after leaving Old Drovers Inn, bear left onto Dutchess County Route 26. A quarter of a mile later, bear left at the "Y" intersection onto New York State Route 55. This stretch here is a long, straight downhill. This is also a section with several restaurants, among them il Compare (offering Italian lunch and dinners) and the Riverview Tavern.

Less than a mile later, turn left onto Dutchess County Route 22. You are now at the Webatuk Trading Company craft village, where you might want to lock your bike and walk around to watch the old water wheel. Or peek into the showroom of Hunt Country Furniture, watch some artisans at work in the pottery studio, or sample some homemade soup and the assorted teas and coffees at the Pepper Mill Cafe. True to its name, the Pepper Mill has on display pepper mills imported from around the world.

Continue north on Route 22 (also called Dog Tail Corners Road), which will bend right and then begin climbing. Steeply. Well, at some point you have to make up for the generally downhill route up to now. But the steep climb lasts only about a quarter mile before you get a bit of downhill relief again. Soon a little sign informs you that you have left New York State and have passed into Fairfield County, Connecticut. Ahead of you is a lovely prospect of beautifully wooded hills; be thankful you are not going to climb them.

Now you are riding downhill through a stunning and steep rocky gorge over the Housatonic River, through a small pine forest whose needles perfume the air. Put on the brakes to enjoy this short but rather wild descent, gazing at the island in the river to your left. This area is a park with hiking trails, which I encourage you to take into the woods and over boulders to see an impressive waterfall.

Best of all, at the base of the hill is an ancient, wooden covered bridge over the river: Bulls Bridge. The narrow, one-lane structure is 109 feet long and was built by one Jacob Bull, a farmer who operated a gristmill and an iron forge. There is some controversy over its date, but historians agree it had to be sometime during the first four decades of the 19th century. Built before the age of steel and the automobile, wooden bridges were essential to the rural highway system: they were covered to protect the wooden trusses and floors from moisture and rot. Now on the National Register of Historic Places, Bulls Bridge is one of three remaining in Connecticut, which used to have more than 60. From the bridge, the view to the north is of water tumbling down a dam built in the early 20th century by the Connecticut Light and Power Company.

Here you have a choice of how to cover the four miles to Kent: you can either ride through Bulls Bridge and make an immediate left onto U.S. Route 7 heading north past various shops, or you can stay on the western side of the Housatonic to travel along an obscure forested road past an Indian reservation (including a mile of hard-packed dirt). Alan Wolf and I decided to do both.

Alan took Route 7 north, and reported that although the traffic was moderate, the road was essentially level with a narrow but usable shoulder. Immediately on the other side of Bulls Bridge is the Bull Bridge Inn and Restaurant and a Country Mart with a gas station. A mile and a half north of the bridge is a real treat: Fellerman Glass, a studio where the prizewinning master craftsman Stephen Fellerman will give tours and fascinate you with demonstrations of glassblowing Tuesdays through Saturdays. In the store Alan saw entire lamps made from glass, as well as other sculptures. Three miles north of the bridge is Country Things, a store selling all kinds of crafts items for country homes. Route 7 takes you directly through the Main Street of Kent, with all its antiques and gourmet shops and cafes.

I opted to take the road less traveled, retracing our route from Bulls Bridge half a mile back up Route 22, and making the first right onto the unmarked Schaghticoke Road. This road is narrow and flat, with zero traffic its whole way, and so quiet that the loudest sound was the croaking of frogs in the underbrush. Soon you're riding even with a line of pines 50 feet high, their trunks bare except for their uppermost branches. Between their trunks to the right, you'll catch glimpses of the placid Housatonic River. The road dips right down to the river, where fishermen may be snoozing, and shortly thereafter its pavement turns into hard-packed dirt. Occasionally to your left are sheer rock walls and boulders.

The road bends right, and a sign informs you that you are entering the Schaghticoke Indian Reservation. On your left is a cart with great iron-spoked wheels (kind of putting your bicycle tires to shame). Further on, on your left, is a campground complete with a white, blue, red, and yellow wigwam. A bit beyond is an ancient graveyard, with tiny, weathered stones. The most remarkable one that struck me was to "Eunice Maumee, a Christian Indian princess, 1756-1860." What a wealth of questions are begged by that short legend!

Shortly thereafter, the pavement resumes. You'll pass the Kent Water Pollution Treatment Location Septage Lagoons on your right, and then emerge from the forest into a meadow that in late July was alive with birds. The road bends left and ends at Connecticut State Route 341. To visit Kent, turn right at the stop sign onto Route 341 and coast downhill for three-quarters of a mile, crossing the iron bridge over the Housatonic River.

Kent, Connecticut, is one of those towns that, like Woodstock, New York or Chester, New Jersey, has been made into a kind of craft and boutique village. Buy a homemade ice cream cone at the Cobble Court Cookery and then stroll up and down the main street, visiting the various cottage-sized stores tempting you with wind chimes, fragrant potpourri in tiny wicker baskets, straw whisk brooms, carved chairs, ceramic cookie presses, and flavored mustards whose tops are bonneted in gingham squares and tied with yarn. A perfect opportunity to pick up some small items for birthdays and no-occasion gifts—as long as you've brought along enough bungee cords for fastening your purchases onto your bike!

To continue the ride, retrace your route back across the Housatonic River onto Route 341, also called Macedonia Brook Road. About a mile after crossing the river the road begins to climb, first steeply, then more gradually, but generally uphill for a couple of miles. About three miles northwest of Kent, you'll cross back into New York State, and the road changes name to Bog Hollow Road (Dutchess County Route 3). It also becomes a fun rollercoaster up-and-down through field and forest and farmland, wonderful for using your momentum to try and top the next rise. Ride it to the end.

At the "T" intersection, turn left onto Dutchess County Route 4, another rolling road through peaceful farm fields. At the next "T" intersection, turn left to stay on Route 4 (County Route 105 goes to the right), and begin the long grind up Poplar Hill Road. At the crest half a mile later, you're rewarded with the view of several tree-covered ridges paralleling your route. At the next crest, note the trees and moss growing from the huge, bald boulder.

A mile and a quarter later, turn right onto Maple Avenue (McCarthy Avenue goes left) into Dover Plains. Three-quarters of a mile later, you're back at the train station.

NEW JERSEY

OF CONVENTS AND BIKE PATHS

Morris County, New Jersey

Ride Ratings

Length: 8 or 10 miles
Configuration: loop
Difficulty: very easy; mostly flat, 5 miles on paved bike paths; little or no traffic
Surface: good pavement throughout

—Highlights: An almost traffic-free route through beautiful and peaceful wooded preserves; opportunities for picnicking and observing wildlife; touring the grounds of the College of St. Elizabeth, or watching pro football teams practice on the grounds of Fairleigh Dickinson University; this ride can be combined with "Exploring the Great Swamp" for a total of 32 miles.

If you haven't been on a bike for more years than you care to admit, this is an ideal starter ride for the bicycling season. Because the terrain is so gentle and there is so little traffic, it's a great ride for rank beginners to the joys and freedom of bicycle touring, for a parent toting an infant in a bike seat, or for children on or off training wheels. It is also a very beautiful ride, with 60 percent of the riding being on paved bicycle paths and most of the rest on quiet, wooded, older suburban lanes. You will be tempted often to stop and stretch your legs.

The ride is on two levels: flat for the first couple of miles, then gently descending to the level of the Loantaka Brook Recreation Area for another four miles of flat cycling, and climbing back up again for the end. Not to worry: no hill is steep, and with a little patience and a lower gear, you should feel satisfied at the end.

The only services on this ride are the drinking fountains and bathrooms in the Loantaka Brook Recreation Area. For an eight-mile excursion that's hardly likely to be a problem, although you might want to take some raisins from home. Better yet, pack a picnic lunch. Loantaka is so restful, with its picnic tables, barbecue grills, duck ponds, trails, and playground equipment, that you're likely to want to make an afternoon of it and relax. In fact, because of the public grills, you might want to throw in some hot dogs and charcoal.

Strong riders needn't feel left

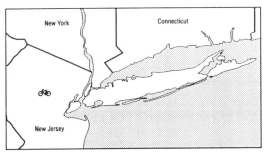

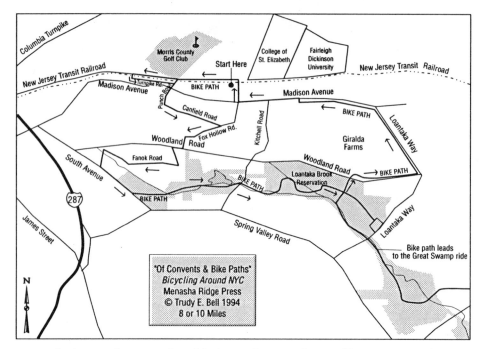

out and give up because the ride is so short and easy. If you want a longer excursion, combine this ride with the longer version of the ride through the Great Swamp Wildlife Refuge for a total of about 32 miles. Specific instructions are given in "Exploring the Great Swamp."

But back to this little gem. The ride begins at the driveway next to the Convent Station railroad station. If you're taking the train from New York City, consult the preface for restrictions and other details about taking a bike on New Jersey Transit trains. If you drive, on weekends and holidays you can park your car for free in the parking lot. According to the signs, during the work week you need a Morris County resident sticker to park at the meters (which cost an unbelievable 25 cents for 12 hours of time!) During the week the station house is open, giving access to restrooms and machines dispensing drinks and snacks.

Turn left out of the train parking lot and cross the tracks. Immediately, you are facing the entrance to the College of St. Elizabeth. The manicured grounds are so inviting that you would be remiss if you passed the opportunity to explore. So, enter the gates. The majestic stone administration building on the road that curves to the right is styled like an Old World cathedral. If you ride a couple tenths of a mile down the main road to your left, at the greenhouse you'll see a sign that reads ENTRANCE TO NAZARETH: A PLACE OF PRAYER AND REFLECTION.

And so it is. Up on a rise to your left is a narrow asphalt walking path that meanders through the trees, with benches before stone icons of the Madonna and Child and of several saints. Marked on trees are the stations of the cross. A quarter of a mile later the path comes to an end in a little round plaza with a seven-foot-high crucifix under a sheltering tree. The quiet and contemplation of the place can't help but seep into your spirit, no matter your specific religious background.

When you return to the bike path—either now, or when you come back at the end of the ride—you might want to explore the unpaved section that heads off to the east (to the left as you emerge from the college or to the right as you approach from the train station). That is opposite the way you'll be heading for the main ride. Its hard-packed dirt and gravel dips under heavy shade trees in the most delightful shady lane that, unfortunately, peters out into a stony track less than a mile down the way. But it is a pretty detour while it lasts, and for me the path less taken evokes the best appeal of the open road.

In any event, for the main ride, head west (right out of the college grounds, left from the train station) onto the paved section of the bike path. Officially called the Traction Line Recreation Trail, it was dedicated in June 1986 and resulted from a cooperative effort among the Morris County Park Commission, Jersey Central Power & Light, and the New Jersey Department of Transportation. It parallels the railroad tracks, which are to your left, and various neighborhoods are behind fences and hedges to your right. The bike path is punctuated by the stations of one of those fitness circuits, where you can try your strength at leaping over railroad ties or doing sit-ups. A jogger may pass you on your travels; wave in the courteous custom.

After half a mile on the path, at the second miniature stop sign on this bike path (I think those tiny stop signs are so darling), turn left, cross the tracks, and make an immediate left onto Turnpike Road. (The bike path actually continues for another mile ahead and its peace and beauty and its traverse under a stone bridge are worth continued exploration to its end. But then you should retrace it to return to this spot; there is no way, in a reasonable distance, to use side streets to do a loop without pedaling on at least one extremely busy highway.) Turnpike Road parallels the train tracks, taking you back the way you had just come.

Where Turnpike Road dips, turn right at the stop sign onto Punchbowl Road. Cross the extremely busy Madison Avenue (New Jersey State Local Route 24) onto Canfield Road, noting the castlelike brick building to your right labeled The Abbey. Shady Canfield Road curves left beneath stately maples, the street marked by old-fashioned gas streetlamps that are aglow even during the day. Enjoy these gas street lamps: even though a product of a bygone age, you still find them occasionally in the oldest neighborhoods. Note the four stately brick mansions on your right, followed by a cool wooded hollow.

In half a mile, turn right onto Foxhollow Road. Enjoy your descent on this narrow, quiet, winding road. Turn left at the "T" intersection onto Canfield Way, and then right at the end onto the moderately busy Woodland Avenue. Make an immediate left onto Symor Drive. Now you're back on the level for a while, riding through a quiet neighborhood that is neither old nor new.

Take the second right onto Fanok Road, turning left at the end into the parking lot of the Morris County Recreation Center. Ride straight through the parking lot and out through the other side. The swimming pool looks so inviting with all its boisterous children that I wish I could tell you to bring your swimsuit and join the fun. Alas, it's only for Morris County residents and their guests. And although you'll see the Seaton Hackney Stables, which do give riding lessons, you must sign up for a course of 10 weeks at a time. Oh, well, you're on a mount of a different type.

At the end of the parking lot, turn left at the stop sign onto moderately busy but wide South Avenue. Pass Bell Communications Research, one office of the entity split off from Bell Laboratories in 1984 with the breakup of the Bell Telephone System, and now charged with researching advances for your local phone service. Don't despair of the traffic on South Street, for you're on it for only a short stretch.

In a quarter mile turn left into the Loantaka Brook Recreation Area, making an immediate right onto the paved bicycle path. If you feel the need for water or a bathroom, then ride through the parking lot to the picnic area straight ahead. Here there are picnic tables, a picnic shelter with a fireplace, and barbecue grills, where you can relax with the hotdogs and fixin's you may have brought. The bike path that begins there joins the one you were on in a few hundred yards.

When you're ready, continue along the path. Eventually you'll emerge into the open at another parking lot with grassy areas and more picnic tables overlooking a popular and large duck pond a partially dammed area of Loantaka Brook. Ride through the parking lot to its entrance, turning left onto the unmarked Kitchell Road, then turning right onto the continuation of the paved bike path.

This path meanders through the sunlight that filters down among the slender trees. Depending on the time of year, I've seen broad-leafed plants, soft grasses, wild violets, and even bright orange mushrooms. At one point the path dips and crosses a shallow creek bed, just like old colonial roads used to do. You can either ride through the flowing water (just test your brakes on the other side) or avoid the wetness by lifting your bike and walking across the nine concrete stepping stones on your left.

Where the path is intersected by another paved bike path, turn left. (If you turn right, you may continue on the longer version of the Great Swamp ride.)

Cross the busy Woodland Avenue to continue on the bike path straight ahead, which curves right around a large field and parallels Woodland. Cross the entrance driveway into the industrial park Giralda Farms; signs bill it as the ultimate corporate environment, which is easy to believe when you're gazing at the grassy swards and wooded copses. Not too shabby to have this nice bike path for a lunchtime spin around the 310-acre grounds, either.

Begin climbing a gentle but steady rise. (You do have to make up for the descent at the beginning of the ride, after all!) Follow the bike path as it turns left to continue around the periphery of Giralda Farms, this time along Loantaka Way. The gentle climb continues, but when you reach the crest don't zip too fast down the other side, for you must walk your bike across the next road crossing.

Follow the path as it turns left again, this time to parallel Madison Avenue (Local Route 24) heading west; aren't you glad you are not riding in that busy traffic?

Unfortunately, your friendly bike path ends at Treadwell Avenue. Carefully cross the very busy two-lane Madison Avenue. Be patient, as it may take a minute or two before there's an adequate break in the stream of cars. Now, you must brave riding west with the traffic for a bit, but have no fear: you have a civilized, lane-wide painted shoulder all to yourself.

A hundred yards later, you'll be pedaling alongside the walls of Fairleigh

Dickinson University. FDU, founded in 1942 by one man (Peter Sammartino) with $60,000 and 60 students, is now the largest private university in New Jersey; its main specialities are liberal arts, business administration, dentistry, engineering, and education and it has an enrollment of 12,000 over several campuses.

If the gate is open, ride inside and turn left onto the one-way road paralleling your westerly travel on Madison Avenue. If you're a football fan, you can come here in the summer to watch the San Francisco Giants or some other pro team practice (unless the teams get so paranoid about spies from opposing teams that they close their practices to the public, as periodic flaps threaten). This road through the university will dump you back out onto Madison Avenue at the end of the campus, where you will turn right to continue your westerly travels.

Turn right at the light onto Convent Road; this intersection is absolutely unmistakable as it is marked by the arresting, greenhouse of the sprawling, white, Southern-plantation-like structure of the Madison Inn. Behind the hotel, not readily seen from the road, is Rod's 1890s Restaurant.

If you have the time and money (for it is moderately expensive), bring a change of clothes and stop at Rod's for dinner. The ambience alone is worth it, as some of the dining rooms are made from converted Pullman dining cars from gracious old trains. The culinary specialties, which are superbly prepared, include a 16-ounce prime rib, Maryland crab cakes with big bites of sweet crab, and garlic-dripping escargot. And the moist date-nut bread included in the bread basket is simply scrumptious. Yum!

Stomach full, you're now just a hop away from the New Jersey Transit train back to New York City. Turn right out of Rod's (or, if you haven't gotten there yet, ride down to the end of Convent Road and turn left) into the parking lot of the Convent Station railroad station.

RAHWAY RIVER RAMBLE

Union County, New Jersey

Ride Ratings

Length: 12 or 20 miles
Configuration: a long, skinny figure 8
Difficulty: flat with virtually no traffic
Surface: good pavement throughout; 3 miles on paved bike paths

—Highlights: This route, winding along the Rahway River, is an ideal early-season ride, and is very shady even during a hot summer day; plan to combine it with canoeing, fishing, swimming, or picnicking.

Some of the best cycling alongside the Rahway River is so little known that you'll not only see few cars, you'll be surprised to see another cyclist. Since the route is so pretty—and about as rural as a suburban ride can get—its obscurity is a complete mystery. I happened to discover it completely by accident, simply by following BIKE ROUTE signs posted on suburban streets and setting out to explore an enigmatic green road paralleling the Garden State Parkway on the Hagstrom map for Union County.

What a delightful find! (At first, because of its history, I was tempted to call it my Serendipity Ride.) It since became a popular first ride for the students in my adult-school introduction to bicycle touring.

If you like rivers (and my own prejudice in favor of water shows in the selection of rides in this book), you'll enjoy the many bridges crisscrossing the lazy Rahway River, and the quiet roads hugging its shores. Three miles into the ride, you may rent a canoe to paddle along its quiescent banks. At the far end of this long, skinny route, you can relax in Rahway River Park; either bring a picnic lunch, or—on weekends between Memorial Day and Labor Day—buy a hotdog in the park's snack bar. The park also features playground equipment, a swimming pool, and a few modest hiking trails. There is so little traffic and so many parks along the way that

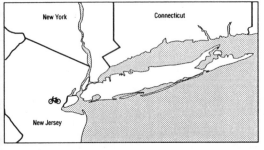

New York

Connecticut

New Jersey

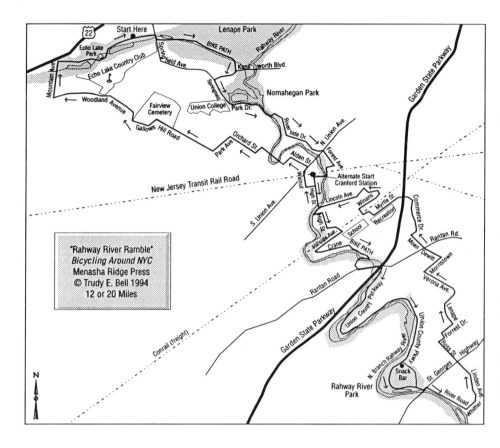

"Rahway River Ramble"
Bicycling Around NYC
Menasha Ridge Press
© Trudy E. Bell 1994
12 or 20 Miles

this flat ride is also an excellent adventure for children, and indeed was tested and enjoyed by my own daughter Roxana at age 22 months.

The ride starts at Echo Lake Park, where there are restrooms and drinking fountains for topping off your water bottles. If you drive from New York City, get on Route 22 East, exit onto Springfield Avenue heading south for half a mile, and turn right at the traffic light onto Mill Lane, which enters Echo Lake Park. A quarter of a mile later there are parking spaces on your right, where you may park your car for free and refresh yourself at the public rest rooms (open during the summer).

If you're using public transportation, take a New Jersey Transit train to Cranford (see the introduction for information on taking your bicycle on the train). This option will require you to pick up the ride in the middle. But you also have a choice on length: If you do only that section south of the train station, the ride will be 12 miles long; for the full 20 miles, follow it all the way north back to Echo Lake Park and then south again to end at the train station.

From Echo Lake Park, start your adventure at the entrance to the park, where Mill Lane intersects Springfield Avenue at the traffic light. Before you put on your helmet, though, look across Springfield Avenue to your left; there is Geiger's Bakery, locally known for its superb cheesecake, which you may feel you've earned at the end of your trip.

From Mill Lane, turn right at the light onto the busy Springfield Avenue, cross the short concrete bridge over the creek, and make an immediate left between the vertical wooden logs onto the paved bike path next to the gravel parking lot of Williams Nursery. This huge nursery is one of the best in the area, with a staff very knowledgeable about all kinds of fruits, flowers, vegetables, and trees.

Eventually, the path will take you along the top of an earthen dike, and on lovely sunny days is populated with dozens of joggers, strollers, dogwalkers, and children on BMX bikes. You've now entered Lenape Park. You'll pass a pond to your left. On an October ride with my students, one sharp-eyed woman spied a gray heron in graceful stance among the cattails in the marshy land at the base of the dike. And late one March, during an early season warm-up ride, I saw boys chopping down those very cattails, whose tops were fuzzy with going to seed. In answer to my curiosity, they explained that if the cattail stems were stuck into the ground and the dried tops set afire, the cattails made long-lasting patio torches. You learn something new every day.

After a bit less than a mile, you'll pass a target-practice range, from which gunshots may punctuate the silence. The path ends in a short distance at busy Kenilworth Boulevard; cross the boulevard, turning right on the paved bike path on the far side. Follow the path through a small parking lot, past the playing fields of Nomahegan Park on your left, wandering through the trees paralleling a fitness circuit with its various exercise stations. Continue on the path as it curves left to parallel Springfield Avenue instead of Kenilworth Boulevard, passing the picnic tables and barbecue grills, always following the fitness circuit.

Cross the entrance of a small parking lot, continuing on the bike path ahead. The path now curves around a pond with two spray fountains. In the springtime, the lily pads in the pond sport bright yellow and purple blossoms. You may even see people fishing; one time I saw a man reclining with a beer, watching the lines of four rods neatly propped in a row. Life is tough!

The path ends at a quiet road whose double yellow line will lead you to a quiet dead-end court—a dead end, that is, to automobiles. Cyclists, on the other hand, may pass through the two metal posts to continue on another paved path into the forest, with a few houses to the right and a creek to the left.

After only a fifth of a mile, the path will slope down abruptly to join unmarked Ballmere Parkway. Make a sharp left, and another immediate left onto a new path, up across a wooden bridge over the placid Rahway River. Hello, river. This lazy watery expanse will be your nearly constant companion for the next eight miles. If you're lucky, you might see a couple paddling a canoe under the bridge.

Head right at the fence at the edge of the bridge and coast down the short ramp onto Riverside Drive. Now a big earthen dike hides the view of the river to your right, but that will change. Follow Riverside Drive for a quarter mile until you reach a small park resembling a town square, one block before busy Springfield Avenue (which you can see just beyond). Linger here a moment to read the plaque on a boulder to your right, commemorating the site of Crane's Ford across the river. Light horsemen crossed here during the Revolutionary War while General George Washington's army was encamped at Morristown. The name of today's town of Cranford is a shortening of the name Crane's Ford.

Now turn left, leaving the river briefly, to continue on the unmarked one-way Riverside Drive. Cross Central Avenue and Orange Avenue, both marked with stop signs. If you're up for canoeing, turn right onto Orange Avenue and ride one block to the Cranford Boat and Canoe Company (250 Springfield Avenue, Cranford, New Jersey 07016, 201-272-6991). The place is open every day but Tuesday, including Sundays from May through September, and the hourly rate is about the cost of a deli lunch. You can lock your bike up on the bridge for safekeeping while you're drifting down the gentle current.

To keep cycling on the main Rahway River ride, though, do not turn on Orange Avenue, but continue straight on Riverside Drive. In a short distance, the river will resume being your companion. Look for white ducks as you pedal, either on the road or on the paved bike path right along the water's edge, eventually passing a small waterfall.

Turn left at the "T" intersection onto North Union Avenue, and make an immediate right at the majestic, white-columned mansion onto Forrest Avenue. Note that in this older neighborhood the sidewalks and curbs are not made of ordinary concrete. Instead, the sidewalks are slabs of slate and the curbs of chipped granite blocks carefully mortared together. Similarly, the street names are carved into vertical stone posts. Such unobtrusive, comforting reminders of bygone days are like a touch of time travel.

At the end of Forrest Avenue, turn right at the stop sign onto North Avenue, where you will have to put up with a couple of unavoidable minutes of traffic through central Cranford. Turn left at the light onto the busy Centennial Avenue, pass under the railroad tracks, and turn right at the light onto the busy South Street. Here, if you're hungry or thirsty, you can grab a snack at Krauszer's (a deli and convenience store), or stop at the Exxon station across the street. As you continue riding on South Street, you'll cross over the Rahway River, and the Cranford train station will appear to your right. Here, if you've chosen instead to ride the New Jersey Transit train from New York City, you can begin the ride.

Turn left at the light onto High Street (or, if you started from the train, come out of the south side of the train station and head straight south on High Street), which begins directly in front of the train station. Now, you're back to the quiet suburban streets and bike route signs. In a few blocks, Droescher's Mill Park appears to your right; dismount to walk over to the Rahway River to admire the waterfall. Here are some highly interesting signs pointing out that the river is kept stocked with trout, so if you enjoy fishing, unpack your collapsible rod (I hope you have a fishing license!). Note also how the bridge to your right is constructed at an odd angle on top of an earlier roadway.

Remount your bike, cross up and over that bridge, and make an immediate sharp right onto Bluff Street, riding with the river to your right. Follow the road as it bends left after a block and becomes Elm Street. In one more block, turn right at the stop sign onto High Street. A few blocks later, turn left onto Hickory Street, opposite a shady park.

Now you're in for a little surprise. Ride only a couple of blocks, slowly, and turn right onto the bike path (just before Mansion Terrace appears on your left). Walk your bike through a small round corrugated culvert under the railroad tracks! It's so compact that if you're tall, you may have to duck. Climb the four short stairs at the other end and you'll emerge at the back of a school, facing a small geodesic dome.

Ride right onto the unmarked Hillside Avenue, following it as it bends right. (Ignore the BIKE ROUTE signs pointing left; the way I'm guiding you is a prettier choice). After a third of a mile, Hillside Avenue will bend sharply left to follow the elbow of the Rahway River, and becomes Crane Parkway. The river itself is secluded in trees to your right, but there is a chance at Mendel Avenue to pedal over to a wooden bridge to watch mallards preening themselves on rocks, and to explore some walking trails along the bank.

Continue on Crane Parkway until it intersects with Wall Street. No, you can't make your investments here, but there is a big payoff: a paved bike path. Turn right onto the path, and soon the river once again emerges into view. I love this little secluded section. Follow the bike path left where it splits in a "Y" to make a circuit of the pond just ahead. The busy highway beyond the pond in front of you is the Garden State Parkway. Circle the pond clockwise; along one stretch on the return, you're riding between two bodies of water—the pond to your right and the Rahway River to your left. You're also likely to see young fathers showing their small sons and daughters how to fish.

Make a sharp left where the path makes a "T," passing the basketball half court. Ride a wooden bridge over the Rahway River, to join the quiet Johnson Avenue. A small playground is on your right. Turn left onto Johnson Avenue (in spite of the BIKE ROUTE sign pointing right), make an immediate left onto Mohawk Drive, and ride to the stop sign at the end.

This is the only other busy section of the ride, so follow the directions carefully. Turn left onto busy Raritan Road, up over the Garden State Parkway. Immediately at the end of the overpass railings, make a sharp right onto the unmarked Union County Parkway. This will look like a highway on-ramp, and every instinct will tell you it's the wrong turn. But do it, for if you continue ahead to the light at the next intersection, you will have gone a block too far.

And now, relax. Union County Parkway is a quiet, winding road of remarkable, undiscovered loveliness. To your left are humble homes, some very boxy, some even trailers. But to your right the tall, misty trees almost resemble a primordial forest. Ride leisurely for a bit less than a mile. At the first really sharp left turn, where there appears to be a wide parking area, dismount for a few minutes and walk into the woods to see a waterfall off a dam and a small, forested island 20 feet across. To me, this is magic. I always associate islands with adventure, probably because of overdosing in childhood on *Peter Pan*, *Treasure Island*, and *Huckleberry Finn*.

Continue your ride for another mile, taking a sharp right at the first stop sign to stay on Union County Parkway. Eventually the Rahway River becomes two or three times as wide as at the ride's start. Every time I pedal along this broad expanse of sun-glinting water, my mind starts playing "Moon River, wider than a mile . . ." You'll pass a few small parking areas, and at the next stop sign (at the unmarked Valley Road) a couple of miles after the first, you'll see an engagingly secluded little place to your right, with a lone picnic table overlooking a waterfall. Think twice about stopping here, though, for if you cross Valley Road and continue straight, you'll enter Rahway Park. You have now traveled a tad less than halfway through the ride (9.5 miles out of 20.5 total).

In the park, bear right at the "Y" to follow the one-way signs. The building immediately on your left after the "Y" houses a snack bar, which is open seven days a week between Memorial Day and Labor Day, and on weekends in April, May, September, and October; in addition to the usual hotdogs, it also offers hot meatball heroes and chicken-steak sandwiches. That building also houses serviceable but not-very-sanitary public rest rooms with running water. The rest of the park offers picnic tables complete with public barbecue grills, playing fields, and playground equipment for big kids and infants.

Meander on around the park on the one-way road (or ride on the paved bike path to your left) past the Walter E. Ulrich Memorial Pool—a large, clean and inviting Union County swimming pool that is open to the public in the summer for a few dollars per person. Just past the pool at the crosswalk, where the right-hand curb is painted yellow, turn right off the road onto the paved bike path to follow the fitness circuit around the duck pond. Here the Rahway River is babbling over stones to your right. Stay on the bike path as it circles around the duck pond on your left, eventually joining the road exiting the park to your right.

At the park exit, cross the very busy four-lane Saint George's Avenue onto the quiet River Road, which parallels the Rahway River to your right. Note yet another lovely forested island a few yards from the shore, just begging for a treehouse and kids lounging with fishing rods.

At the end of River Road, turn right at the "T" intersection onto Whittier Street—here saying farewell to the Rahway River, which has been your companion now for eight miles. You won't see it again for a while. Cross the busy Scott Avenue at the light.

Make a diagonal left turn at the next intersection onto Linden Avenue. You'll stay on this road for nearly a mile (it becomes Ross Street where you cross the busy Saint George's Avenue), through older family suburban neighborhoods with towering maples.

Turn right onto Durham Drive. Here you'll make several turns in fast succession: left at the "T" intersection onto Rose Terrace, and an immediate right at the next "T" intersection onto Forrest Drive. Then cross the busy North Stiles Street—being careful not to rush out into traffic as the signal is a delayed green —onto Princeton Road ahead and a little to your left. Take the first left onto Lenape Road, which gently curves around through the quiet tract of newer, ranch-style homes. Turn left at the "T" intersection onto Amherst Road, and then make an immediate right onto Verona Avenue. Here you'll go through a number of stop signs, turning right at the dead end sign onto Morristown Road. After a quarter mile, turn left at the stop sign onto DeWitt Terrace.

At the busy Raritan Road make a right, watching carefully for traffic as you make the first left onto Moen Avenue; there is a dry cleaners and a luncheonette on this corner. Now you'll ride on wide, traffic-free roads through some industrial parks with glass-and-steel office buildings that are virtually untenanted on weekends.

Head right at the "T" intersection onto Commerce Drive, which curves around to the left. The steady traffic noise you hear is from the unseen Garden State Parkway. Ride all the way to the end, turning left at the next "T" onto Myrtle Street to pass under the Garden State Parkway. Ride past the playing fields of a small park on your left to make a right onto the unobtrusive residential Park Street, following the BIKE ROUTE sign.

Now, pedal the one short block into what appears to be a small parking lot, heading left at the end onto a rather unkempt paved bike path alongside the railroad tracks. Take the path behind a number of back yards, heading right at the "T" onto the busy Centennial Avenue. After pedaling under the railroad overpass, make the first right onto Winans Avenue.

Here it will appear you are going down a dead-end street. Well, you are. Pass the factory building to the right, with its picnic tables out front until, lo and behold, another short bike path leads you to the left between houses onto Ann Street, which begins at a courtyard before an apartment building. Turn left to ride out the only way you can, turning right onto Woodside Avenue and then left at the "T" intersection onto the wide Lincoln Avenue.

Stay on Lincoln Avenue for more than half a mile. You'll know you're doing it right if suddenly you find yourself approaching that bridge oddly built over the preexisting road, which you passed over a few hours ago after gazing at the waterfall at Droescher's Mill Park just south of the Cranford train station. But this time you're heading toward the bridge from the opposite direction. Cross over the bridge, bearing right onto High Street. Once again, on your right is the Rahway River.

If you continue straight at this point you'll dead-end into the Cranford train station, and can return to New York City, if you're so inclined. If you want to complete the ride, one block short of the station turn left onto Chestnut Street and then make the first right onto the rather busy Walnut Avenue under the railroad bridge. Bear right onto North Union Avenue into downtown Cranford.

Cranford is a cute New England-style town with ye olde shoppes and brick sidewalks and street lamps made to look like old gas lamps. Turn left at the second light onto unmarked Alden Street. If you pass the brick New Jersey Bell building half a block later on your right, you've done it correctly; if you've remained on North Union until you pass the Cranford Bicycle Shop and a white steepled church on your left, you've gone too far: turn around and come back. Alden Street has a pizza parlor (whose concoctions, when I was there, were utterly forgettable, so don't bother), a deli, some other shops, and a wonderful second-hand book store called Linda's Book Exchange.

A quarter mile later, turn left at a stop sign onto Holly Street, following the bike route signs. At the next block, turn right at the flashing yellow light onto Eastman Street. This road is neat because within a couple of blocks you'll cross the Rahway River twice! Nestled in the curve at your left where the river makes its sharp bend, you can relax in the grassy miniature McConnell Park.

Turn left at the "T" intersection onto Pittsfield Street, and make a right at the next "T" onto Orchard Street. Ride another quarter mile, making a left onto Park Avenue. Turn right at the next "T" intersection onto Gallows Hill Road.

You'll stay on Gallows Hill Road until it ends in about a mile, past a cemetery on your right and the Holy Trinity Church on the left, where birds in the trees are likely to be making a very unholy racket.

You'll also pass the back entrance to Union College on your right. If you choose to explore the college, ride through the large parking lot until you reach the two domes of the William Miller Sperry Observatory on your left. Here you can rest for a few moments on the flat round concrete sun dial in the front lawn.

The Sperry Observatory is the headquarters of the Amateur Astronomers Inc., (AAI). From September through May at 8 P.M. on the third Friday of the month, the group holds a free public lecture meeting at one of the college auditoriums. All other Friday nights between 7:30 and 10:30 P.M., visitors—including you!—are welcome to view the heavens through the telescopes at the Sperry Observatory and see a slide or lecture presentation on a variety of astronomy-related topics.

AAI has a soft spot in my heart because in the early 1970s, shortly after I first came to the east coast from California, I spent a lot of time here. As a teenager I'd wanted to be an astronomer. I'd studied physics and astronomy in college and spent my early journalistic career writing and editing articles on astronomy and its history. In 1973, AAI chartered a plane and organized an expedition of 225 members—including me—to observe the century's longest total eclipse of the sun from the Sahara Desert. The group still runs such fantastic expeditions for its members, keeping the cost as low as humanly possible. For more information, call (908) 276-STAR or (908) 709-7520.

When you're ready to resume pedaling, leave the campus the way you came in, turning right to continue on Gallows Hill Road. You'll climb a slight rise—the first "hill" of any description on the trip—and then turn right at the "T" intersection onto moderately busy Broad Street. Make the first left onto Woodland Avenue, riding past a golf course on your right. After three-quarters of a mile, turn right at a light onto Mountain Avenue. Half a mile later, turn right into the rear entrance of Echo Lake Park.

On your right you'll pass a small building on the shore of Echo Lake. Here you'll find restrooms and a snack bar with the usual hotdogs and chips; during the summer you can also rent pedal boats (if you haven't had enough pedaling) for drifting out onto the lake itself. The lake is particularly lovely in the autumn, with the fiery gold and vermilion of the trees reflected like a painting in its placid surface.

If you started here, you'll be at your car in a few minutes. If you started at the Cranford train station, go to the beginning of this description to continue your ride. Enjoy!

NETCONG GETAWAY

Morris, Sussex, & Warren Counties, New Jersey

Ride Ratings

Length: 17 miles
Configuration: loop
Difficulty: first half is gently downhill; second half uphill; traffic is light
Surface: some good pavement, some roads roughly paved or dirt

—Highlights: This ride's prime attractions are solitude, back-country vistas, camping, a restored colonial village and abandoned sections of the Morris Canal; in late July, you can pick blackberries along the side of the road.

Want to get away from the heat, grime, noise, rush-hour crush, and panhandlers of the city? This ride may well be the prescription for urban claustrophobia. It's about as far removed and rustic as any you'll find within a couple of hours of midtown Manhattan, and it will remove you both physically and spiritually from urban sprawl.

It's a particularly good ride if you have a mountain bike or a cross (hybrid) bike, because some of the roads are dirt and even some of the paved roads are rough. But it's quite do-able on a thin-tire bicycle (my bike has 1-1/8-inch tires and it did fine). But before you grouse about the road conditions think of the payoff: absolute solitude for certain portions, with hardly any traffic. Perfect for a solo rider to collect his or her thoughts and restore some calm . . . or, perhaps, for a couple to have a romantic tryst in the open air . . .

American history buffs, canal lovers, crafts hobbyists, or curious families will also enjoy exploring Waterloo Village, a reconstructed colonial town where people in period clothing demonstrate trades and crafts typical of the 18th century. There is also a restored incline plane from the 19th-century Morris Canal, showing some of its engineering marvels, which were more remarkable than those for the more famous Erie Canal.

If you love camping as much as I do, bring a small tent and cook

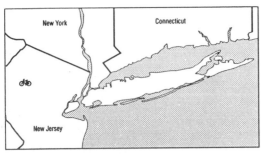

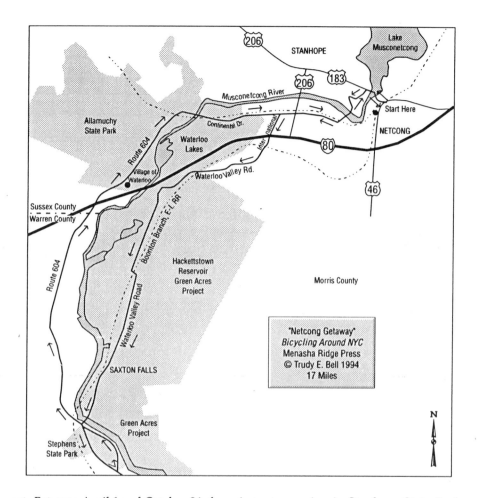

set. Between April 1 and October 31 there is tent camping in Stephens State Park for a modest fee. If you drive, you could even park there and make that your base of operations. Or, if you're a bit more adventurous, load your camping gear into panniers hooked to your bike and take to the road (in my view, the single best book on bicycle camping is the classic *Bike Touring: The Sierra Club Guide to Outings on Wheels* by Raymond Bridge, Sierra Club Books, 1979).

The Netcong getaway is one of the more distant rides in this book, nearly a two-hour drive from the city. It begins and ends at the Netcong station of the New Jersey Transit railroad, the westernmost end of one of NJT's lines (see the preface for information on taking your bicycle on the train). It's also easily accessible by car: from the George Washington Bridge, take Interstate 80 west to Exit 27B. Follow Route 183 north half a mile to the traffic circle, follow the circle halfway around to continue north on Routes 206 and 46. In half a mile, at the lake, turn left onto Main Street. One-quarter mile later, the Netcong station will be on your right.

Western New Jersey is quite hilly, and so designing a ride as relatively flat as this one took some doing. Other bicycle touring books have some beautiful rides leaving from Allamuchy Mountain State Park, just a mile farther west. So if you're a strong hill-climber, you might want to check out those as well. This ride is suitable for more average cyclists, including older children.

The Netcong train station is in the middle of the town. There are no services elsewhere on this ride, so take the opportunity to fill your water bottles and buy lunch at one of the local shops (there's Carmine's Pizzeria & Restaurant, a Quick Chek convenience store, a Chinese restaurant, a deli, and a number of other eating stops nearby). If you're camping, you also should load up on supplies for dinner and breakfast.

Turn left out of the train station onto the busy Main Street, watching carefully for traffic. A quarter mile north, turn left at the "T" intersection onto State Routes 206 north and 183 (Ledgewood Avenue).

You're now at the southern shore of Lake Musconetcong, the highest point on the course of the Morris Canal, built in 1831. In its heyday, the Morris Canal ran for 102 miles over hill and dale from the Delaware River on one edge of New Jersey to the Hudson River on the other. During its peak year of 1866, it transported 889,229 tons of freight—more than the famous Erie Canal. Even Mrs. Frances Trollop, whose candor often stung in her 1832 classic *The Domestic Manners of the Americans*, admired the canal as a "noble work" that proved "the people of America to be the most enterprising in the world."

At Lake Musconetcong there is a small park with a playground and geese wandering over a grassy slope. If you pull your bike up onto the sidewalk next to the lake, you'll see a waterfall below the bridge. At times of very low water, you can catch glimpses of the earthen towpath along which mules pulled the barges. In the park next to the dam, you can see the capstones for Lock 1 West. The dam was built after the canal was abandoned in the 1930s.

After you've gazed your fill, continue across the bridge and turn left at the first opportunity across from the Hess gas station just past the park. A brief section of the Morris Canal—looking much as it must have in its prime—is carrying water below you to your left. You're now riding on another Main Street because you've crossed the invisible boundary of Morris County into Sussex County, and this Main Street (Sussex County Route 601) leads into the historic village of Stanhope with all its antiques shops.

Now there are some quick turns after only one or two blocks riding each, so pay close attention. They're worth it to avoid traffic and to see some local color. Ride briefly along the Musconetcong River. Just after Main Street curves right, make the first left (at the Pampered Pet dog and cat grooming house) onto Kelly Place, and an immediate right onto the narrow Plane Street, which is a gentle one-way downhill. After one block, turn left at the stop sign onto the unmarked New Street. At the "T" intersection in front of the stone wall, turn right onto the unmarked Waterloo Road. Ride slowly over the metal bridge grating to enjoy the pool in the babbling creek to your left and the white and purple wildflowers. At this point you've reentered Morris County.

At the cemetery entrance at the end of the road, turn right onto the unmarked Love Road, which eventually becomes Continental Drive. Let the gentle downhill carry you at a slow coast past tall maples and open fields bordered by white boulders.

In half a mile you'll cross an overpass over four-lane U.S. 206. At the first intersection, turn left onto the broad International Drive, which is paralleled by a paved bike path. Just after International Drive crosses over Interstate 80, turn right at the sign for AREA 3 onto Waterloo Valley Road.

Now you just stay on this road, through all its incarnations, for the next five miles. Take your time to enjoy it, for it will be the most isolated section of the route—your ticket to solitude and adventure.

Shortly after turning onto the road, you'll cross over railroad tracks and pass the sprawling United Parcel Service building on your left. Less than a quarter mile beyond, the road narrows into a back country lane and becomes quite rough: you are now wending your way through forest, past abandoned houses and vegetable gardens long overgrown. Coast down the gentle incline slowly, to minimize the bumpiness and to harken to the birdcalls. I rode after a July thunderstorm, and the vine-hung forest was dripping, the air heavy with moisture and drifting fog; the forest was transformed into a place of shaded mystery and rustling animals.

At the next set of railroad tracks dismount to walk your bike, as the tracks are diagonal to the road and could catch one of your tires and throw you in a nasty spill. The tracks will then parallel your road for some distance as you plunge back into the forest. At this point, your ears will be hearing the traffic on nearby parallel Interstate 80 and the road surface grows briefly better as the landscape opens and you catch sight of the distant forested hills straight ahead.

The interstate highway will soon recede west as you curve south. Daisies, white filigree Queen Anne's lace, clover, thistles, and the miniature sunflowers of black-eyed Susans bob in the breeze. Soon the chirp and chatter of birds fill your ears as you pedal back into the forest—where the zipping of a nylon shell evokes the memory of the dawn unzipping of sleeping bags in the great outdoors.

Soon you begin climbing. After you top a small rise, look to the right to glimpse two small lakes formed in the Musconetcong River in the valley below. When I was there the weekend after Labor Day, bulldozers were digging up the ground for gravel, in support of endless Progress, the bane and illusion of Western Civilization in its perception of land only as real estate, to be turned into shopping malls and highways.

Continue straight where Bell Road heads off to the right—no relation to your guide here, as no one yet has seen fit to name a road after me. This intersection is preceded by rusted iron junk and an ancient, tumbledown house on your left, from which was issuing country western music and is apparently the habitat of aforesaid Bell. In less than half a mile, the road will make a sharp left, cross the railroad tracks, and make a sharp right. The tracks will now be your companion to your right.

In another half mile, the road begins to climb and gets more covered with sand and gravel—no surprise, since this area is dotted with several sand and gravel pits, and you may be passed by a dump truck along the way. Almost guaranteed, though, that's the most traffic you'll encounter. Keep your eyes out to the right, because soon you'll see a brilliant aqua lake, its surface lazily rippled by the breeze, flanked by a steep ridge paralleling the one you're on.

Where the road widens at the next gravel pit, pull over and walk to the boulders at the edge and take in the view. Here you'll see the entirety of the strikingly bright blue-green lake in the gravel pit. (Could it be colored so by copper salts?) As you continue, you'll also pass by the cranes and funnels of Saxton Falls Sand & Gravel; note the piles of gravel sorted according to the size of the stone.

The bumpy road improves as you pass the Intercounty Paving Asphalt Plant. Soon you'll see the mailboxes of houses tucked away in the woods, after which you'll coast on a nice mile-long downhill. Ride on a bridge over a creek and suddenly you're at the idyll's end.

At the "T" intersection marking the end of your solitude, turn left onto Warren County 604, heading south (yes, you've switched counties again). Although suddenly you may be plunged into moderate traffic, the painted shoulder is comfortably wide.

Don't get up a good head of steam, though. Less than half a mile on your left, past the brick Hackettstown Armory of the New Jersey Army National Guard, is the entrance to the shady Stephens State Park campground—just the cooling refreshment needed on a hot summer day eight miles into the ride. If you're carrying panniers, why not stop now to select a campsite and check in at the park office? Or at least relax on the benches thoughtfully placed on the islands in the boulder-strewn Musconetcong River and watch the fly fishermen cast their hooks.

When I was there, a warm and perfect Saturday afternoon the weekend after Labor Day, the place was only a quarter full. Even on the July 4th weekend, the place was half empty, and there was a pick of campsites carpeted with soft pine needles—one of the best surfaces for a good night's sleep under the stars. Although there are flush toilets and running water, there is no hot water and no showers. For more information about the park, call (201) 852-3790.

When you're ready to continue the ride, exit the campground following the one-way signs, and turn right onto Warren County Route 604 headed north, retracing half a mile of your route down.

After crossing over the railroad tracks, the wide painted shoulder ends, so ride carefully in the moderate traffic. The Musconetcong River parallels your course on the right. After three quarters of a mile, turn right at the sign for the Morris Canal Guard Lock No. 5 West for a bit of local history.

It took me a few minutes to realize that the lock was the grass-filled rectangular concrete depression that looked like a filled-in swimming pool, with the mules' towpath between it and the Musconetcong River. The Morris Canal was chartered in 1824, and opened for business in 1832. For the next half century it was the chief means of transporting coal and iron across New Jersey, a journey that took five days.

As freight left the Musconetcong River and resumed its course in a "cut prism" in the earth, it passed through Guard Lock 5 West, one of the 28 locks on the Morris Canal system necessary for climbing the steep hills of Western New Jersey. In this depression here in the parking lot are the capstones of the lock with recesses that once held the gates.

Continue north on Warren County Route 604, and in another three-quarters mile you can stop to try and find Lock No. 4. At the site, there is an abandoned restaurant called Elsie's; when I was standing photographing some ducks and geese, old Elsie herself appeared on the back deck and told me that she had opened the restaurant in 1940, but was long since retired. Nothing there now resembles a lock, although Elsie said that the long, overgrown gully just north of the restaurant paralleling the river for several tenths of a mile was once part of the canal. She was old enough to have seen the canal still working before it was abandoned in 1933, in the midst of the Great Depression.

Continue north on Warren County Route 604, where you'll pass a playing field. There you may be lucky enough to watch radio-controlled model aircraft doing barrel rolls and other aerial acrobatics behind the trees.

Just past the Concert Field at Waterloo, you'll reenter Sussex County. The wide, painted shoulder resumes and you pedal beneath Interstate 80, past the entrance to the Allamuchy Mountain Reservation. The road bears right. The split rail fence to your right heralds your approach to the entrance of Village of Waterloo.

Although the admission fee is a bit stiff—about the same price as a first-run movie—exploring everything takes a good four hours, and so it is eminently worth the afternoon. It also has several places for lunch and snacks, and it is fascinating for children as well as adults. Lock your bike, pay your admission, get the map, and wander around for the rest of the afternoon.

Here in the restored village, you can watch a blacksmith in period dress hammering away over his fire, forging hooks, candle sconces, and other implements; or observe the chandler hand-dipping wax candles; or watch a weaver producing multicolored fabric on a colonial loom; or note the efficiency of waterwheels powering a gristmill and a sawmill; or sample some old-fashioned candy at the village apothecary. You can also explore restored homes from the Colonial and Victorian eras, ranging from mansions with period furniture to the longhouses of the Lenape Indians on a nearby island.

Founded in 1740 as Andover Forge, the village was a prime supplier of armaments for George Washington and the Continental Army in the Revolutionary War. But its economic high point came in 1831 with the opening of the Morris Canal, making the village a major port stop on this bulk freight transportation channel. Canal buffs can slake their thirst for more knowledge at the Canal Museum. More fun, though, is to gaze at the full-scale restoration of one of the canal's inclined planes.

To cross the mountainous terrain of western New Jersey, the Morris Canal carried freight up and down the greatest change in altitude of any canal in the world: 914 feet up from the Hudson River and down 760 feet to the Delaware River. Note: the Erie canal is only the most famous because it was the first (finished in 1825) and the longest (some 400 miles). It hoisted loads up only 700 feet; the Panama Canal only 85 feet. The Morris Canal was as long as the Suez and twice as long as the Panama.

Such huge vertical distances made locks impractical in the steepest sections—so the loaded canal cars were hauled by mules and underground water turbines up tracks on inclined planes. The inclined planes were hailed as the engineering marvel of the time, and no wonder: they could raise 70 tons of coal 100 feet in 12 minutes. Here at Waterloo Village you have the chance to see how it worked.

By the way, every year from May through October, Waterloo Village hosts a six-month Festival of the Arts: alive with music, dance, song, and poetry under a huge performance tent. Performers ranging from folksinger Arlo Guthrie to "Mostly Mozart" conductor Gerard Schwarz delight the crowds with classical and popular events. Time your trip to the performance of your choice. For information on performances or for ordering tickets, call the Waterloo Box Office at (201) 347-4700. Waterloo Village is open from 10 A.M. Tuesday through Sunday mid-April through the end of December; for specific hours, particularly around holidays, call (201) 347-0900.

When you're done eating, walking, and looking your fill, unlock your bike and turn right out of Waterloo Village parking lot to continue on Sussex County Route 604 east. Note the well-kept grounds of lawn, boulders, and stately trees on your left with a gazebo nestled to the rear. On your right is the Musconetcong River, whose low verdant islands and blooming lily pads must make wonderful canoe hide-and-seek.

Make your first right at the signs for I-80 onto the unmarked Continental Drive, with its promising BIKE ROUTE signs. Cross the road to the paved bike path on your left. The path dips down below the road, then back up again; after that July thunderstorm, I had the adventure of lifting my bike over a small tree that had fallen across the path. The path ends at International Drive.

Cross International Drive to stay on Continental Drive, but don't ride too fast! On the right, hidden under the trees, are blackberry bushes! The berries are abundant and flavorful in late July, but bring a long-sleeved shirt and pants and gloves to protect your arms, legs, and hands from their cats' claws of thorns.

Turn left onto the unmarked Waterloo Road across from the second entrance to the Stanhope Union Cemetery and just before the Federal Express warehouse. Stay on it as it bends left and becomes New Street. Turn right at the white clapboard First Presbyterian Church onto Main Street (Sussex County 601) through Stanhope. Follow the double yellow line through this wonderful old town, relatively untouched and spared the "cutesing up" of a restored town. Where Main Street curves left, the Morris Canal is immediately to your right below you, and you may see people fishing.

Turn right at the "T" intersection onto the busy Routes 206 and 183 (Ledgewood Avenue), and your first right onto the Main Street of Netcong, then right into the Netcong train station.

Detailed guided tours of the Morris Canal or the Delaware and Raritan Canal are offered by the Canal Society of New Jersey, P.O. Box 737, Morristown, NJ 07953-0737; for information, call (908) 722-9556. At least three books have been published on the Morris Canal. The definitive work is the 700-page *A Hundred Years, A Hundred Miles: New Jersey's Morris Canal* by Barbara N. Kalata, Morris County Historical Society, 1983. A wonderful picture book is James Lee's *The Morris Canal: A Photographic History*, Delaware Press, 1988. And for oral history and old-time songs, enjoy James Lee's *Tales the Boatmen Told: Recollections of the Morris Canal*, Delaware Press, 1991. In addition, see the lively article "Coal, Canallers, and Conches . . . New Jersey's Inland Canals," by Donald H. Lotz, in the Spring 1990 issue (vol. 3, no. 1, pages 1-10) of *Portfolio: A Quarterly Review of Trade and Transportation*, published by the Port Authority of New York and New Jersey.

EXPLORING THE GREAT SWAMP

Morris County, New Jersey

This tour in and around the 6800-acre Great Swamp National Wildlife Refuge is so rustic you can hardly believe that the grubby, noisy, crowded steel canyons of New York City are only 25 miles east. Actually, we're lucky the swamp even exists. In 1959, when everyone was so enamored of Progress, there were plans afoot to drain the region and turn it into an international jet airport. A group of farsighted local citizens defeated the effort by buying up land through the North American Wildlife Federation and deeding it to the U.S. Department of the Interior.

Exist it does, and it's enchanting in all seasons. Like all wildlife areas, you'll see more animals in the spring and fall, particularly at dawn or dusk. Especially in spring, after heavy rains, it's the fairy-tale embodiment of "swampiness," complete with blooming lily pads, purple irises, and hummocks of long grasses rising out of the water with mosses at their base. Listen, and in the late afternoon and early evening you will hear a chorus of peepers and frogs.

Pack a small pair of binoculars and walk out on the wooden boardwalks to the bird blinds to watch great blue herons standing majestically in the marsh or swallows swooping for insects while tiny caterpillars drift through the air on fine webs. In fact, make a point of arriving well before you intend to ride in order to explore the boardwalks and let the magic of the swamp seep into your

Ride Ratings

Length: 14 or 22 miles
Configuration: longer or shorter loops
Difficulty: half flat, half gently rolling; traffic generally light
Surface: good pavement with 1.5 miles of gravel and 1.5 miles of paved bike path

—Highlights: A traffic-free route through the Great Swamp National Wildlife Refuge; utilizes the paved bike paths of the Loantaka Brook Reservation and includes a picnic at Bayne Park; the swamp offers 16 miles of wilderness hiking trails.

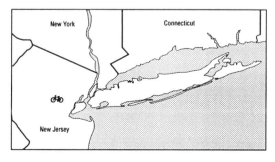

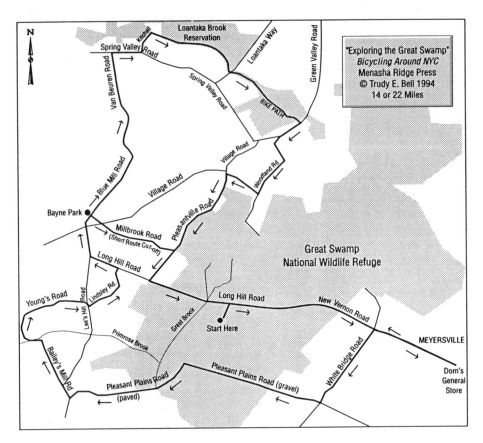

"Exploring the Great Swamp"
Bicycling Around NYC
Menasha Ridge Press
© Trudy E. Bell 1994
14 or 22 Miles

spirit and set the mood for your tour. To best enjoy the day's whole experience, take advantage of the modest mileage: bring boots or waterproof shoes and some insect repellent and plan to spend a couple of hours hiking along some of the trails deep into the swamp as well as biking around it.

Nature lovers who want to find out more about the swamp's ecology can visit three separate nature centers. One, on the eastern side of the swamp, is the Great Swamp Outdoor Education Center, operated by the Morris County Park Commission, off Southern Boulevard in Chatham; open seven days a week from 9 A.M. to 4:30 P.M. (closed July and August). Among other activities, it features guided nature walks into the swamp at 2 P.M. on Saturdays and Sundays. For information, call (201) 635-6629. The other two centers are short detours off the bicycle route itself.

The swamp and its immediate vicinity are enormously popular with cyclists. Guaranteed, even in winter, you'll get a wave and a smile from lone riders. And on summer weekends you're very likely to be overtaken by a club ride, or even group pedaling with the New York City-based commercial Brooks Country Cycling and Hiking (formerly Country Cycling Tours). It has also been a winner as the second of the two day rides for the people enrolled in my "Bicycle Touring: An Introduction" class that offered I've in the spring, summer, and fall at the South Orange-Maplewood Adult School in Maplewood, New Jersey since 1989.

Terrain on this ride ranges from flat to gently rolling, with about a mile and a half of gravel. Both the longer and shorter versions begin in the parking lot of the wildlife observation area on Long Hill Road, where there are bathrooms with flush toilets, potable water for your water bottles, and wooden board-walks leading out to bird blinds in the swamp. The two rides diverge after Bayne Park, where my bicycle-touring students enjoy lounging in the shade near a brook to eat lunch. Facilities on the shorter ride are virtually nonexistent, so take advantage of the restrooms and deli at Dom's General Store at the beginning. On Sunday you must pack a lunch, for the deli is closed.

For riders wishing to take the shorter swamp ride, I'm afraid there's no alternative to driving and parking at the Long Hill Road wildlife observation area.

Stronger riders have the option of relying on public transportation, coming into the New Jersey Transit train station is at Convent Station seven miles north (see the preface for information about transporting your bicycle on the train). Then follow the first half of the route described in "Of Convents and Bike Paths," joining the longer Great Swamp ride two-thirds of the way through, for a total of 32 miles. On this combined ride, you'll have two options for picking up lunch: one at the Green Village Deli where you turn from Green Village Road onto Meyersville Road about 9 miles into the double ride, or Dom's General Store 14 miles into the double ride. The suggested lunch stop in Bayne Park falls 23 miles into the combined ride.

After checking your bike and locking your car in the wildlife refuge park-ing lot, make your way back out of the lot onto Long Hill Road, riding with care on the large gravel. Turn right out of the lot onto Long Hill Road, which at the first intersection changes name to New Vernon Road. Ride around the traffic circle marking the intersection with Meyersville Road, and buy lunch at Dom's General Store. You may find it fun to read the newspaper at the table in the back where locals come to sip coffee and banter with the proprietors. There are also restrooms and potable water. Dom's is open Monday through Friday 6 A.M. to 6 P.M., Saturday from 6 A.M. to 5 P.M., and closed Sunday (the Green Village Deli has even more limited hours).

Dom's is also a popular hangout with cyclists full of on-the-road tips, as you'll discover if you relax for a few minutes on the front stoop. When I was there on a cool sunny Saturday morning with one of my spring classes, two long-distance touring cyclists stopped by for a mid-morning pick-me-up to break up their informal century ride (100 miles in a day). One, a man in his 50s, amazed us by pulling out a cold baked potato for his snack; he claimed that for the "tetchy" digestive systems of older cyclists a baked potato was mild but tasty and full of wonderful complex carbohydrates, complete in its own wrapping.

By the way, across from Dom's is Casa Maya, a superb Mexican restaurant to which people migrate from 20 miles or more away. You might remember it for carbo loading after your ride (for a group of cyclists, be there before 5 P.M. if you want to get a seat together—and bring your own beer or wine).

You also might enjoy wandering across the road to poke around Archie's Resale Shop and Martin Urbanski's Trading Post Antiques. The wooden exteri-ors of Trading Post Antiques is absolutely covered with outdated street and merchandise signs and in the front yard is a cyclone fence enclosing several munching deer. Archie's, decorated by an antlered hunter's trophy, features glass cases of certain collections, such as rare ice skates dating back to the 18th century. Urbanski specializes in animated animals and pinball machines and amusement park wares: put in a coin, and a mechanical seal twirls a ball on its nose. Trading Post Antiques is open 10 A.M.-5 P.M. seven days a week; Archie's Resale Shop the same hours on weekends only.

After leaving all these attractions of Meyersville, ride back around the traffic circle to retrace your route on New Vernon Road, making the first left onto White Bridge Road. After another mile or so, stop at the first intersection, which is Pleasant Plains Road. If you want to keep on the main route, turn right to follow Pleasant Plains Road into the swamp itself and skip down to the double asterisks (**).

If, on the other hand, you're game for a little detour to learn more about this area's ecosystem and wildlife, continue straight ahead on White Bridge Road for another 1.3 miles, including over the metal bridge to the gravel of Lord Stirling Road. The modern building off to your right is the Somerset County Environmental Education Center (908) 766-2489, located on the 425-acre Lord Stirling Park adjoining the swamp to the east. The 18,000-square-foot building is solar heated and cooled—the first environmental center in the country to be so energized.

The environmental education center, which is open 365 days a year from 9 A.M. to 5 P.M., is worth a detour for its programs for children and adults, especially if you love wildlife books. Not only can you buy from a wide selection (and even pick up some novelty nature gift wrapping paper), but there's a very large collections of wildlife books in a public library to browse or consult. You can also learn more about the harrowing story of the swamp's history in Cam Cavanaugh's book *Saving the Great Swamp: The People, the Power Brokers, and an Urban Wilderness*, which is available at the center.

You can also pick up a map to guide you on the eight miles of hiking trails that traverse the acreage. Fully a quarter of that mileage is on wooden boardwalks, so you can explore the wetlands even at high water. When you're done browsing, retrace your route back to the intersection with Pleasant Plains Road, and turn left into the swamp.

(**) A quarter of a mile ahead on your right is the Great Swamp Wildlife Refuge headquarters (908) 647-1222. It has a few exhibits and a lot of leaflets on the birds, mammals, reptiles, amphibians, fishes, and wildflowers of the swamp, plus maps of the trails. Unfortunately, it's open only Monday through Friday from 8 A.M. to 4:30 P.M., so weekend visitors are out of luck. When you leave, exit to your right to continue the ride.

Shortly after you pass through the gate into the refuge, the road degenerates into gravel for the next 1.4 miles—gravel that eventually becomes chunky stones. But the gravel, plus the occasional speedbump, reminds you why you're here: to take your time to stop, listen, and watch for waterfowl. If you prefer, walk your bike. One October my bicycle touring class and I were lucky enough to encounter several dedicated birders, who pointed out cedar waxwings, chickadees, red house finches, indigo buntings, and even a bluebird—which, despite its prevalence in song and legend, is a borderline endangered species.

All this is in Great Swamp Wildlife Refuge's western half, which the refuge staff intensively manages to maintain an optimum habitat for a wide variety of wildlife. Water levels are regulated, grasslands and brush are periodically mowed to encourage a diversity of species, shrubs are planted, and nesting structures erected for wood ducks, bluebirds, and other fowl.

The gravel road bends left, eventually ending in a turnaround before a bridge across the Great Brook. But even though the signs say it is not a through road, that message pertains only to cars, which are turned back at the gate across the bridge. However, the gate is designed to admit a pedestrian and a bicycle (even one with a child seat), which can be wheeled under it to the far right. But don't overlook the almost prehistoric scenery photo opportunities from this bridge: vine-hung trees and marshy wetlands, ready for a pterodactyl to wheel overhead.

Once over the bridge, you're back on pavement—which feels deliciously smooth—and abruptly into farm country. Note the gracious farmhouses to your left.

Turn right at the "T" intersection onto Lee's Hill Road. Ride briefly alongside the Passaic River tor your left, looking at the back of one of the AT&T Company's office buildings on the opposite bank. At the first fork, make a left and begin climbing and coasting along Bailey's Mill Road—a narrow, bumpy back road that feels undiscovered. Undiscovered it's not, though; those enormous modern mansions on the right I saw at various stages of construction. Now they're fully landscaped. But what's always struck me about these huge homes in New Jersey is that I've never seen them occupied; seems that the folks who can afford to own them spend their time elsewhere in the world.

After you've meandered awhile, make a right at the first intersection onto Young's Road, another undulating country lane with plenty of trees and meadows. Ride it until it ends. Turn right at the "T" intersection onto the moderately busy Lee's Hill Road, and then make an immediate left onto Lindsley Road. Continue your rolling exploration of the forest and an occasional pond until the road ends. Turn left at the "T" intersection onto Long Hill Road. Coast down a gentle hill to your old friend, Lee's Hill Road—the third and last time you'll encounter it.

Pedal straight across Glen Alpin Road; you'll discover that at that intersection Lee's Hill Road changes name to Blue Mill Road. Now, be careful on the descent—that green acreage on your left means lunch. Turn left into Bayne Park, opposite the road sign proclaiming GOOSE XING, taking care on the gravel.

Bayne Park is a beautiful little oasis with a pond and fountains, but it has no facilities—not even garbage cans. Even though the sign says it's for residents, unobtrusive bicyclists are welcome if they take their lunch litter with them when they leave. The geese and ducks there are quite tame—to the point of being insistent on sharing your lunch. Lie back in the dappled shade on one of the benches or dabble your toes in the refreshingly cool freshet of the small creek or photograph your companions standing on the miniature stone bridge.

It is at Bayne Park that you must decide whether to go on for the full 22-mile long ride or the shorter 14-mile ride. You have already ridden just under 11 miles, so judge your energy and time from that.

If you opt for the shorter ride, cross Blue Mill Road onto Millbrook Road, directly across from the park. After one uphill, the rest is all flat or downhill. Turn right at the "T" intersection onto Pleasantville Road, left at the next "T" intersection onto Long Hill Road, and straight for the last mile or so until you see the sign directing you right into the Great Swamp refuge parking lot. Watch for the gravel as you head back for your car.

If you want to continue on the longer ride, turn left out of Bayne Park onto Blue Mill Road. After about three-quarters of a mile, turn left onto Van Beuren Lane, a wonderfully narrow, winding country lane where you'll see cattle and sheep grazing in fields to your left. One early evening in late May, I also coasted by a pair of deer, and a woodchuck hurried across the road in front of me bearing a pup in its mouth.

Turn right at the "T" intersection onto the moderately busy Spring Valley Road. Ride slowly here, gazing into the bushes to your right: in late July or early August you may find the branches heavy with ripe raspberries.

After a short quarter mile, turn left onto Kitchell Road and glide down the short hill into the Loantaka Brook Reservation. To your left is a parking area with playground equipment and a picnic shelter with public barbecue grills, which overlook the sparkling Kitchell Pond; at the far end of the parking lot are restrooms. It's a beautiful and well-appointed park, where you may well wish to spread out a blanket and drowse the afternoon away to the laughter of children feeding the ducks or flying a kite.

To continue the ride, take the paved bike path opposite the Loantaka Brook Reservation sign (after your descent down Kitchell Road, you'll turn right onto the path).

This path is one of the best parts of this entire ride, meandering through the sunlight filtering through the slender trees. Depending on the time of year, I've seen broad-leafed plants, soft grasses, wild violets, and even bright orange mushrooms. A quarter of a mile after you join it, the path dips and crosses a creek bed, just like old colonial roads used to do. You can either ride right through the shallow flowing water (just test your brakes on the other side) or avoid the wetness by lifting your bike and walking across the nine concrete stepping stones on your left.

Three-quarters of a mile later, where a second paved bike path intersects yours at right angled, you have a choice. Turn left, and you can return to the New Jersey Transit railroad station at Convent Station (see "Of Convents and Bike Paths"). Turn right to continue back to the swamp. If you turn right, the path curves left until you reach the moderately busy Loantaka Way, which you cross on foot to continue on the paved path directly ahead of you. Soon you'll be following the meandering Loantaka Brook babbling alongside to your left.

Now you have another mile of wandering through fields and forests on the path. Take time to enjoy the ferns and flowers and to read the labels describing the vegetation (with a remarkable number of typographical and grammatical errors). Eventually the path comes to an end at a set of low parallel bars that compel most cyclists to dismount and walk their bikes through. I say "most" cyclists, because one of the teenagers in my bicycle touring class simply lifted his legs and rode right through. No fear. (*FYI:* Even a child seat and low-rider front panniers can be maneuvered through these bars—so until you try, don't assume you have to dismantle your equipage.)

Turn right at the path's end onto Green Village Road; a small fire station is on your right. You'll soon pass The Farm at Green Village, a nursery-cum-farmstand on your left where you can buy perennials or melt-in-your-mouth fresh corn.

When you see the Sunoco gas station and the Green Village Deli on your right—the only other deli besides Dom's on this tour—turn left onto Meyersville Road (another one by the same name). This is a nearly untraveled country lane from back in time, so pedal slowly and enjoy the rural feel.

If you are in the mood for a hike, take Meyersville Road to its end; in a mile it dead-ends into a parking area that is the head of about 8 miles of foot trails into the eastern half of the Great Swamp. Lock your bikes together or to a nearby fence before entering a trail, as bicycles—even mountain bikes—are not allowed. This eastern half of the swamp was designated a wilderness area by an act of Congress in 1968. As such, it is unmanaged, and is left to the course of its own natural evolution. To researchers, the area serves as an outdoor laboratory. To you, it offers a more pristine outdoor experience than the relatively manicured western half of the refuge.

To resume the ride, retrace your path back a mile along Meyersville Road, eventually turning left onto Woodland Road. Take the next right at the dead end sign onto Miller Road, another relaxing farm lane. At its end, turn left at the "T" intersection onto rolling Pleasantville Road. Now you'll just stay on Pleasantville Road for more than a mile and a half, enjoying its shady dips, until it ends.

Turn left at the "T" intersection onto Long Hill Road, and a mile and a half later turn right into the gravel parking lot of the Great Swamp wildlife observation area. Sneak a peak at the birds' evening activities before saying farewell to this wilderness.

BLACK RIVER RETREAT

Somerset & Hunterdon Counties, New Jersey

Ride Ratings

Length: 23 miles
Configuration: figure 8
Difficulty: flat along the river, gently rolling elsewhere; traffic is very light
Surface: 2.5 miles of dirt road; the rest is good pavement

—Highlights: This gentle ride features life's simple pleasures: quiet and lush riverbank scenery, a picnic lunch, and nonexistent traffic.

Sometimes you simply have to get away—away from all other people and any sign of civilization. If you want a day of solitude, a retreat if you will, to commune with nature and refresh your spirit, this quiet pilgrimage through the forest along the banks of the Lamington River may be just the Rx for peace.

This ride, along the border of Somerset and Hunterdon counties in New Jersey, is one of the two farthest west in this book (the other is the "Netcong Getaway"). It is also one of the most rural—as indicated by the astonishing fact that even in the 1990s, many of the important town roads through the woods and farm fields are still graded dirt and fine gravel. What a change from New York City, which is less than two hours' drive to the east!

In fact, it was quite a challenge to design a ride in this area that minimized the travel on unpaved roads. But don't let the few in this ride concern you. The unpaved roads are well-maintained, some of them with a remarkably smooth and hard surface. Once you get used to them, you'll find yourself handling the bike virtually as you do on asphalt. Although they are easiest if you have a mountain bike, the roads are suitable even for a thin-tire touring bike like mine. I happened to do this ride just after a rain, and found that the slight dampness actually helped compact the road surface and settle dust.

It was also a challenge to design a ride in this area that minimized hills. Western New Jersey is

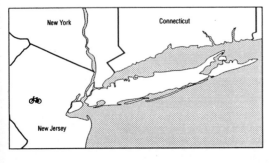

New York

Connecticut

New Jersey

characterized by parallel ranges of hills stretching northeast to southwest. While diminutive by West Coast standards—the highest point in the state, appropriately called High Point, is all of 1500 feet altitude—these rollers are nonetheless prevalent enough and steep enough to challenge even an animal cyclist. The secret to avoiding them is to stick to the river valleys. And that's what this ride does in its course up and down the meandering Lamington River, following the suggestion of literature from the state bicycle coordinator of New Jersey. So the most change in altitude you'll encounter are some gently rolling rises for variety.

As this is one of the few rides in this book that is not near a commuter rail line, you must drive to its start. From New York City, you want to end up heading west on Interstate 78; take exit 26 south onto Rattlesnake Bridge Road (County Road 665), which changes its name to Lamington Road. After a couple of miles, turn left into the campus of Raritan Valley Community College, and park in Parking Lot 5 for nonstudent visitors. This free parking area seems to be open to considerate folks all year round; the campus also seems to be a gathering place for local bicycle-club rides, at least judging from the sheer number of colored arrows painted on the ground.

One more suggestion: fill your water bottles at home and bring your own snacks. There is one deli in Pottersville about 10 miles into the ride where you can buy lunch, but there are no other services. Even the couple of miles down Rattlesnake Bridge Road passes no shops. After all, this is a solitary retreat from civilization . . .

To start by taking a quick tour of the college campus, turn right out of Parking Lot 5 and head left at the stop sign where the road forks. Coast downhill past the college buildings, around to the right past the pond with its geese, to the campus' main exit facing County Road 523 Spur.

Turn left onto the wide shoulders of County 523 Spur, checking out all the bike club arrows painted on the ground! You're in good company! Some of these arrows will be your companions on some of the roads, although I didn't follow them in designing this route.

After half a mile, turn left at the BP service station to head north on Burnt Mills Road (County Road 641). This is the last opportunity for 10 miles to fill your water bottles, so smile pleasantly when you ask for the restroom key.

A mile up this slightly rolling, quiet road is a sign that informs you you're on an official bike route—and a nice one it is, too, through the quiet woods. Shortly afterward, you'll reach the crest; enjoy the view of the distant hills to your right as you coast down. At the bottom, you'll cross the wonderful one-lane iron Burnt Mills Bridge, built in 1928. This ride will take you over several such antiques, well worth an examination stop and a photo.

At the stop sign, go straight even though Burnt Mills Road turns left; now you're on Cowperthwaite Road. In half a mile turn left onto River Road, just before the overpass for Interstate 78. During my ride in mid-July, the highway's embankments were blanketed in soft, multicolored wildflowers. River Road parallels the interstate for three-quarters of a mile, then mercifully turns away from its traffic noise and heads off into the woods.

At the stop sign, turn right onto the wide shoulders of moderately busy Rattlesnake Bridge Road (County Road 665), heading north over Interstate 78. After you pass the two traffic lights, the road gets narrower and less busy, and suddenly you'll find yourself riding through very beautiful farmland.

Make a right at the "T" intersection onto County Road 523, then an immediate left onto Black River Road. The few houses you just passed make up the town of Lamington. Note the wonderful sign, WATCH FOR HORSES, JOGGERS, BICYCLES—this is my kind of place! Ride slowly; in July you'll hear the singing hum of cicadas.

Relax . . . You'll meander along Black River Road for the next four miles. After spending a little time in flat, open farmland, the road will then dip into a wooded hollow and the Lamington River itself will appear in the shade to your left. It's a small river, more like a wide creek, but its burbling is companionable. And don't ask me why the road that goes along the Lamington River is called the Black River Road; it's a mystery to contemplate as you watch how the river parts around a narrow island, and then rejoins a tenth of a mile further north.

When you cross the concrete Vliettown Bridge Number 2 (built in 1931), you might want to pause for a while to enjoy the unobstructed view and babbling of the river. Then continue on, perhaps seeing cattle resting in the fields up to your left. Soon you'll cross over the river again on Vliettown Bridge Number 1 (also built in 1931). At a third river crossing, note the United States Geological Survey stream-gauging station in what looks for all the world like a birdhouse. By the way, since the river marks the boundary between Somerset and Hunterdon counties, each time you cross over a bridge, you're also switching counties. So, if you're with a lover, you could say that you're wanted in two counties!

Eventually you'll be riding along the white fence of Oak Hollow Farm, which marks the southern limit of the town of Pottersville. North of here pleasant houses make up a rural residential community. Continue pedaling past the stone-lined pond to your left and the Pottersville Reformed Church (1866) and cemetery to your right.

Just past the church, follow the left fork of the "Y" intersection at the yield sign onto Pottersville Road (County Road 512), and continue left around the curve. Opening up to your left is a parking lot before a post office, a liquor store, and a deli—this last conveniently open seven days a week (7 A.M.-8 P.M. Monday through Saturday and 7 A.M.-5 P.M. on Sunday). There's also a pay telephone, and a couple of picnic tables in the shade of some trees. If you like sitting on furniture while you eat, this is your only opportunity on the ride. If, in the spirit of your solitary retreat, you want more privacy, then just buy your lunch and pick whatever tucked-away spot appeals to you. For soon you'll be embarking on an even more rustic portion of the ride.

Turn left onto McCan Mill Road just past the deli's picnic tables, and begin a gentle climb. Although this road starts off paved, by the time you reach the long plateau it has degenerated into rather rutted dirt. About a mile after the deli, you'll cross over an exceptionally stony creek. You'll continue to pass an occasional house, and eventually a school in the crossroads town of Vliettown. Shortly thereafter, the Lamington River will reappear to your left, and you'll cross it via an undated iron bridge.

Turn right at the "T" intersection onto the pavement of unmarked Black River Road to retrace just half a mile of an earlier section of the route. Take the first right onto Vliettown Road, continuing right at the "T" intersection a hundred yards later.

Now you're climbing between the cleared, rounded hills of farms. Don't let the humble appearance of the terrain fool you; you're now entering the playgrounds of the rich and famous who wish to remain incognito, and may catch a glimpse of how the other 0.01 percent of us live. As I was repairing a flat bicycle tire for a local damsel in distress, she informed me that the late Jacqueline Onassis liked to go horseback-riding over these hills and to stay at the Tewksbury Inn farther west.

There are also some unusual hobbyists here: on the July afternoon I was here, I had to pull over to the side to let pass a dozen horses and buggies carrying gentlemen in top hats and women in long, 19th-century period costumes carrying parasols. When I asked whether it was an outing for a club or society, they replied: "No, just some neighbors getting together!"

In a quarter mile the road makes a sharp left, giving you a wonderful view before you start your descent. Just after crossing a bridge over a small creek called Cold Brook, turn left onto Cold Brook Road, which is of high-quality graded dirt. Shortly after I made this turn, a tiny brown rabbit with a perfect white cottontail hopped frantically alongside me for 20 feet before disappearing into the grass.

After about a mile, turn left at the "T" intersection onto paved Lamington Road (County Road 523), and make an immediate right onto Felmley Road. In a little less than a mile, turn left onto Gulick Road; by this time you can hear Interstate 78, and as Gulick Road takes you under it you can also smell the car exhaust. Ugh. Eventually Gulick changes its name to Cedar Road.

About a mile after the interstate underpass, turn left onto Meadow Road—

aptly named, you'll agree, for the wide farm meadows through which you'll be pedaling. Turn left at the "T" intersection onto Lamington Road (a different one; there are at least three by this name in this area) and coast downhill over another iron bridge. But even though it's a lovely downhill, don't race across the bridge; pause to enjoy the placid water of the Lamington River and the wooded island to your right.

With this river crossing, you're back in Somerset County for good, and the road has changed name to River Road West. On your left is the manicured golf course of the Fiddlers Elbow Country Club. The day I was riding, a deer crossed right in front of me even though it was 1 P.M.!

Turn right at the stop sign onto Rattlesnake Bridge Road; even though it's moderately busy, you'll have plenty of room on the wide paved shoulders. In a quarter mile you'll pass over the river one last time; I waved to late afternoon fishermen. Here you'll begin climbing and eventually lose the wide right shoulder, so pedal with caution. But you don't have much farther to go.

Turn left into the well-marked entrance of the Raritan Valley Community College; note that this lane is designated an official bike route. Bear left at the "Y" intersection, and then turn left into Parking Lot 5. Want to do it again?

DELAWARE & RARITAN CANAL RIDE

Somerset County, New Jersey

The real way to enjoy this ride is to prepare for its end. Pack in the trunk of your car a cooler filled with ice, hotdogs, hamburgers, beer, soft drinks, and all the fixings for a full-fledged cookout after you've finished the route. Guaranteed you'll be in the mood.

I first devised this ride for the students of my "Bicycle Touring: An Introduction" class offered through the South Orange-Maplewood Adult School in Maplewood, New Jersey; it now includes some lovely modifications suggested by my Morristown cycling companion Alan Wolf and some mapping help from one student Eileen Serow of Maplewood.

Since it is featured as the first ride of each class, I took great care to ensure that it was flat, beautiful, largely free of automobile traffic, and had many attractions—a combination of four characteristics that are a challenge to find all together in the greater New York metropolitan area. But the enthusiasm and exclamations of the dozens of students I've brought here have been reward and testimony enough of its success.

The ride begins and ends at Colonial Park in Manville, about 15 miles north of Princeton. Colonial Park has everything for all ages: picnic tables, barbecue grills, teeter-totters, slides, swings (even baby swings), nature trails, tennis courts, a fitness circuit, a pond with paddleboats, the Spooky Brook golf course, an

Ride Ratings

Length: 17 or 22 miles plus optional 7-mile detour for ice cream
Configuration: line with two optional loops
Difficulty: flat to gently rolling; longer route has one significant climb; portions of the ice cream loop features moderate to heavy traffic
Surface: good pavement with off-road riding on canal towpath

—*Highlights: This ride features truly rural cycling through cornfields, canoeing on the Delaware & Raritan Canal, hiking, picnicking, golfing; the 7-mile detour will lead to the best homemade ice cream in creation.*

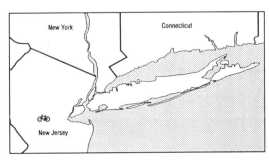

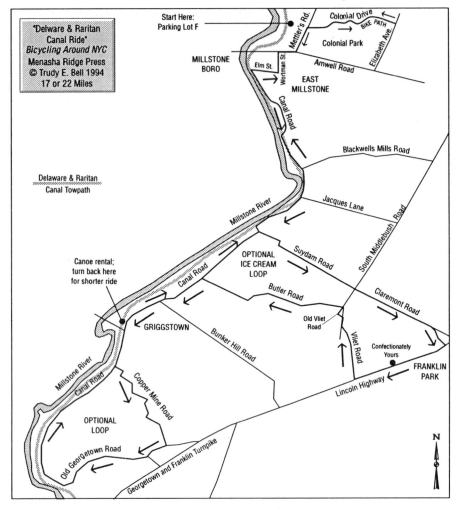

"Delware & Raritan Canal Ride"
Bicycling Around NYC
Menasha Ridge Press
© Trudy E. Bell 1994
17 or 22 Miles

Start Here:
Parking Lot F

Mettie's Rd.

Colonial Drive
BIKE PATH

Colonial Park

Elizabeth Ave.

MILLSTONE
BORO

Elm St.

Wortman St.

Amwell Road

EAST
MILLSTONE

Canal Road

Blackwells Mills Road

Delaware & Raritan
Canal Towpath

Jacques Lane

Millstone River

South Middlebush Road

Canoe rental;
turn back here
for shorter ride

OPTIONAL
ICE CREAM
LOOP

Suydam Road

Canal Road

Butler Road

Claremont Road

Old Vliet
Road

GRIGGSTOWN

Bunker Hill Road

Vliet Road

Confectionately
Yours

Millstone River

Canal Road

FRANKLIN
PARK

Copper Mine Road

Lincoln Highway

OPTIONAL
LOOP

Old Georgetown Road

Georgetown and Franklin Turnpike

N

arboretum, a fragrance and sensory garden, a bridle path, a softball diamond, and plenty of soft green grass for laying out a blanket and relaxing pleasantly exercised muscles.

The park also seems to be popular with the matrimonial crowd—the first day I scouted out this route in June, I saw two weddings, one in the lilac garden and one in the rose garden. You may even see the van of Brooks Country Cycling and Hiking, a New York City-based commercial bicycle touring organization (formerly Country Cycling Tours), parked nearby, but they take a different route.

The ride itself goes through scenery about as rural as you're likely to find in northern New Jersey, mostly along the Delaware & Raritan canal. When I first scouted it in early June, white wild roses festooned bushes, trees, and embankments and their fragrance filled the late spring breeze. Also, I kept noticing abundant small creeks, probably on the average of one per mile, babbling alongside or across the road.

The entire shorter ride is virtually flat—an ideal starter for the season, or for someone new to the beauties of bicycle touring. The longer ride has one climb up to a plateau. It is well worth the low gears or walking the bike, for at the top are some wonderful horse farms and cornfields. And at the end of the longer loop, there is a glorious extended downhill coast back to the canal.

For either ride, one attraction of Griggstown is the opportunity to rent a canoe to paddle along the slow-moving canal. You also have the choice of pedaling back either the way you came along Canal Road (a generally quiet country lane with the canal on one side and farm fields on the other) or along the unpaved towpath between the canal and the Millstone River.

The Delaware & Raritan Canal's course wanders through river valleys between Bordentown on the Delaware River and New Brunswick on the Raritan River—a distance of 44 miles; in addition, a 22-mile feeder channel was built from Trenton north along the Delaware River (which marks the Pennsylvania-New Jersey border) to supply water to the canal. With the exception of a few sections around Trenton and New Brunswick, the entire Delaware & Raritan Canal still flows through the open countryside.

The towpath, from which the barges were towed by mules, is a wide, hard-packed surface, generally suitable for bicycles although it can be muddy the day right after a rain. Sections of it are cobbled, sandy, or bumpy with tree roots, so some kind of a hybrid or fat-tire bike makes for the surest riding.

There is one caution for this ride: try this route sooner rather than later. Dread Progress is on the march in this part of the world, and each time I've taken this route, something old has been effaced by something new. Especially on the optional seven-mile detour for homemade ice cream, large attached houses seem to be rapidly replacing cornfields. I cannot vouch for how long the ride—particularly the ice cream detour—will remain charming and rural.

Near the beginning of the ride, after you leave Colonial Park, you will have the chance to pick up lunch at one of East Millstone's two delis. The only other opportunity for real food is on the optional seven-mile ice cream detour, as there are quite a number of ethnic restaurants and a pizzeria on the busy Lincoln Highway, as well as the ice cream and chocolate confectionary. Other than those options, you can buy granola bars and juice at the Griggstown General Store, where you also rent canoes.

The ride begins from the gravel Parking Lot F in Colonial Park. There you'll find restrooms, a drinking fountain, a pay telephone, and a park office, in addition to widely scattered picnic tables and BBQ grills.

To drive to Colonial Park, take Interstate 78 west to Interstate 287 south; get off at Exit 7 (Weston Canal Road). At the end of the ramp, turn left at the "T" intersection onto Weston Canal Road, keeping the canal on your right and never crossing it. After a mile or two, make a sharp left at the little white building onto Weston Road (do not follow Weston Canal Road as it curves right and crosses over the canal). Continue another half mile or so and make the first right onto Mettlers Road. Turn right into Parking Lot F.

Alternatively, take U.S. Route 22 west to the Finderne Avenue, Manville exit (there is no warning sign; coming from New York City, the two exits just beforehand are Thompson Avenue, Bound Brook, and Chimney Rock Road).

Once on Finderne Avenue, drive seven miles south to Manville, where the road changes name to Main Street. Turn left at the light (at the Getty gas station) onto Amwell Road, over the canal; about a mile later, turn left onto Mettlers Road; 0.5 mile later turn left into gravel Parking Lot F.

Unfortunately, this ride is one of the few in this book that is not within easy access of public transportation. About the best you can do is take the New Jersey Transit Railroad to the Finderne Avenue, Manville station stop seven miles north of Colonial Park; then follow the directions above for driving south from Route 22. (See the Introduction for information on taking your bicycle on the train.)

To begin the ride, we'll try a little warm-up tour of the park itself. Turn right out of Parking Lot F onto Mettlers Road, heading south. After 150 yards or so, just past the entrance to Colonial Road (the main road through the park), turn left onto the park's 1.3-mile paved bike path. At first you'll skirt Spooky Brook pond on your right and follow a fitness circuit. At 0.6 mile the path crosses Colonial Road and you'll pass a children's playground, another pond with paddleboats to your left, a bridle path, the entrance to a hiking trail, and a golf course.

At the end of the path, turn around and retrace your route back the entire length of the bike path. Take this opportunity to survey the grounds and decide what you'd like to do the rest of the afternoon when you return!

All warmed up? Okay, let's hit the road. At the end of the path, turn left to continue your southward ride on Mettlers Road. After half a mile, turn right at the "T" intersection onto Amwell Road (Somerset County Route 514); as this road may be moderately busy, keep an eye out for cars.

In a quarter mile, take your first left onto Wortman Street. Suddenly you're in the sleepy hamlet of East Millstone, which is all of four blocks on a side. I felt as if I'd been transported to the setting of *To Kill a Mockingbird*. Ride around the town for the local color; you may be lucky enough to happen upon a church bazaar or supper.

At the end of Wortman Street, turn right at the dead end sign onto Elm Street. Four blocks later, pause at Market Street, for here you have a choice. Go straight to continue your ride onto Canal Road. If you want to buy lunch, though, turn right down Market Street to Chester's Market, open 5 A.M.-5 P.M. Monday through Saturday and 5:30 A.M.-1 P.M. on Sunday. If you want something a little fancier, go a hundred yards farther down Market Street until it intersects with Amwell Road; there you'll find PK's Country Kitchen and Deli, which is open Saturdays 7 A.M.-2 P.M. and closed on Sundays.

To continue the ride, return to the intersection of Market and Elm. Continue straight onto the unmarked Canal Road, which bends sharply left. Look to your right: now you are riding south alongside the placid Delaware & Raritan Canal.

Built in the 1830s, the Delaware & Raritan Canal was intended as a smooth way of transporting freight between New York City and Philadelphia. Remember, at that time the railroads were in their infancy and the few horse-cart roads that did exist were difficult at best and impassable at worst. The canal opened the way for farm products and coal from Pennsylvania to reach the Atlantic coast, and fancy dresses and furniture from New York City to reach the country's interior. And when it opened, the Delaware & Raritan Canal served for a century as one of the country's busiest navigation canals. In 1871, its busiest year, it actually carried more tonnage (80 percent of it coal) than the much longer and more famous Erie Canal ever saw.

By the end of the 19th century, though, the railroads came into their own. The Delaware & Raritan Canal never showed a profit after 1892, but still stayed open until the winter of 1932-33, when it was closed for good. Even then, it enjoyed continued life as a source of raw water for farms, industry, and homes, and was used for recreation. In 1973 it was included on the National Registry of Historic Places, and the next year the New Jersey State Legislature passed a bill establishing the 60-mile-long canal as a state park.

Canal Road is now shaded by tall maples and oaks, and portions of it to your right open into flat land wide enough for corn and other crops. To your left, up on the rise, are more cornfields, whose sweet green fragrance fills the summer air.

A couple of miles south of East Millstone, at the four-way stop at Blackwells Mills Road, pause a few moments to gaze at the lovely garden of the Canal House, dating from the 1830s. There is also the small shack of the bridge-tender's station. To the right, across the bridge, is an opportunity to join the towpath if you wish; beyond the towpath is a small park with picnic tables and two portable chemical toilets.

Continue your southward wanderings along Canal Road. A mile later, you'll see the rather elegant round windows of the Township of North Brunswick Water Treatment Facility directly in front of you. Here the road will bend sharply left to meet Suydam Road. If you wish to continue the main ride, turn right just after this bend to stay on Canal Road to Griggstown, and skip down to the double asterisks (**).

But here also is the first of two opportunities to take the seven-mile detour for home-made ice cream (the second opportunity is at this same intersection on the return). If ice cream is your choice, do not turn right onto Canal Road, but continue straight on Suydam Road and ride it until it ends. Suydam will make several bends as it carries you through cultivated farm fields.

After a mile and a half, turn right at the "T" intersection onto the busy South Middlebush Road (Somerset County Route 615 south), and a hundred feet beyond—opposite a rather ramshackle general store—make an immediate left onto Claremont Road. Claremont Road can have moderately heavy traffic, so watch carefully for cars and trucks. You are now riding through the outlying suburbs of Franklin Park. After about a mile, bear right at the "Y" intersection onto Pleasant Plains Road (Somerset County Route 611).

Turn right at the "T" intersection onto the very busy four-lane Lincoln Parkway (New Jersey State Route 27). In spite of the heavy traffic, much of the Lincoln Highway is edged with painted shoulders almost a lane wide. Stay with it for three-quarters of a mile. You will first pass a giant shopping center on your right with a deli and other services. Continue farther to the small shopping center called The Village Shopper, also on your right.

This is the home of Confectionately Yours, center of the best ice cream this side of heaven. This shop is the discovery of my Morristown bicycling companion Alan Wolf, who firmly believes ice cream and chocolate are necessities of life. (Alan also suggested modifying this route to include the ride through Colonial Park.)

Unlike Alan, I'm not a big fan of ice cream; most types I find so cloyingly sweet and mild-flavored I end up sugar-saturated and disappointed. But at Confectionately Yours the peanut butter flavors taste unmistakably of salt and nuts, the pumpkin pie flavor is full of nutmeg and cloves, and the Grand Marnier flavor includes the real liqueur. So generous are the servings that a single scoop is the size of a standard double; moreover, for a few cents more you can ask for a single scoop incorporating two flavors! Yum! The store—which also has cute cards and gifts—is open seven days a week until 10 P.M. in the summer, opening weekdays at 10 A.M. and weekends at 1 P.M.

To resume the ride, turn right out of The Village Shopper to continue south on Lincoln Parkway, making the first right onto Vliet Road. At the "T" intersection, turn right onto South Middlebush Avenue, and then make the first left onto Old Vliet Road. Here new construction is rapidly changing the placement of old country lanes, but you may still be able to capture some of the flavor of a quieter era.

Old Vliet Road will bear sharply right and come to an end at Butler Road, where you should turn left. If you're feeling adventurous, turn left onto the abandoned and secluded Old Butler Road just beforehand; it's only a quarter mile long but has the feel of the road not taken, left to languish as part of history bypassed by faster times. In this case, pick your way around the guard rails at the end to continue the ride onto Butler Road heading left, taking your time along this quiet, shady lane. Once when I was riding, I was lucky enough to see a woodchuck waddling forth out of the brush to cross the road ahead of me.

Turn left at the "T" intersection onto Canal Road.

(**) The north edge of Griggstown is marked by a small but official-looking yellow sign declaring DUCK CROSSING and portraying a silhouette of a mama duck and her ducklings. When I've been there, the area has been complete with actual ducks quacking and placidly pacing around the hummocks and stones of the small creek to your left.

Now you're in true bicyclists' territory—a dozen or more may pass you with cheery waves while you consult your map. A mile later, on your right, are the Griggstown Causeway and the Griggstown General Store, home of canoe rentals and some welcome cold soda and juice. But do not be deceived by the name: although it was once indeed a general store, in 1982 the building was converted to a two-family house and the canoe-renting concession kept the name for historical purposes. You can rent a canoe Saturday and Sunday from 9 A.M. to 7 P.M., at least during the summer; call (908) 359-5970 for more information.

It's at this point that you also need to decide whether you want to go on for the longer 22-mile route or begin your return for the shorter 17-mile route. If lack of time or energy dictate the shorter route, skip down to the quadruple asterisks (****).

If you're game for the longer journey, continue south along Canal Road, turning left in half a mile onto Copper Mine Road. Here is the one significant climb of the ride, and it is reasonably steep. Gear way down and get the old pump working there, or walk your bike. After three quarters of a mile, it levels off at a higher plateau of cultivated fields, gorgeous giant rhododendron bushes, and absolutely no traffic.

Turn right at the "T" intersection onto Old Georgetown Road. At the "Y" intersection, veer to the right to stay on Old Georgetown Road. Now comes a long, wonderful downhill coast, your reward for the uphill—but descend with caution, for at the end the road bends right and ends steeply on Canal Road.

Here at this "T" intersection you have another choice. If you want to stay on paved road for the entire ride, turn right to ride north on Canal Road; three miles north is the Griggstown Causeway and general store. Once there, skip down to pick up the description at the quadruple asterisks (****).

If you're game for trying your skill on the canal's dirt towpath, turn left to ride south on Canal Road. The mileage is essentially the same either by road or by towpath, but the scenery is different—and both alternatives are beautiful. There are also several chances to switch from one to the other, so you haven't committed your life irrevocably to one alternative. I recommend you at least try the first three miles of the towpath.

If the towpath it is, take Canal Road south for less than a quarter mile. Turn right at the "T" intersection onto Somerset County Route 518 (the Georgetown and Franklin Turnpike), cross a short bridge, and make an immediate right into the little gravel parking lot. You will see the wooden gate barring motor vehicles from entering the wide, hard-packed towpath (bicycles are allowed).

Now you're in the sun-dappled woods riding along a raised dike with the placid canal to your right and the Millstone River to your left. You'll see people fishing for the stocked trout, large-mouth bass, bluegill, pumpkinseed, catfish, perch, and pickerel.

After just under two-and-a-half miles you'll come across one of the 14 locks in the canal. Back in the 19th century, from a quarter mile away, barge captains would signal their arrival by blowing on a conch shell, signaling the lock tender to open the lock for the barge. The lock now is no longer in use, but the lovely plashing miniature waterfall through its open gate invites you to sit on the concrete edge and enjoy a snack. Here you can also cross the bridge and switch between the towpath and Canal Road.

If you want to take the towpath for the entire return, you will ride on it for 9.3 miles, until you come to Amwell Road (Somerset County Route 514). Turn right, ride half a mile, turn left onto Mettlers Road at the sign for Colonial Park, pedal another half a mile, and turn left into Parking Lot F. The directions below are for those electing to ride on the paved Canal Road.

(****) At the Griggstown Causeway, you have one more chance to pick up some snacks or rent a canoe. Then continue north past the duck crossing and past the intersection with Butler Road. Now Canal Road has become a true quiet country lane, with barns and farmers loading bales of hay, and the lazy water of the canal to your left—sometimes close by, sometimes a few hundred feet away. The towpath is almost always in sight, so if some of your party want to separate from you and explore their own route in parallel, you can still keep an eye on one another.

Turn left at the "T" intersection where Suydam Road joins Canal Road. You can't miss this intersection—the tanks of the water treatment plant are to your left. This is your second opportunity to try the seven-mile ice cream detour.

A bit farther north, you'll cross Blackwells Mills Road, whose bridge will allow crossing between Canal Road and the towpath. Remember that just west (left) of the bridge and towpath there is a small park with picnic tables and two portable chemical toilets. This four-way stop gives you your second and last chance to admire the 19th-century canal house and bridge tender's station.

A couple of miles north, Canal Road abruptly rises and bends right, ending at the intersection of Market and Elm Streets in East Millstone. Continue straight on Elm Street. Turn left at the "T" intersection onto Wortman Street. Turn right at the next "T" intersection onto Amwell Road (Somerset County Route 514). Then make the first left onto Mettlers Road at the sign for Colonial Park. Half a mile later, turn left into Parking Lot F. Enjoy your cookout!

MOUNTAIN LAKES RIDE

Morris County, New Jersey

One of the greatest attractions of this ride is its apparent contradictions: plowed farm fields only minutes from some of New Jersey's busiest highways, and a bed-and-breakfast home where a modern house was turned antique. I've done my best to link the wonderful parts together in a single thread; but with dread Progress on the loose in New Jersey, my sense is that portions of this ride are fragile: so enjoy your cycling here sooner rather than later before the beauties are paved over.

If you're a bird-watcher or nature lover, take binoculars and prepare to rise before dawn's dew or stay out in gathering dusk: birds cry their sweetest calls before first light during their busy search for breakfast, while deer and raccoons and other nocturnal fauna begin their foraging around dinnertime. For communing with nature, the route offers you a choice of several parks: on even the short ride, there is Grace Lord Park with its gorge and its two beautiful waterfalls plus there is rustic The Tourne County Park; on the longest ride there is also Old Troy Park.

One last note: the town from which the ride starts is called Mountain Lakes. Like many names in areas with some history, this is a description of the geographical features. The more mountainous portions are in the two loops making up the short and middle-length rides; the additional third loop for the long ride is relatively flat. The interior of The Tourne County Park is very hilly indeed.

Ride Ratings

Length: 6, 17, or 25 miles
Configuration: 3 adjoining loops
Difficulty: rolling to moderately hilly, the longest loop is flat; traffic is light to moderate
Surface: good pavement throughout; 2 miles on paved bike paths

—Highlights: This ride features several lovely parks that offer a bird sanctuary, hiking trails, and a remarkable waterfall; also a bed-and-breakfast near good restaurants.

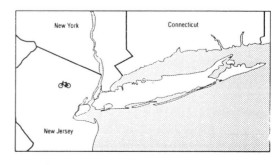

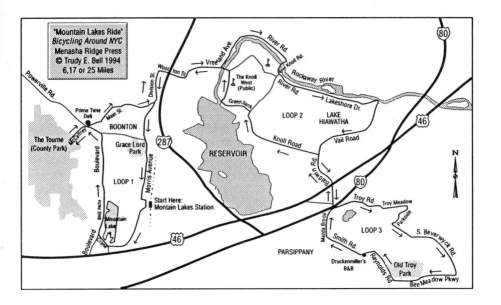

This ride starts from the Mountain Lakes station of the New Jersey Transit railroad (see the preface for information on taking your bike on the train), where you can also park your car on weekends. Alternatively, you can leave your car in the public lot of The Tourne, and pick up the ride from there. The Tourne has pit toilets; at either the train station or the park, there is no ready source of water or food, but not to worry: at about four miles into all the rides you'll come across a fantastic deli.

Before leaving the Mountain Lakes station, take a peek at Phoebe Snows Restaurant in the former station house, noted for its savory hot breads, fresh crisp salads, and creamy quiches. When you're ready to roll, cross the railroad track, going away from the stone building and sheltered bench, and ride left through the parking lot; this is the unmarked Romaine Road. Make a right at the stop sign at the end onto Midvale Road; you've done it right if straight ahead of you there's the brick building of Master Printers.

A quarter of a mile later, turn left onto Morris Avenue and begin climbing. At the crest of the hill, note the three-story house on the left with its whimsical purple shutters. Morris Avenue curves gently right. Soon you'll catch a glimpse of Mountain Lake. To fully enjoy the view, you may want to stop at the log benches near the little cove on your right and admire the sailboats in the distance.

Turn right at the "T" intersection onto Crane Road. A quarter of a mile later, cross the busy Boulevard and make an immediate right onto the paved bicycle path. You'll stay on this path for nearly two miles. This is a lovely stretch, so enjoy its pastoral splendor, keeping an eye out for patches of sand, cars in driveways, and cross streets. Mountain Lake stretches sparkling to your right, protected by massive anchor chains draped like silken cords between concrete stanchions. A bit over a mile up the path is Island Beach Park, although car parking is only for Mountain Lake residents. A little north of the park, smile at the boulder in the grass to your right that is painted to look like a grinning green frog.

At the end of the bicycle path, turn left onto the busy Elcock Avenue, crossing to the far side with care. In a few hundred yards, bear right at the "Y" intersection onto West Main Street, then make an immediate left onto Hawkins Place. You'll be right at Del's Village Shopping Center, with a Food Town grocery store, a drugstore, a restaurant, and other services.

My recommendation is the Prime Time Deli, which is extraordinarily good, even by the standards of New York City, the U.S. capital of delis. The sandwiches are fresh and huge: I ordered a smoked turkey on rye, size medium, and the thing was made on a slice of rye the size of a dinner plate, which was then folded in half. The large uses the full surface of two such dinner-plate-sized slices! For small appetites, even the medium was hearty enough to feed two people.

Get your lunch to go, for you have only a couple hundred yards before the ideal picnic spot. Continue the half-block farther down Hawkins Place, turn right at the "T" intersection onto Elcock Avenue, and an immediate left onto McCaffrey Place, following the signs to The Tourne County Park.

The Tourne is a couple of miles long by more than half a mile wide, making it bigger than New York City's Central Park. More rustic and not so manicured as smaller parks, it offers delightful solitude: on the late June Friday I was there, I saw only one or two people in the whole park lying on blankets and reading. Its hilly main road is deliberately blocked to cars halfway through by a small fenced-off stretch of gravel, but is quite passable to cyclists.

The word "Tourne" comes from the Dutch meaning "lookout" or "mountain"—an apt description: on a clear day, from the top of a rugged trail that winds its way through forest and large rock outcroppings, you can glimpse the skyline of New York City 30 miles to the east. Munch on your wonderful deli sandwich in one of the picnic areas, and then try one of the gravel hiking trails winding through stands of hemlocks or fields of wildflowers; one has the fascinating-sounding destination of Balancing Rock. There are also horseshoe courts, a baseball field, and the Eleanor Hinricksen Bird Sanctuary—an idyllic retreat from "the city that never sleeps." For further information, call the Morris County Park Commission at (201) 829-0474.

Retrace your way back out McCaffrey Place and turn right onto the busy Elcock Avenue. Take the first left onto Hawkins Place past Del's Village Shopping Center again. Hawkins Place joins the moderately busy West Main Street at the stop sign. Keep going straight on West Main.

A quarter of a mile later, at the base of the gentle downhill, is Grace Lord Park, given to the town of Boonton by as a memorial to one Grace Lord Nicoll by her family. This park is worth a stop not so much for what you see, but for what you cannot see from the road. There is a grassy lawn with a gazebo and a lake, a children's playground, and a placid pond. Dismount and walk on the trail that goes along the right side of the pond. In a minute or two you'll see a large, artificial waterfall where the water of the Rockaway River rushes over the dam creating the pond and then courses through a surprisingly deep gorge.

Keep walking down the trail next to the gorge, and claim your reward: a wild, cascading, natural waterfall plunging torrentially over boulders and crashing so loudly you must yell to be heard even two feet away. When I was there on a late June morning, a solitary fisherman was casting his line to try his luck in catching lunch. I find the sound of water—any water: burbling creeks, roaring waterfalls, breaking waves—so relaxing that it would be easy to sit on one of the ledges and lean back against the stone for the whole day through . . .

When you're ready—and only then—climb back up the trail and remount your bike to continue past the park on Main Street (the park will be to your right). But don't go too far. Just on the other side of the bridge over the pond, bear right onto the bicycle path into Helen Boesche Park. Ride through the basketball courts and tennis courts, keeping an eye to your right to gaze down into the gorge of Grace Lord Park and its waterfalls. Continue riding through the parking lot.

You are now riding on Plane Street behind the shops on the Main Street of Boonton. In short order, Plane Street will give you a choice: either you can continue your way down Plane Street, or you can turn left to exit from the lots, turning right onto Boonton's busy Main Street.

Main Street is narrow with a lot of traffic and is a steep descent. But it also has a bakery, a bicycle shop called the Crankers Cycle Shop, antiques shops, a map store that among other things sells envelopes made from recycled U.S. Geological Survey topographic maps, and even a store for selling and repairing player pianos. Plane Street, with virtually no traffic, also has its charms, among them the tucked-away Bethel AME Church—and it joins Main Street with a right-hand turn at the bottom in a quarter mile.

The traffic light just before the iron bridge marks the intersection of Main Street with Division Street heading left and Morris Avenue heading right. It is also a decision point between the shortest ride and the longer two. If you want the shortest ride, turn right here onto Morris Avenue and pick up the instructions near the end of the chapter at the double asterisks (**) for a total ride of 6.4 miles.

For either the middle or longest ride, turn left onto Division Street. You'll pass abandoned railroad cars on your right, and extra parking for Kelly's Station Restaurant, which was built in some of the sided train cars. Continue pedaling past abandoned factories and vacant lots, keeping the railroad tracks on your right—trust me, the industrial ugly scenery does improve. At the first stop sign, turn right onto Wootton Street, take the bridge over the railroad tracks, go through the light, and pass under Interstate 287, continuing straight until Wootton Street ends. Turn left at the "T" intersection onto the busy Lathrop Avenue. The inviting grounds ahead of you are part of the New Jersey Firemen's Home.

Turn right at the next "T" intersection onto Vreeland Avenue, a name that made me nostalgically recall my college dating of one astronomically inclined Albert P. Vreeland. Wonder whatever became of him? Vreeland Avenue is a wonderful downhill coast past cultivated fields, although you should take care to avoid the bicycle-tire-eating grates on the side. Half a mile later, turn left at concrete triangle at the "T" intersection to stay on Vreeland Avenue.

Right around here there are two white frame clapboard houses that might not necessarily catch your eyes, but the markers tell of their quite ancient history (by American standards). On your immediate left is the Miller-Kingsland House, whose west wing was originally built by Johannes Miller in 1740 and whose large Federal-style addition was built in 1808 by Isaac Kingsland. On your right is the Johannes Parlaman house, whose original western section was built around 1755. Can you imagine what this road might have looked like around the Revolutionary War, with these two houses?

Continue on Vreeland Avenue, which will carry you through flat, plowed farm fields; in late June, the succession planting of corn on your left was evident in neighboring fields by the different heights of the maturing corn plants. Turn right at the "T" intersection onto River Road. Now you're pedaling alongside the lazy Rockaway River, which looks more like a large creek visible through the trees to your right. To your left, across from it, you might want to buy some of the scrumptious fresh produce at the sprawling Condurso's Garden Center and Farm Market.

At the first left turn after Condurso's—Church Lane—you might want to pause and consider a pleasant option: picking up a bottle of excellent wine for dinner or the ride home. If that appeals to you, turn left onto Church Lane, turn left again at the end onto Change Bridge Road, and ride a mile or so until it dead-ends at U.S. Route 202. Diagonally to your right across the busy Route 202 is the Red Barn Plaza.

The plaza includes Red Barn Wines & Liquors, run by Orville Druckenmiller and his son Craig. The spacious, airy, immaculately kept Red Barn Wines & Liquors was the first gourmet wine store to be opened in the Parsippany area. Featuring 50 different domestic and imported beers plus a wide selection of wines, all at discount, it might tempt your wallet and bungee cords. But never fear. Orville happens also to be the husband of Janet Druckenmiller, hostess of Druckenmiller's bed-and-breakfast guest house, where you just might have decided to stay the night. The advantage of that connection is that you might ask Orville whether he would be so kind as to take your purchases back to the inn in his car, freeing you to continue your ride unladen. Before you leave, you might want to visit the deli in the Red Barn Plaza, which Janet notes features tasty scrambled-egg sandwiches, homemade soups, and sloppy joes.

When you're ready to resume riding, retrace your way back on Route 202, left onto Change Bridge Road, a mile later turning right onto Church Lane, and left at the end onto River Road.

In maybe half a mile, take your first right on the bridge across the river onto the unmarked Knoll Road. Knoll Road climbs for a quarter of a mile. At the yellow blinker, turn left onto North Beverwyck Road. In less than a quarter mile, make another left onto Cayuga Avenue; this turn is easy to miss, so watch for it—it is opposite the fourth group of brick apartment houses, which are designated 199C.

Now your route is blessedly free of traffic. Turn right onto the end onto River Drive. You are now riding along the other bank of the Rockaway River, whose placid waters you can glimpse between the quiet homes to your left. I envied these people; how nice it must be to live right on a river or creek.

Turn left at the stop sign onto Hiawatha Boulevard and then take an immediate right to continue on River Drive. In a quarter mile, bear left at the "Y" intersection to continue on River Drive, past the massive concrete retaining wall that silently vows "never again" to floods. A bit beyond, turn left at the stop sign onto Lake Shore Drive, riding past a small children's playground and the Lake Hiawatha Community Club. Long ago there really used to be a Lake Hiawatha that attracted summering New Yorkers. To your right, all the cross streets bear the names of Indian tribes: Mohawk, Pawnee, Seminole, Ute.

Turn right at the "T" intersection onto Vail Road, climbing uphill to cross the busy North Beverwyck Road at the light. The blinking yellow light at Knoll Road is another decision point: if you want the middle-length ride, turn right at the blinking yellow light onto Knoll Road and pick up the instructions at the quadruple asterisks (****) for a total ride of 17 miles.

For the longest ride go straight, continuing on Vail Road, but take care: in a few hundred yards bear left at the "Y" intersection onto Baldwin Road. In half a mile, you'll cross the major divided highway U.S. Route 46 at the light. Just before that intersection, there are shops allowing you to refuel on Gatorade or to stuff yourself with seafood at the North American Lobster House. The bagel shop in the little mall is notable for selling not only standard-sized bagels and miniature cocktail-appetizer bagels, but also giant party bagels weighing up to four pounds!

Shortly after crossing Route 46, Baldwin Road will bear left and to carry you over Interstate 80, where the overpass is painted dark blue with white stars and the smiling yellow faces of Mr. Sun and Mr. Moon—a cheerful gift of the students from Central Junior High.

Turn left at the "T" intersection onto Troy Road (Mazdabrook Road goes right). Now you're coasting in the cooling shade of trees past and some lovely meadows. In two-thirds of a mile, turn right at the "T" intersection onto the moderately busy, unmarked South Beverwyck Road and begin climbing uphill. At the crest, not a tenth of a mile later, turn left onto Troy Meadow Road, where a sign pointing left reads Troy Meadows Trap Club.

When I first scouted this ride, I saw on the map that this road led to a huge green area called the Troy Meadows Green Acres Project. That sounds promising as a picnic spot for the bike book, I thought, imagining something as wonderful as the Great Swamp Wildlife Refuge (see "Exploring the Great Swamp"). The road got bumpier and I kept hearing shotgun reports, but I persisted; it ended about a mile later in a gravel parking lot strewn with empty gun cartridges where lots of burly men in fuzzy black-and-red buffalo-plaid jackets were introducing their gawky 11-year-old sons into the Rites of Manhood. So there I was, a lone female in black Lycra, pedaling into this all-male sanctuary with my innocent questions about hiking trails and picnic tables. They stared, but very courteously told me no such things existed.

So, I departed, and am now advising you not to pay the place a visit, but instead to make your first right turn onto Parkside Drive. Pedal through the swooping S-curve, and then turn left at the stop sign to rejoin South Beverwyck Road (Reynolds Avenue goes right). This is a pleasant, winding descent through shady woods past pre-Revolutionary homes, although again you should watch for the bicycle-tire-eating grates (in the autumn, especially, avoid riding through piles of leaves, which may have collected over the dangerous grates). You'll pass the Parsippany Board of Education Transportation Department, home to a fleet of yellow school buses, and then you'll ride under some high-tension power lines.

Turn right at the light onto Bee Meadow Parkway, a wide highway obviously intended for heavy traffic, although on Labor Day morning there was scarcely an automobile in sight. Turn right again at the flashing red light onto Reynolds Avenue, following the small painted arrows on the ground—happy signs that this road has been deemed attractive by local bicycle clubs. Reynolds Avenue narrows to two lanes.

A quarter mile later, across from the Reynolds Avenue Soccer Facility is the Old Troy County Park, a quiet little out-of-the-way park with hiking trails to a pond with bullfrogs and water lilies, a softball diamond, picnic tables with barbecue grills, and—dear to cyclists' heart—restrooms with flush toilets and running water. Since this park falls about half-way through the longest ride— 12 miles from the start at the Mountain Lakes railroad station—it is conveniently situated as a rest stop.

It is also less than half a mile from Druckenmiller's bed and breakfast guest house, if you're making this trip an overnighter. When you emerge from the park, turn right to continue north on Reynolds Road. Make the first left onto Smith Road, right after the yellow school BUS STOP AHEAD sign. Druckenmiller's guest house is the brown shake house surrounded by a split rail fence on your left (880 Smith Road), the second house after Deauville Drive.

I have the distinction of having been their first guest ever when they opened for business in September, 1990. Now, the hostess Janet Druckenmiller explained, there is a one-bedroom suite with private bath occupied for months at a time by one or another short-term corporate client, with a shared-bath bedroom (where I stayed) reserved for drop-in travelers. The home, which is quite modern, has been made to feel comfortably antique by Janet's careful redecoration, and my bicycle was safely stored in the garage.

Janet serves a full breakfast on the lattice-shaded deck outside that overlooks the large lawn and a profusion of flowers continuously in bloom from April through October—a testimony to her impeccable landscaping. She's also a notable chef. You could have just a continental breakfast if you wish, but I'd suggest her full breakfast, which may include shirred eggs stratta or mouthwatering fruit frappes or fruit-filled muffins, along with fresh-squeezed juice and heavenly coffee. With notice and for a modest extra charge, she would also be happy to pack you a lunch for the road. Children are also welcome, with no age limit, if space is available. For reservations, please contact Bed & Breakfast Reservations, Inc., in Chatham, New Jersey, by calling (201) 635-6777.

Leaving the Druckenmillers', turn left onto Smith Road to continue the ride. At the "T" intersection, turn right to stay on Smith Road (Dunkirk Road goes left), past the gas station and past the sheep in the pen to your left. Immediately over the small bridge, bear right at the "Y" intersection onto Mazdabrook Road, coasting down through the woods. Then take the first left onto Baldwin Road to cross the whimsical astronomical overpass over Interstate 80, following the bike club arrows painted on the pavement, which also point left. Cross

Route 46, and turn right at the stop sign onto Vail Road. At the yellow blinker, turn left onto Knoll Road.

(****) On Knoll Road you'll be cycling first through residential areas, then through forest, which all but obscures the reservoir of the Jersey City Water Works on your left. First you'll be climbing a gentle uphill, which turns into a gentle downhill coast sweeping to the right.

At the first stop sign, turn left onto Greenbank Road, and continue your downhill coast, past the reservoir's big earth-fill dam as you glide by. A quarter mile later, you can halt in your climb to see the bubbling circular tanks of the sludge-thickening facilities used for water-pollution control by the Rockaway Valley Region Sewerage Authority. It does not smell, and the whole place with its weird clean architecture looks like something out of a science fiction movie.

At the "T" intersection, turn left onto Vreeland Avenue, a pretty stiff climb, paying for the earlier glorious coast. For the next mile, you'll be backtracking some roads you took on the way out. Make the first left onto Lathrop Avenue, and then the second right onto Wootton Street. After passing under Interstate 287, crossing U.S. Route 202, and riding over the railroad tracks—all in quick succession—make the next left onto Division Street, through industrial suburbia again.

(**) At the iron bridge of Boonton's Main Street, ride straight through the light to continue on Morris Avenue. At first you'll descend but soon you'll start climbing a reasonably challenging hill. In half a mile or so, bear left at the "Y" intersection about a mile later to stay on Morris Avenue (Bellvale Road goes right). To your right is a beautiful wooded area and then a gazebo.

At the Mountain Lakes Public Library, turn left onto Elm Road, then right at the end onto the unmarked Romaine Road to Mountain Lakes railroad station. Cross the tracks to wait at the sheltered bench for the next train back to New York City.

Sandy Hook: A Day at the Beach

Monmouth County, New Jersey

Pack your swimsuit and a small drink cooler for this ride, for it features a day at one of the tri-state area's most popular series of beaches: those along Sandy Hook, a sandbar peninsula jutting nearly 6-1/2 miles north into New York Harbor.

Actually, Sandy Hook is the northern end of a 10-mile-long barrier beach peninsula along the Jersey shore. Its strategic location at the harbor entrance made it an important navigational landmark in the 18th and 19th centuries and a key defense site to protect New York City from enemy attack from the American Revolution until the Nuclear Age. In the last quarter of the 19th century and the first quarter of the 20th century, it was also remote enough to be used as a location for testing military weapons.

Only in 1973 did the National Park Service assume possession of Sandy Hook, as the New Jersey unit of the Gateway National Recreation Area created by Congress the year before—so named because New York Harbor was the "gateway" through which millions of immigrants entered the New World. Because of Sandy Hook's strategic history, there are fascinating ruins ranging from 19th-century gun batteries to Nike missile sites. So for military history buffs or just plain explorers, this is the trip for you.

Bring money—there are plenty of places on the beach to spend it: not only for food, but also for renting umbrellas, chairs, and sailboards. If you like saltwa-

Ride Ratings

Length: 12, 30 or 47 miles
Configuration: 3 adjoining loops
Difficulty: the short ride is flat, the middle-length is rolling, the longest is a steady climb; traffic is light off-season but heavier in summer
Surface: good pavement throughout; optional gravel detour

—Highlights: All three of these rides include swimming at the beach and visiting military history museums and the oldest continuously operating lighthouse in the U.S.; the longest tour includes Holmdel Park with its working historical farm.

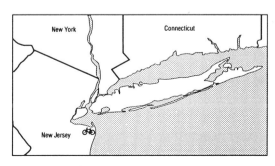

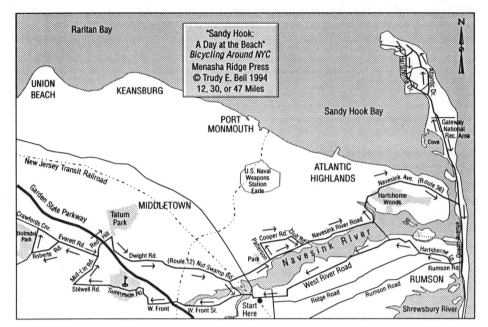

ter fishing, you can fish for free in the ocean without a license, so consider taking along a collapsible fishing pole. Also, pack your sunglasses and high-SPF sunscreen; on sunny summer days, parts of these rides are devoid of the merciful shade of trees and are hot, HOT, HOT.

To the taste of those like me (a fair-skinned redhead who hates crowds), any of these rides would be most delightful in either off season. For New York City area denizens, that means before Memorial Day at the end of May or after Labor Day at the beginning of September. Alternatively, these rides would also be wonderful any summer morning at dawn's first rosy glow. Or try it on a weekday instead of Saturday or Sunday. The later in the summer, the warmer the water will be, helped by the Gulf Stream. At the end of the summer and in early fall, many beaches have water whose temperature approaches that of a bath.

Depending on how fit you are, or how much you want to bicycle versus lounge on a beach towel and check out the local cheese- and beef-cake, you have the three following options.

The shortest ride is just of the Gateway National Recreation Area on the peninsula of Sandy Hook; for this option, park your car in Parking Lot B, just after passing through the toll booths into the park. This short ride is suitable also for novice riders or young children, during offpeak hours and in the off-season; the two longer rides have too much traffic.

The bad news about the short ride is that you have no option except to drive there, taking Exit 117 on the Garden State Parkway and following the signs to Sandy Hook. Think carefully about that if you're coming from New York City on a summer weekend, because the beach traffic on the Parkway can move as slowly as 15 to 20 miles per hour—the hot roadway was so slow and sweaty one July Sunday that I stayed overnight at a friend's place in Aberdeen and drove back 5 A.M. Monday. On the other hand, with a fun companion or some good tapes and no evening plans, the beach crawl could be just part of the weekend's leisure.

For the middle-length or the longest ride, you have the option of taking the New Jersey Transit train to Red Bank (see the preface for information on taking your bicycle on the train). If you drive anyway, take the Garden State Parkway to Exit 109; turn left at the end of the ramp onto Newman Springs Road; left onto Shrewsbury Avenue; right onto Oakland to the train station; park in the metered spaces next to the station building in Lot 1B.

The middle-length ride will let you see some of the local beach communities, with the possibility of exploring some of the still surprisingly rural backroads. The longest ride also takes you west of Red Bank through some of the prettiest farm scenery you'll find anywhere, with the reward of an exploration of Holmdel Park (introduced to me by my first cycling companion in adulthood, John F. King). If you're game enough to commit yourself at the outset to the full 47 miles including a climb at the end, you could park your car at Holmdel Park. (To do that, take Exit 114 off the Garden State Parkway onto Red Hill Road south; turn right at the first intersection onto Everett Road, left onto Roberts Road, right onto Longstreet Road, and an immediate left into the park).

This description starts from the Red Bank train station, treating the Holmdel Park extension as a long option at the end. Although there are no restrooms available at the Red Bank train station on weekends (when the station house is closed), the route passes a park with public restrooms where you can fill your water bottles. Meanwhile, near the train station in the center of town there is a convenience store, a bagel shop, and a TCBY (The Country's Best Yogurt) yogurt and waffle shop for buying a snack. Don't bother stocking up on food for lunch; there are plenty of options all along this ride, including at Sandy Hook.

Turn right out of the Red Bank train station Lot 1B onto the unmarked Oakland Street and immediate cross the railroad tracks. At the second stop sign, turn right onto the rather busy Shrewsbury Avenue (Monmouth County Route 13), crossing the tracks a second time. Turn left at the first light onto West Front Street, dipping down under the tracks and watching carefully in the busy traffic. Immediately, swerve to the right up onto the wooden walkway of a small metal-grate bridge over Swimming River, which feeds into the Navesink River to your right. To best appreciate the watery view, walk your bike across the bridge.

On the other side, turn right at the first intersection (at the traffic light) onto Hubbard Avenue (Monmouth County Route 12). The road will wind a little, past some shady woods and then past a small earthen dam on the left, behind which is the serene Shadow Lake. In late May, a fisherman slid down the embankment and called to his fishing buddy that he had caught nine bass that morning.

At the next major intersection, turn right onto Navesink River Road (Monmouth County 12A). Glance to your right; you'll catch a quick glimpse of Poricy Brook, along with a magnificent stand of wild rose and rhododendron, which bloom in late May and early June. Over the railroad tracks again, then cross the very busy Coopers Bridge Road at the light. One block later begins a three-foot-wide painted shoulder—not the widest in the world for cyclists, but certainly better than no shoulder at all.

Half a mile later, after crossing another creek, you'll see the entrance to Bodman Park to your left. This town park has public restrooms with running water, playing fields, picnic tables, and barbecue grills, plus some nice tree-lined roads for some tame but pleasant exploration.

Continuing on Navesink River Road, keep your eye out for Cubbage Farm on your left: a surprising Spanish style white house with a terra cotta tile roof on the corner of Navesink River Road and Patterson Avenue. Stop here for a moment to figure out what you want to do.

The main bicycle route continues straight ahead on Navesink River Road (skip down to the quadruple asterisks ****). But if you have a spirit of adventure and a mountain bike, you may want to turn left and hie yourself up Patterson Avenue instead for a beautiful little detour. It's sand and gravel, but it's an traffic-free trip back in time past farms hardly touched by Progress and curses "modren."

If you decide to go up Patterson Avenue, ride all the way to the end (about a mile). Turn right at the "T" intersection onto the paved Cooper Road. Pedal past the Navesink Country Club stables, keeping your eyes out to the fields to your right for sheep and geese.

As you coast down Cooper Road past the Luffburrow Lane entrance into the country club, look left: there are at least two ridges of green hills between you and the horizon. But better yet, the split rail fence along the road is festooned with luxuriant wild rose and dotted with thousands of white petals in a hot May or cool June.

Just before the road dips down to cross McClees Creek, take a right onto Club Way, ignoring the NO OUTLET sign; the reason for this sign is that Club Way is one way toward you for the brief stretch just before it rejoins Navesink River Road. Walk your bike the wrong way down this one-way street and turn left onto Navesink Road, coasting down to cross an inlet where McClees Creek feeds into the Navesink River. You're now back on the main ride.

(****) If you'd elected to stick with Navesink River Road all the way, the golf course of the Navesink River Country Club will appear above you on the hill to your left as you climb a rise. As you coast down the other side, look to your right for your first view of the broad Navesink River, dotted with sail-boats. After crossing over a small inlet where McClees Creek feeds into the Navesink River, the climb on the other side will give you the opportunity to watch the sailboats and other river traffic. The painted shoulder, however, grows narrower.

After the better part of a mile, the road heads downhill, makes an abrupt left, then a sharp right, and then the shoulder disappears altogether. The road climbs and drops several times, past the large lawns of estates that certainly I, and possibly you, will never be able to afford. At least the river view is nice through the trees. The road becomes narrow and winding, but the traffic is lighter than it was at the start. At last it bends left and descends steeply; brake carefully and watch for sand as you coast straight through a flashing yellow light at a three-way intersection.

At this point you have joined Locust Point Road (Monmouth County Route 8A) and are riding through the historic district of Locust. Locust, settled in

1797, was an early center of oyster farming and shellfish catching. Later it became a summer colony of *émigré* performers prominent in the arts.

Less than half a mile after the flashing yellow light, you'll see a white false-fronted building selling antiques. Turn right here onto Locust Avenue, across a metal bridge over the water (you may prefer the wooden walkway to the right). At the next intersection—it will look as if you're about to ride straight into a stone church—turn right onto Navesink Road (Monmouth County Route 8B). Here the traffic is moderately heavy, so watch for cars.

About half a mile after this turn, you'll pass the dirt parking area of Hartshorne Woods county park, which rises up on the hill to your right. Peek into the trees and you'll see some benches and public barbecue grills.

Continue straight as the road rises. This road will take you onto the on-ramp of State Highway 36 toward Highlands. This busy, four-lane highway has a lane-wide painted shoulder in excellent condition on the right, perfect for cyclists. After all your climbing, you can now lean back and coast: it's downhill or flat the rest of the way to Sandy Hook.

As soon as the highway crosses the water of the Shrewsbury River, you may prefer to pull your bicycle up onto the sidewalk to your right. That will leave you free to pedal slowly and savor the panorama in a leisurely fashion instead of dodging the beach blanket bingoes in their four-wheeled motorized pounding Altec Lansing stereos. That's the Atlantic Ocean there in front of you; ain't nuthin for 2000 miles now between you and Portugal . . .

Continue on the sidewalk as it carries you around right, following the signs to Sandy Hook. Where the sidewalk abruptly ends, carefully rejoin the main pavement, which has become a narrow on-ramp rising to an overpass around to the right. There is no shoulder, and watch for the bicycle-tire eating grates. Just take it slowly, up over the overpass and down the other side to the toll booths marking the entrance to the Gateway National Recreation Area at Sandy Hook.

Bicycles are always passed free through these booths, but a rather hefty parking fee is in effect for cars between Memorial and Labor Days. I visited the park one sunny weekend before Memorial Day when cars were still admitted free, and I had the beaches virtually to myself. But on Memorial Day weekend seven days later, when drivers were charged $5 per car, the place was a boombox, oiled-flesh zoo. Whether you prefer solitude or full beach swing, you have your pick.

Just past the toll booths on the right is Parking Lot B, the starting place for the shortest ride. A stone seawall blocks a full ocean view on your right, but is necessary since the erosion of the beaches is so great. Because Sandy Hook has been built up by the ocean's longshore current carrying sands in a northerly direction, its contours have been ever changing.

To your left, you may see windsurfers skimming along in Sandy Hook Bay. When I was there in late May, there were also people flying the most exotic assortment of multicolored kites, including one that looked like a flock of birds rising and dipping one after the other in close formation. Continue your leisurely pedaling another 1-1/2 miles along the rock seawall, past Parking Lot C.

If your thoughts are turning to lunch, head right into Parking Lot D and roll your bike up to the huge wooden double-deck structure labeled Seagull's Nest. On the ground floor you'll find hotdogs and souvenirs; on the upper floor there is a complete bar, plus a selection of seafood sandwiches. When I was there Memorial Day weekend, I kicked back with some other cyclists from a formal tour of Brooks Country Cycling and Hiking (formerly Country Cycling Tours, a commercial bicycle touring company based in New York City), recognizable by the triangular red flags waving above their bikes. You can also wheel your steed out to the nearby sands to enjoy your lunch next to the Atlantic surf.

When you leave Parking Lot D, turn right onto unmarked Hartshorne Drive to continue the ride. Make a point of hanging the next right into the lot of the Spermaceti Cove Visitors Center, where you can pick up some detailed maps and a booklet that recounts some of the major historical sites and stories of Sandy Hook. The visitor's center is open 8 A.M.-5 P.M. seven days a week in the summer, and on weekends the rest of the year. Then ride past the ranger station, where the road divides into two one-way lanes. Soon you'll see the water of Sandy Hook Bay almost at road level to your left.

At the first intersection, make a right at the sign to Gunnison Beach onto Atlantic Drive. On a summer day, the sun can beat down on this unshaded road so that shimmering heat waves envelop you from the ground up, but don't miss gazing at the wildflowers that peek from underneath the beach scrub. Ride right around the road divider; the changing rooms, restrooms, and phones on your right serve Gunnison Beach.

Gunnison Beach is named after Battery Gunnison, the ruins of which are off in the brush to your right. Battery Gunnison was built in 1904 to house a battery of rapid-firing, 6-inch disappearing guns—guns counterweighted so that the recoil from shooting swung them back below the protective concrete wall into reloading position. During World War II, they were replaced by pedestal-mounted guns of the same caliber. Battery Gunnison's two Model 1900 6-inch guns remain the only remnants of all the guns that made up the Fort Hancock defenses on Sandy Hook.

At Parking Lot G, turn right to continue on Atlantic Drive, following the signs to North Beach. Now you're riding through Fort Hancock, the name given in 1895 to the fortifications on Sandy Hook in honor of Major General Winfield Scott Hancock. Hancock was a Union fighter during the Civil War and a presidential candidate in 1880 (losing to James A. Garfield by fewer than 10,000 popular votes). Most of the buildings you're now passing were built in the half-century before 1945, when Fort Hancock's population peaked at 18,000.

Turn right at the signs to Parking Lot I to ride out to North Beach, a wide sweep of sand overlooking the Atlantic and all of its boats. You certainly won't dehydrate or starve if you decide to hang out here for a while: the concessionaires will be happy to take your money in exchange for soft drinks and hotdogs and rental of beach paraphernalia. There are also outdoor showers here for washing off the salt and sand before you remount your bike, plus restrooms where you can refill your water bottles.

Continue along the one-way road, past concrete fortifications and barbecue grills and picnic tables. The vine-overgrown battery to your left is one end of a proving ground that first heard blasts in 1874, when giant 16-inch caliber cannons were test fired at targets set up on Sandy Hook's oceanside beaches and dunes. The weapons tested here helped make the U.S. Army a powerful military force during the Spanish-American War and World War I. As guns became bigger and more powerful, the firing range at Sandy Hook proved to be too short, and in 1919 the Army's proving ground operations were transferred to Aberdeen, Maryland. Huge shells—some still live—are even now occasionally discovered on the beaches as the shoreline erodes; should you sight any ordnance, do not touch it, but report it immediately to a park ranger.

At the main road, turn right toward Parking Lots J and K, where you can view the huge, long concrete fortifications that still surround the northern end of Fort Hancock. (They are fenced off from public access.) Follow the road as it makes a sharp left at the end. At the stop sign, where you are now facing the abandoned three-story tan house whose first-floor windows are boarded and painted green, make a left. At the end of this short road, jog right and make an immediate left onto Hudson Drive, passing hulking Battery Potter on your left.

Completed in 1893, Battery Potter housed two 12-inch caliber guns. Each 52-ton gun barrel was mounted on a large elevator platform powered by steam-pressure driven hydraulic machinery—the first and only steam-powered lift-gun battery to protect an American harbor. However, Battery Potter was obsolete almost as soon as it was built because of the development of faster-firing counterweighted disappearing gun carriages. So, in 1906 Battery Potter was disarmed and its roof converted into target-spotting stations for Fort Hancock's other gun batteries.

Continue pedaling past Battery Granger, which is vaguely suggestive of a colonnaded Greek ruin. It was the first of Fort Hancock's counterweighted gun batteries, and mounted two 10-inch caliber disappearing guns that were in use from the Spanish-American War to World War II.

The road will carry you right, heading toward the Sandy Hook Lighthouse, the oldest continuously operating lighthouse in the United States. By 1761 shipwrecks threatened the merchants of New York with financial losses they could not afford. They petitioned the New York Colonial Assembly to pass an act to raise money by lottery (perhaps the origin of today's popular state-run lotteries?) to build a lighthouse. Actually, the project required two lotteries to raise enough money to buy the land and build the lighthouse, which was lighted for the first time on June 11, 1764.

At that time the lighthouse was only 500 feet from the tip of the hook. But in the next two centuries, ocean currents carrying sand up the coast elongated the hook so that now the tower stands almost 1-1/2 miles from the present tip. Maintained and operated as a navigational aid by the U.S. Coast Guard, the steady light of the automated lighthouse is visible for 19 miles on a clear night. Since 1964, the bicentennial of its first lighting, it has been a National Historic Landmark.

Immediately past the lighthouse, bear right and make your way through the various driveways, past the building with the sign BROOKDALE COMMUNITY COLLEGE ENVIRONMENTAL STUDIES; then turn right onto Kearney Road. The second building on your right is worth a stop. Formerly Fort Hancock's jail, it is now the Sandy Hook Museum, and has a room-sized relief diorama of the entire hook as it appeared in its military heyday. Lovers of miniatures and model railroads will enjoy the little trees, roads, and buildings.

Leaving the museum, turn right to continue north on Kearney Road, at the end making a sharp hairpin left turn onto Hartshorne Drive. Now the placid water of Sandy Hook Bay is on your right, and on your left you'll be approaching a long row of 18 Georgian Revival-style homes that used to serve as officers' quarters. Stop at the first one, the one with the modest sign reading HISTORY HOUSE. Local veterans have volunteered to restore it, and you can wander through its kitchen to see the grand old 1920s-era, four-legged refrigerator (which still works) and vintage photographs and uniforms of the day. Look up, also, to admire the patterned tin ceilings. The veteran there that day will most likely be eager to give you an inside tour.

When you leave History House, turn left to continue south on Hartshorne Drive, past rock barriers where you may see people baiting and casting their fishing line. In half a mile or so, the grassy sward of Guardian Park opens to your left, with its display of two Nike antiaircraft missiles—a monument to the last descendents of America's coastal defenses.

These post-Korean War missiles were designed to intercept and destroy fast, high-altitude jet warplanes before they reached the metropolitan area. The smaller missile, the Nike Ajax (based at Sandy Hook from 1954 to 1959), had a range of 30 miles and a maximum altitude of 60,000 feet. The larger, the Nike Hercules (based at Sandy Hook from 1958 to 1974), could carry a nuclear warhead more than 100 miles to an altitude of more than 150,000 feet—almost to the edge of space. The Nike Hercules was rendered obsolete as a defense by the development of offensive intercontinental ballistic missiles. In fact, when the Nike Hercules was phased out of nationwide service in 1974, that ended Sandy Hook's long role of guarding the New York Harbor.

Now continue straight on Hartshorne Drive for several miles, past the ranger station, to exit the park. If it is the late afternoon of a busy beach day, this part of the ride is not for the fainthearted; cars can creeping along bumper-to-bumper, requiring good balance to pass them on the right on the shoulderless road. Be alert and patient.

After the toll booths, where most of the cars will be curving right toward the Garden State Parkway, continue riding straight on Highway 36 South toward Seabright. Now, as if by magic, you'll have left the heaviest traffic behind as you pedal straight south on the narrow southern panhandle of the Sandy Hook peninsula. A thick stone-and-concrete seawall to your left unfortunately blocks your view of the Atlantic, but the road has enough automobiles to occupy your concentration anyway. There are also a number of seafood restaurants and motels along this stretch that may be worth checking out, such as the Chuckling Oyster and the Fairbanks Motel and Marina.

After a mile and a half, turn right at the first light onto unmarked Rumson Road (Monmouth County Route 520), up and over the Seabright-Rumson Bridge. Just after leaving the bridge, make the first right onto the unmarked Ward Avenue: it's just before the Holy Cross Church. At the end of the road, turn left at the "T" intersections onto the unmarked Hartshorne Lane, blessedly quiet and free from traffic.

Cycle leisurely past manicured lawns and well-kept hedges. At Navesink Road, Hartshorne Lane becomes Ridge Road (still unmarked) and bends a couple of times. At the flashing yellow light, turn right onto the Avenue of Two Rivers, past a couple of cute cafes and gourmet shops. Ride almost to the end, turning left onto the very last street: the narrow Meadowbrook Avenue. After one block, turn right at the "T" intersection onto the moderately busy East River Road, which will curve left and become West River Road.

Now, just enjoy the ride for 3-1/2 miles, catching glimpses of the Navesink River to your right between houses. This road is dotted with a number of antiques shops, frame shops, and chichi stationery shops. If you're still hungry, you can also stop for a slice of pizza en route. Although the speed limit is 40 miles per hour and on a summer weekend the traffic can be moderately heavy, the road is wide enough for a cyclist to share it with the cars. After about three miles, it changes name to Front Street.

As your next landmark, watch for the sign saying LEAVING FAIR HAVEN. Half a mile later, right after crossing a very short bridge, turn left onto Spring Street. Ride three blocks and turn right onto one-way Linden Place. At the end, turn right onto Broad Street, and make the first left at the light onto Monmouth Street. None of this wins a prize for light traffic, but it avoids the worst of the very heavy beach traffic entering Red Bank.

When you reach the train station, if you're satisfied with the middle-length ride you've just completed, turn left into Parking Lot 1B and enjoy your drive or train ride back into New York City.

(**) If you're game for the longest ride, though, head out again as you had for the original ride. Turn right out of the Red Bank train station Lot 1B onto the unmarked Oakland Street, immediately crossing the railroad tracks. At the second stop sign, turn right onto the rather busy Shrewsbury Avenue (Monmouth County Route 13), crossing the tracks a second time. Turn left at the first light onto West Front Street, dipping down underneath the tracks and watching carefully in the busy traffic. Immediately, swerve to the right up onto the wooden walkway of a small metal-grate bridge over Swimming River, which feeds into the Navesink River to your right.

On the other side of the bridge, go through the traffic light and continue straight on West Front Street. After less than a quarter mile you'll pass a deli on your left. A mile later, the road has become so rural you're riding alongside cultivated farm fields. In a short distance you'll be shaded by woods again, and will coast down past a creek into a gully.

At the bottom is a traffic light at the intersection of an incredibly appealing, traffic-free, wooded road paralleling the railroad tracks—a road simply beckoning to cyclists. But it is my regretful duty to direct you to pass by this road. This is a U.S. Government road that runs for about 10 miles, which ultimately joins a pier in Sandy Hook Bay belonging to U.S. Naval Weapons Station Earle down to the main part of Earle. Posted at each intersection of this government road are signs with dire warnings of the horrible consequences that will befall unauthorized personnel trying to travel on it. So sigh for the road not taken (I didn't have the nerve to even try to explore it) and continue straight on West Front Street, under the Garden State Parkway.

At the next light, 3/4 mile later, turn right onto the wide Middletown-Lincroft Road (on the signs, designated MID-LIN ROAD for short). This is also Monmouth County Route 50, and has wide painted shoulders and plenty of room for cyclists. Half a mile later, take the first left onto Sunnyside Road, through the green golf courses of the Bamm Hollow Country Club. As soon as you cross Everett Road (the Sunnyside Deli is on the corner), the name changes to Stilwell Road, and the country opens up into farm fields.

Turn right at the triangle onto Middletown Road and begin a steady climb, enjoying the sight and fragrance of the bushy, white-petaled wild rose. At the second light, turn left onto Everett Road, and here keep watching to the left. Far away, across the huge manicured acreage, is the reflective bronze-mirrored-glass building of AT&T Bell Laboratories at Holmdel.

It was at Bell Telephone Laboratories in 1948 that Bardeen, Brittain, and Shockley invented the transistor, the solid-state analog to the vacuum tube that has made possible most of today's computers and miniaturized electronic devices. Note that the pale green water tower at the entrance to the property has been built on three slender legs to look like a transistor—or, rather, to look the way a transistor looked in the days when it was a discrete component soldered onto a circuit board instead of traced out as metallic lines on a chip.

At the next intersection, turn left onto Roberts Road, past a Christmas tree farm. Continue climbing. At its end, turn right onto Longstreet Road and then make an immediate left into Holmdel Park.

Holmdel Park is 340 grassy acres crisscrossed with 8 miles of hiking trails and a fitness circuit for joggers. In the winter Holmdel Park's hills are favorites for cross-country skiing, and there is ice skating on the pond. In the summer the pond is stocked with bass, trout, and various panfish species. An arboretum features flowering crab-apple and cherry trees, rhododendrons, and hundreds of shade trees.

Nine acres of Holmdel Park are devoted to the preservation of the historical Longstreet Farm, and the bucolic grounds are really worth a stroll. During the 19th century, Longstreet Farm was among the largest and most prosperous farms in Holmdel. The original 495 acres were assembled in 1806 from several existing farms, and were used to raise cereal grains, livestock, and potatoes. But by the 1890s farm practices in Monmouth County were changing in response to competition from midwestern farmers and greater mechanization. General farms that used primarily horse power, such as Longstreet Farm, were being replaced by farms using steam and gas power. The farm remained in the family until 1967, when Monmouth County bought it to preserve a slice of the county's rural past; it has been open to the public since 1972.

Now there are 18 buildings to visit, including the original farmhouse, corn crib, wagon house, hen house, workshop, pump house, and privy. Park employees dress in period costumes and give tours of the buildings, animals, and fields as they were in the 1890s. The activities change from season to season, ranging from plowing and sheep shearing in the spring to grain harvesting and blacksmithing in the summer to cooking and cider making in the fall and ice cutting and food preservation in the winter. The farm is open daily 10 A.M.-4 P.M. year round; for information on farm activities, call (908) 946-3758 between 10 A.M. and 2 P.M.

After your picnic and exploration, leave Holmdel Park the same way you came in, turning left to continue up Longstreet Road. Pass the Monmouth County Historical Society's Holmes-Hendrickson House (open Tuesday, Thursday, Saturday, and Sunday), climbing and then coasting down to the end of the road. Turn right onto Crawfords Corner Road, once again passing Bell Labs, this time on your right.

At the light, turn left onto Red Hill Road (note, the soil is red!). Ride the overpass over the Garden State Parkway, taking the first right onto Dwight Road, which descends through very beautiful houses and curves to the left. When you cross MidLin Road, Dwight Road changes name to Nut Swamp Road (Monmouth County Route 12), which once again crosses that enviable traffic-free U.S. Government road. Eventually Nut Swamp Road changes name to Hubbard Avenue; continue straight on Hubbard Avenue to the end.

Turn left at the light ("T" intersection) onto Front Street, cross the bridge and pass under the railroad tracks. Make the first right onto Shrewsbury Avenue, and the second left onto Oakland Road. At the Red Bank train station, turn left into Parking Lot 1B.

For suggestions of entertainments and accommodations to make a long weekend out of your visit to Sandy Hook, see the first chapter "The Bayshore and Sandy Hook" in Robert Santelli's *Guide to the Jersey Shore from Sandy Hook to Cape May*, The Globe Pequot Press, Chester, Connecticut, whose second edition was published in 1991.

FOOD FOR THE MIND AND BODY RIDE

Essex & Morris Counties, New Jersey

Ride Ratings

Length: 20, 28 or 48 miles
Configuration: an out-and-back line to the south; a long and skinny loop to the north
Difficulty: gently rolling to rolling with 2 significant climbs; traffic is moderate on weekends, but heavy during the week
Surface: good pavement throughout

—Highlights: This ride features stops at the Montclair Art Museum, Thomas Edison's laboratories, a world-reknown iris garden, and the best croissants and cookies anywhere.

This ride is full of well-kept local secrets. The southern half, from Maplewood to Chatham, is part of a suburban route I often ride from my home either to the Great Swamp Wildlife Refuge—or simply to stretch my legs and justify the reward of some of the sweetest, creamiest, flakiest croissants that you've ever dipped into cappuccino.

The northern half, designed by one of my former bicycle-touring class students Sandy Coffey, winds through some quiet residential areas of older money, passing by two remarkable museums that are unjustifiably eclipsed by the greater fame of the many in New York City. It also passes an iris garden that rivals portions of the Brooklyn or Bronx Botanical Gardens, and ends with a circuit around a forested reservoir. At only 40 minutes from the heart of midtown Manhattan, this ride is perfect for that spontaneous weekend when you want the feeling of getting away from it all without spending all kinds of time and logistical effort to do it.

The full 48 miles can be pedaled by a strong rider in one day, although probably at the expense of visiting all the neat sites and eateries. A more relaxed one-day ride to most of the sights (with cookies but sans croissants) is just the shorter 28-mile round trip heading north to Montclair.

Come hungry on this trip. In fact, skip breakfast and arrive early. Since this is my stomping

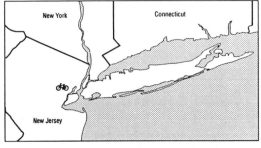

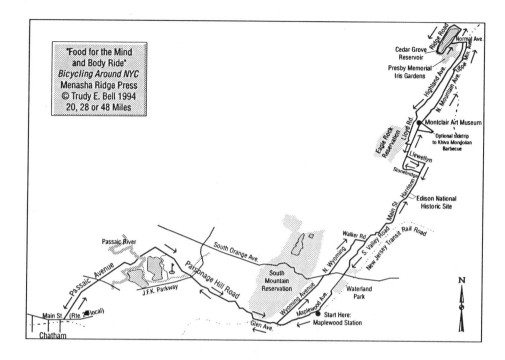

ground, I'm going to clue you in on some of my favorite grazing places along the side of the road.

If you love a bargain, you might also want to bring empty panniers or an extra backpack. Yard sales are one of the favorite fair-weather pastimes of many New Jersey residents—to the point of even advertising them in the small local weekly papers such as the *News-Record* of Maplewood and South Orange. On a sunny summer afternoon you may pass up to a dozen, and who knows what clothing or antiques you might be able to find for a dollar or two. In various New Jersey bike rides, I've picked up everything from an old-fashioned meat grinder to (yes!) wire baskets for carrying groceries on a bike to a walnut double-door armoire (a couple with a pick-up truck saw me gazing at the five-foot-high piece of furniture and offered to cart it home for me as their good deed for the day).

The southern portion of this ride to Chatham has one long climb in each direction, as the route takes you over a relatively low section in the series of ridges running north-south in this part of New Jersey (the ridge lines are defined by the Garret Mountain, Mills, Eagle Rock, South Mountain, and Watchung Reservations). It also has noticeably more automobile traffic than the northern half—although you can avoid much of it by the usual technique of riding early on Sunday morning. But this southern leg is also a gateway to some of the more rural Morris County rides in this book should you wish this ride to be the beginning of a multiday trip. The northern leg is flatter, principally because much of the route runs along the side of a major ridge.

The ride starts from the Maplewood train station of the New Jersey Transit railroad (see the introduction for information on taking your bike on the train). If you drive, from the Lincoln Tunnel head south on the New Jersey Turnpike;

at Exit 15E take Interstate 280 west to the Garden State Parkway south; get off the parkway at Exit 143 (Springfield Avenue, Irvington). Drive straight. At the third stop light (the Irvington Bus Terminal will be on your right), turn right onto Clinton Avenue. A mile later, at the Exxon station at the top of the hill, bear left at the "Y" intersection onto Parker Avenue, which you'll take a mile and a half to its end. Turn left at the "T" intersection onto Maplewood Avenue. Half a mile later, just at the beginning of the village, turn left into the train station parking lot. There is also a municipal lot for public parking a few hundred yards farther down to your left.

By the way, for another six miles of pedaling, you can free yourself of hassling with either New Jersey Transit or a car. Take the PATH train under the Hudson River to the Newark station (see the preface for information on obtaining a permit for taking your bicycle on the PATH). Once you're above ground, turn right out of the train station to ride west on Broad Street. After about a mile, take a left fork onto the four-lane Springfield Avenue. In another four miles or so, just after passing the Irvington Bus Terminal on your left, turn right at the light onto Clinton Avenue and follow the remaining directions above to the Maplewood station.

From the Maplewood train station, look straight ahead up Durand Road: there is the Burgdorff Cultural Center, which features three Broadway plays a year at a quarter the price of Broadway. Now, mount your bike and turn left onto Maplewood Avenue to enter Maplewood village. The village is only a few blocks long, so don't rush through it. You can also begin your culinary tour here by making reservations for dinner at Terra Cotta (201-763-1176), an intimate restaurant whose exotic offerings and exquisite preparation will compare with any of the finest places in New York City. The menu changes with the season, offering venison or medallions of pork in the winter and lighter vegetarian dishes in the summer. At any time, it features perhaps half a dozen entrees, each of which is superb. Be aware: Terra Cotta's prices are comparable to what you would pay for similar fare in the city, so I tend to save a visit for a truly special occasion; Sunday brunch is more modest in cost. You may also want to shop for a wine from one of Maplewood's two liquor stores. Although Terra Cotta does not have a liquor license, its waiters are happy to uncork your selection.

If you're hungry or thirsty right now, Maplewood village has shops offering yogurt, bagels, ice cream, and lighter fare (Arturo's down the street is my favorite). For a full breakfast, stop at the Maple Leaf coffee shop across from Terra Cotta; its food is fresh and well-prepared, and it prides itself in keeping prices as low as humanly possible. And Celebrated Food, behind the store fronts between Highland Avenue and Baker Street, is a cafe and caterer specializing in exotic combinations that will delight the most discriminating or jaded palate.

When you've fueled up for the trip, continue south on Maplewood Avenue, out of the village. The train tracks parallel your path on your left. Where Maplewood Avenue ends and Mountain Avenue heads right, continue straight onto the one-block-long paved bike path next to the railroad tracks, giving you a peek into a couple of back yards on your right. Watch carefully as you drop off the curb at the end of the path. Bear left at the path's end to stay alongside the tracks and you'll curve around the U-shaped street onto Cottage Court.

Turn left at the "T" intersection onto the moderately busy Ridgewood Road. Just after the large white clapboard complex of farmhouse-looking buildings labeled SLINGERLAND AND SLINGERLAND, and just before the railroad overpass, bear right at the fork onto the unmarked Glen Avenue. After the grassy playing fields, Glen Avenue bends right and the houses become somewhat more gracious.

At the next light, Wyoming Avenue, you must make a choice. If you're doing only the 28-mile northern section to Montclair, turn right onto Wyoming Avenue and skip three pages to the double asterisks (**). If you're in quest of the perfect croissant, however, continue straight on Glen Avenue.

Shortly after crossing Wyoming Avenue, Glen Avenue bends left and then curves right, again paralleling the railroad tracks. Eventually on your left you'll see the rooftops of the town of Millburn along with its train station. On your right are homes tucked into the forest, which rises behind them.

Continue straight at the light to stay on Glen Avenue. At this light you're passing Brookside Drive, which enters South Mountain Reservation; a sign at the intersection informs you that the reservation has two megabytes of acres—2048. The reservation is one of three that the Essex County Parks Commission designed in the early 20th century in consultation with the firm of Frederick Law Olmsted, who is perhaps most famous in his planning of New York City's Central Park. Today, the South Mountain Reservation includes a 25-foot-high waterfall, 19 miles of blazed hiking trails, eight picnic areas, a pond stocked with trout, an indoor skating rink, and the Turtle Back Zoo. Brookside Drive is about the only viable way for cyclists to enter the reservation (the other entrances require climbing steep flights of stone stairs or riding with heavy traffic); either now or on the return, you might wish to make a short exploratory detour.

Now Glen Avenue presents you with a moderate but steady grade. Get used to it, for you will be climbing for the next couple of miles. Follow Glen Avenue as it bends left and ends. Turn right at the stop sign (at the little triangular island) onto the fairly busy Short Hills Road. Climb for about a quarter of a mile to the next major intersection. Turn left here—watching carefully for the two-way traffic—onto Parsonage Hill Road.

You'll now stay on Parsonage Hill Road until it ends, in about three miles. The road has relatively light traffic, and continues to climb gently, past a large pond to your left. At the first light at Harrison Drive, look to your left: the Spanish architecture house looks as if it would be more at home in California, whose front yard sports an impeccable three-story-high cylindrical tower that is also stuccoed and topped with terra cotta tile. I've never been able to figure out what that tower is, although I suspect it holds water.

Now you've reached the crest, and the next half-mile is an exhilarating downhill coast where you can easily pass 30 miles per hour. Be careful, though: the pavement is uneven, gravel is scattered at the side, and there is a light halfway down at White Oak Ridge Road. If you get stopped at that light, look to your right and examine the small two-century-old family graveyard plot fenced by heavy anchor chains. Among the stones of early settlers is one inscribed to Thomas and Nicholas Parsil, who died in battles during the American Revolution 1778-1780.

When the light changes, continue coasting downhill on Parsonage Hill Road. After it crosses over the John F. Kennedy Parkway, the road develops a nice painted shoulder; you'll pass secondary forest on your right and the East Orange golf course on your left.

At the next light, turn left onto Passaic Avenue, taking note of the small working farm that still exists ahead of you at this intersection. Each time I pass, I look to see if they're still raising corn or selling fresh vegetables from their little private stand. When you cross the small Lower Chatham Bridge over the Passaic River, you've left Essex County and entered Morris County.

Three-quarters of a mile later, you'll ride over the four-lane New Jersey State Route 24. Look down at the cars passing underneath you and imagine seeing cyclists instead. Built in the early 1990s to relieve traffic from the congested two-lane local Route 24, for about a year a completed six-mile stretch of this four-lane highway was closed to cars. The stretch became very popular with bicyclists, roller-skaters, dog walkers, and riders of those mini-motorbikes. Even the pacelines of some sanctioned fund-raising bike races could be seen whipping by in their jerseys and black Lycra shorts. More commonly, you'd see parents teaching their kids to ride their first two-wheelers. It was nirvana to pedal along such a long and wide stretch of smooth pavement with absolutely no automobiles!

After crossing over Route 24, Passaic Avenue enters the suburbs of Chatham and traffic becomes a little heavier. Shortly after passing the a town swimming pool on your left, you'll reach the intersection with Main Street—heavily trafficked local Route 24. Here you may as well pull your bicycle up onto the sidewalk and reconnoiter.

Immediately to your left is Arminio's Italian Corner. Although it appears to be simply a pizza joint, it is actually a very good—and very cheap—Italian restaurant where I've often refueled for the eight-mile journey back to Maplewood. Two doors down is F. P. Garrettson and Co., a gourmet tea-and-coffee shop that also sells hand-painted ceramics and other gifts from artisans the world over. My favorites—which I have bought for many a cycling friend as well as myself—are two different hand-painted mugs, one featuring helmeted bicyclists in a race and the other showing a man and woman (no helmets!) pedaling through trees and tulips.

Other shops on this street include Bike Land for buying and repairing bicycles, the Stitching Bee for all kinds of needlepoint, Jabberwocky for educational games and toys for children, a sports shop featuring running gear, and—in case all this shopping has made you hungry yet again—Cafe Beethoven, a coffee house that makes a delightfully relaxing stop for cappuccino, pastries, and classical music.

But remember, we are still in quest of the perfect croissant. From your approach on Passaic Avenue, turn right to head west on local Route 24 (Main Street) through Chatham toward Morristown. This street has heavy traffic, some of which is parking or pulling out of parking spaces, so either ride extremely carefully or walk along the sidewalk. At Fairmount Avenue (which happens to be a main route to the Great Swamp Wildlife Refuge another 10 miles south), Main Street develops a wide painted shoulder on which you can ride. A quarter mile later, turn left into King's grocery store; on particularly heavy-traffic days, a policeman will hold the cars in the opposing lane and beckon you across.

You've reached Mecca. King's is New Jersey's gourmet grocery store chain, equivalent to New York City's Food Emporium. Here lovers of fine cooking can find a dozen or more different varieties and brands of mustards, vegetables from around the world, hard-to-locate specialties such as green peppercorns or squab, and a whole range of meats by the famed Boar's Head including classic New York corned beef (to be boiled at home).

The bakery in this particular King's has some exceptional offerings, whose fragrances fill the aisles. One of them is their croissants. Yes, I know it is not chichi to buy croissants in a grocery store (and you thought I was going to lead you to a French bakery). Trust me. Maybe you'll be lucky and they'll have samples out on the glass counter. But after you try a croissant here, just write and tell me if you didn't buy more than one.

I should add here that with croissants, as with bagels, there are at least two schools of thought. One school says they should be light and flaky, almost shattering like filo dough when you bite into them, and leaving flavorful bits floating in your cafe au lait after dipping. The other school holds they should be light and tender, more like the sweetest and softest imaginable bread, gently pulling apart with each bite and almost melting like butter when dipped. I subscribe to the latter school, and that is the style of these croissants.

Having debated this cosmic issue, which should involve at least two or three croissants and a cup of coffee for considered analysis and testing, go back outside and unlock your bike. When leaving King's, turn right to retrace your route back towards Maplewood. Less than half a mile later, take the second left at Arminio's onto North Passaic Avenue. In three-quarters of a mile you'll cross again over four-lane Route 24, and then you'll pass some tennis courts on your right. A mile and a quarter farther, you'll turn right at the next light onto Parsonage Hill Road. After crossing over the JFK Parkway, you'll begin to climb; take your time, this rather steep hill will last the better part of a mile. On the way up, take the opportunity to gaze left at the white-painted White Oak Ridge Chapel, founded in 1831. (Could it be the reason this is called Parsonage Hill?) Continue riding, all the way to the end.

Turn right at the "T" intersection onto Old Short Hills Road. But don't let 'er rip on this steep downhill; you're going to want to turn left in only a quarter mile down onto Glen Avenue, and that intersection is extraordinarily easy to miss. Personally, I look for the first place on the right where Old Short Hills Road widens into a kind of court for two other streets; there I pull over and stop to wait for the cars to pass before crossing, making sure that I enter Glen Avenue on the right side of the little triangular island.

Now you'll ride Glen Avenue to its end. Take the first rather steep downhill with caution, as the road is narrow and bumpy, once again passing Brookside Drive and its entrance to South Mountain Reservation. The downhill eases and Glen Avenue widens as you swoop left. Just past the Millburn Free Public Library on your right is Lackawanna Place. (For your culinary information, if you should turn right here and go just a block, you'll reach the Millburn Diner. From the outside the diner's stone facade and darkened glass windows look just like a hundred others on Route 22 that must have all gotten modernized at the same time by the same architect. But inside you can get some of the best-prepared Greek dishes around—my favorite is kapamas, a kind of lamb stew—plus superbly flavorful mashed potatoes made from the root itself, not from white powder in a box.)

Continue east on Glen Avenue, following it through its curves, to the next light. Here, turn left onto South Wyoming Avenue.

(**) Wyoming Avenue is heaven for cyclists. Although it is moderately busy, it has painted shoulders as wide as a full traffic lane and is only occasionally partially blocked by a parked car. Now, put your bike in a lower gear and climb this gentle but steady slope past some truly remarkable homes. The white-steepled brick Wyoming Presbyterian Church on your right sets the mood for feeling that you may be cycling in classic New England. On your left you'll pass some impressive stone walls supporting lawns for the houses above you. Note that on certain cross streets the rain gutters along the curb are lined with cobblestones, a relic of an earlier era. As you continue your gentle climb, the ivy-covered houses grow more stately and manicured, with sculpted bushes out front.

Eventually you'll pass a yellow brick building with a terra-cotta roof on your left, built for the East Orange Water Works in 1904. Shortly thereafter is a small sign welcoming you to the village of South Orange. But if you missed the sign, a clearer indication is the gas street lamps. Yes, gas lights, even on the verge of the 21st century. South Orange is one of just a few remaining communities in this country that has them still (another is Convent Station featured in the "Of Convents and Bike Paths" ride). To be sure, there are local political forces that want to pull them all out and replace them with electric. But so far the citizens who love them for their warm distinction have prevented that desecration, so now you can enjoy how their triple mantles are glowing points even in the bright afternoon sun.

At the next light, turn right onto the busy, steep four-lane South Orange Avenue, but immediately move into the left-hand lane. At the next light, turn left to continue on North Wyoming Avenue in the painted shoulder. From crossing steep South Orange Avenue, the topography of this ride should be clearer to you: you are riding along the eastern side of a north-south ridge, climbing gently en route. If the breeze is gentle, you may catch a whiff of the resin from the large pines to your right.

After about a mile, Wyoming Avenue narrows, the shoulder disappears, and the road changes name to Gregory Avenue. A quarter mile later, turn right at the light onto Walker Road, braking carefully on the steep downhill. At the "T" intersection at the bottom, turn left onto South Valley Road, watching carefully for the moderate traffic. Immediately on your right you will pass a small shopping center with a CVS drugstore, a Krauszer's deli, and other shops. But the place to stop and provision up for your ride is Gimmee Jimmy's Cookies on your right.

I, of course, had to check out the place so I could report on it for this book, right? Gimmee Jimmy's turned out to be more interesting than just another bakery. Founded in 1984 by Jimmy Libman, who is deaf, most of the bakery's personnel are also hearing-impaired. The place has been furnished with a high-tech system of lights to alert the employees when the cookies are done or a customer has come through the door.

Regardless of the bakery's social mission, you know you're in immediate trouble when back of the cash register you're greeted by a sign reading THANK YOU FOR NOT DIETING. The cookies are still soft and warm from the oven, and range from the usual chocolate-chip and peanut-butter varieties to pecan sandies and white-chocolate-macadamia-nut selections. You can even buy ones made out of the plain cookie dough. My personal favorite is the raisin-oatmeal, which has a dash of cinnamon. To my taste, all are far better than the much more famous David's Cookies available in New York City, which I find simply to be greasy. Two other nice things about Gimmee Jimmy's: if you have the "won't power" to buy just one cookie, you may. And you can also mail-order gift boxes of cookies to share the calories with your friends by calling the toll-free number (800) 736-5980.

After packing your haul into your handlebar bag, turn right out of Gimmee Jimmy's to continue north on South Valley Road. You'll stay on South Valley for the next mile through all its bends and curves, past a fire station and crossing over Interstate 280. Traffic can be moderately heavy, so keep your eyes and ears alert for cars.

Turn right at the traffic light at the "T" intersection onto Northfield Avenue (Buy Rite Liquors is directly ahead of you). At the next "T" intersection, make an immediate left onto the moderately busy Main Street of the town of West Orange, past Saint Mark's Church high on the hill above you.

Keep going straight through the major intersection with Mount Pleasant Avenue. A quarter mile later on your left is the unmarked Llewellyn Park, a private community with the home of the inventor of the electric light Thomas Edison. A guard in a kiosk at the base of the hill will stop even cyclists from riding along the streets without a permit. But never fear; you can get one soon.

A quarter mile beyond Llewellyn Park, on your right, are imposing red brick factory buildings that have been converted into discount warehouse outlets for carpets and other goods. But watch carefully: the last building on your right is the Edison National Historic Site. Turn right at the little sign directing you down Lakeside Drive; halfway down the block is the entrance to the museum, where you can lock your bike.

Plan to spend some time here. It was here that Edison spent the last half of his life working on motion picture photography, an improved phonograph, storage batteries for electric automobiles, and a fluoroscope used in the first X-ray operation in the United States. The laboratories here were a model for modern private research linking business and technology, and inspired the structure of Bell Laboratories and Westinghouse.

In addition to museum exhibits about the life and work of Thomas Edison, the modest admission charge gives you the chance to go on two hour-long guided tours. One takes you through Edison's library, chemical laboratory, and machine shop and lets you listen to various models of his phonograph. The other is the permit to tour Edison's 23-room red brick and wood mansion Glenmont in Llewellyn Park, perhaps even taking in a nature walk on its 13.5 acres of grounds. Occasional special evening programs screen some of Edison's early movies, demonstrate his machine shop, or even cut a birthday cake in the inventor's honor. For more information, call (201) 736-5050 or 0550.

To resume the ride, turn right out of the front of the museum onto Lakeside

Drive, and half a block later turn right at the "T" intersection to resume riding north on Main Street. Look to your right as you leave the Edison Historic Site for a last glimpse of Black Maria, the rotating movie studio in which Edison filmed the first moving picture. Tucked under the pine trees at your right, in a kind of nonsequitur historic exhibit, is a cement slab from the first concrete highway built in New Jersey in 1912.

Go straight through the first traffic light, but immediately take the right fork at the second light onto the unmarked Franklin Avenue, keeping the big brick school building on your right. Franklin Avenue is blessedly less traveled than the aptly named Main Street. Continue on it straight for about three-quarters of a mile.

Continue straight onto Nishuane Road where Franklin Avenue bends left, riding through quiet middle-class suburbs. At the "T" intersection at Nishuane Park with its playing fields and tennis courts, turn left onto Cedar Avenue. A tenth of a mile later, at the "T" intersection, turn left onto the busy Harrison Avenue, and then make an immediate right onto Sutherland Road, which climbs slightly into a quiet neighborhood of lovely older homes.

Turn left at the "T" intersection at the stone wall onto Stone Bridge Road. Now you'll be coasting past homes that get progressively larger and more stately as the road makes a big circle to the right, and then you'll start climbing gently up the opposite side of the circle. Continue straight onto South Mountain Avenue, continuing your gentle but steady climb. Now you are riding along a wide but sparsely trafficked road ideal for cycling, passing gracious mansions; note the whimsical metal sculpture birds in front of double-columned number 141 on your right.

About a mile after starting on South Mountain Avenue—just opposite a particularly huge specimen of Spanish-Greek architecture on your left with a vast lawn and huge urns on each side of stone stairs—you have a choice. To continue on the basic ride, keep heading straight (north), pausing at the Montclair Art Museum at Bloomfield Avenue; here, resume the description at the quadruple asterisks (****). If instead you'd like take a one-mile detour into the town of Montclair for some culinary surprises, keep reading here. *But please note:* although the detour is only a mile, its end involves some notable traffic and one long climb.

To take the detour, turn right on Hillside Avenue just opposite the stairway of the Hearst Castle wannabe. Coast down the short but fairly steep hill (which makes clear how you've been riding halfway up along the side of a ridge). Cross Orange Road at the light and continue straight onto Church Street.

After crossing Park Street, dismount your bike to walk it past the DO NOT ENTER signs to continue on Church Street, which is now one-way heading toward you. But here you'd want to walk anyway, for the entire brick-paved street for several blocks has been turned into a permanent, open-air street fair. When I was there in late October, a big truck obviously just in from the country had slung down its tailgate and was selling fresh pumpkins for pies and jack-o'lanterns. A four-piece jazz band was plucking, strumming, trumpeting, and drumming "Take the A-Train" as people strolled past, thumbing through the tables of second-hand books and racks of clothing while the fragrance of gourmet coffees wafted out onto the street. Sandy Coffey assured me that many of the craft shops here sold items that would make perfect gifts.

At the end of Church Street, still walking, make a sharp left to head back west along Bloomfield Avenue, past a cheese shop boasting it offers 500 different types of cheeses (I didn't count to make sure). Don't pass by too quickly, for if you want something completely different for lunch, stop in at Khiva for—yes—Mongolian barbecue.

I don't know how authentically Mongolian the preparations are, but the food is undeniably good. Here you scoop up all manner of whatever vegetables, noodles, and shaved meats that you want into one large bowl. Then you stand before a bewildering array of sauces and ladle what you wish onto your choice. Posted on the wall above are suggested recipes for mild, moderately spicy, and very spicy sauce. For overall flavor, I found the moderately spicy selection the best; the spicy one is dominated by the flavor of chili peppers. Then you watch as the white-hatted chef behind a six-foot semicircular grill dumps your concoction sizzling onto the hot metal and turns it over and over with a huge spatula, literally rolling it to the other end in about a minute. He scoops it back into your bowl and *voilá!* your meal is ready. If you don't like the flavor, you have only yourself to blame! *Note:* Khiva is a good choice for ravenous cyclists at the end of a ride because of its all-you-can-eat format. For reservations, call (201) 509-0660.

To return to the basic ride, head west on the four-lane Bloomfield Avenue. You'll know which direction that is, because it goes straight up the steep hill. Ride very carefully here, because Bloomfield Avenue is a main road and the traffic can be fast and heavy. You'll pass a number of restaurants and antiques stores (apparently Bloomfield is known for its antiques). Eventually, the intersection you want is marked not only by a light but also by the large white-marble building on your left: the Montclair Art Museum.

(****) Known for its collection of more than 800 19th- and 20th-century American paintings and more than 2500 pieces of Native American art, the Montclair Art Museum also features lectures, art classes, and children's classes. Admission is free to everyone on Thursday (25 p.m.); otherwise it is open 10 A.M.-5 P.M. Tuesday, Wednesday, Friday, and Saturday, and 2-5 P.M. on Sunday. For more information, call (201) 746-5555.

To continue the ride, head south across Bloomfield Avenue; on the other side, your road changes name from South Mountain Avenue to North Mountain Avenue. (If you've come up from Bloomfield Avenue from Montclair without visiting the museum, turn right onto North Mountain Avenue.) Now you just continue on North Mountain Avenue for nearly two miles until it ends. You'll cross Claremont Avenue at a light, and in a few blocks pass a brick elementary school where you may see flocks of children swarming across the lawn at recess. You'll pass Watchung Avenue at a flashing red light, and Bellevue Avenue at a stop sign; to your right is Upper Montclair station of the New Jersey Transit railroad. You are now in the exclusive community of Upper Montclair, whose residents distinguish their domicile by emphasizing the "Upper."

Follow the road as it bends right at the end onto Lorraine Avenue, and then take an immediate left before the tracks onto Braemore Road. Follow the quiet, narrow street as it winds through intimate homes. At the first intersection, turn right onto the moderately busy Upper Mountain Avenue. In a third of a mile, just past the Mountain Avenue railroad station, the road bends left. Then, opening before you on your left is the multicolored vista of the Presby Memorial Iris Gardens.

Stop here and stroll through this fragrant paradise of more than 6000 varieties of irises. I had no idea that irises came in so many colors, shapes and sizes—some of them, to my untrained eye, actually unrecognizable as irises. For their peak show, plan your visit in May around Mother's Day through early June; but even well into the summer and early autumn, it is worth wandering through the gardens to read their imaginative names: Launching Pad, Licorice Stick, Ballet Dancer, Lute Song, Clear Sailing.

The entire garden is a memorial to Frank H. Presby, a world-renowned horticulturist who lived in Montclair and founded the American Iris Society in the early 20th century. The garden was started in 1927, and many other plots have a plaque dedicating the perennially blooming beauty to a bygone loved one. In fact, each individual flower has a small tag with the name of the hybrid, the date it was hybridized, and name of the hybridizer. Connie Baumann, one of my former bicycle-touring students who introduced me to the garden, said she loved cycling and stopping here with a picnic lunch. Across the street from the garden themselves is the other side of Mountainside Park, where (depending on the time of year) you may find functioning public restrooms and a drinking fountain.

When you've feasted your eyes, continue north on Upper Mountain Avenue to the light. If you wish, turn right here for a little detour to explore the 220-acre campus of Montclair State University. Besides a wide-ranging continuing education program, the college offers art exhibits, lectures, workshops, plays, and concerts. For the astronomically inclined, the college also holds a public star party from 8-9 P.M. on most Wednesday evenings during the academic year, where you can view the moon or planets or other celestial objects through a portable telescope. (For schedule information, call Mrs. Hecht before 4:30 p.m. at 201-893-4166.)

To follow the main ride, turn left at the light from Upper Mountain Avenue onto Normal Avenue and begin climbing. This is a fairly hefty climb, so gear 'er down and take your time, stopping to rest as you wish. The hill is short, though, and you'll reach its crest in a quarter mile. Here a sign informs you is parking for the Mills Reservation, one of the series of park lands preserved across the ridge line from here south.

Continue straight over the crest of the ridge and starting down the other side. But brake and ride slowly, for in a few hundred yards where the main road bends left, you want to go right onto the narrow, unmarked Reservoir Drive.

The next three-quarters of a mile is the most rustic part of the ride, so pedal slowly along the rutted pavement to savor it. Since the bumpy road is closed to automobile traffic, you may come across only an isolated fellow cyclist or jogger from the Cedar Grove Running Club. Otherwise, it's just you and Mother Nature. When I was there in late October, the oaks and maples were aflame in gold and red, and huge black crows were raucous in the trees and the ground, "kind of like the Hitchcock movie *The Birds*," remarked the female cyclist who passed me. You are circling Cedar Grove Reservoir, although you can scarcely glimpse the water through the trees to your left. After half a mile, the road bends left to pass below a small earth-fill dam, and the air is fragrant from the pines.

At the end of Reservoir Drive, turn left at the "T" intersection onto the moderately busy, unmarked Ridge Road, which eventually develops a nice painted shoulder almost as wide as a traffic lane. Now you're below the level of the reservoir, pedaling alongside the grassy earthen dike to your left. In late October, the autumn leaves were brilliantly contrasted against the azure sky, and flocks of gulls wheeled and screeched overhead. Eventually the road climbs to the level of the water, allowing you to see the hundreds of gulls floating on the water or flying and dipping their beaks in search of lunch.

After about a mile, take the first left onto Reservoir Drive. Keep your eyes left, for in a few hundred feet you'll catch for the only good view of the entire body of water and its shoreline. Follow the road right at the traffic arrows onto the unmarked Normal Avenue, up a quarter mile to the crest and down again.

On this rather steep descent, watch carefully. In another quarter mile, at the stone wall on your left, turn right onto the quiet Highland Avenue—one of the prettiest and least-traveled parts of this ride. In half a mile, you'll be riding through the trees of Mountainside Park, above the lovely Presby Memorial Iris Gardens.

After crossing the moderately busy Bradford Avenue at the stop sign (watch for the cars zooming down the steep slope to your right), continue straight on Highland Avenue. You'll pass a magnificent rhododendron on your left, which is stunning in June with its huge blooms. On your left, across the lowlands of eastern New Jersey, on a clear day you can see more than 20 air miles to the Empire State Building and twin towers of the World Trade Center punctuating the Manhattan skyline. In another mile, bear right to stay on Highland Avenue where Edgewood Road descends left. Shortly thereafter, you'll begin a wonderful descent, past stone mansions with greenhouses.

Cross the moderately busy Claremont Avenue at the stop sign, ride through the tiny Graz Park straight ahead, and make an immediate left onto the very busy four-lane Bloomfield Avenue. Use caution on this steep descent, watching not only for the traffic but also for bike-tire-eating grates (avoid puddles or piles of leaves, which often hide these grates).

Ride through the yellow blinkers and make the first right onto the level Lloyd Road—an intersection marked by the sign welcoming you to the campus of Montclair Academy. You'll pedal by some of the stone-faced dorms and other academy buildings, and then abruptly you're back on a narrow, quiet road with its comfortable mansions and views of the New York City skyline.

After about a mile, Lloyd Road bends left in a sharp descent. At the "T" intersection at the bottom, turn right onto Undercliff Road. Across from the entrance to Eagle Rock Reservation (another of the reservations along the ridge line), turn left onto the unmarked Gates Avenue, continuing a steep descent. Take the first right onto South Mountain Avenue, and then the first left onto Llewellyn Road. At this corner is a small, odd concrete shoulder-high obelisk topped with an iron triangle. These "markers" seem to be quite common on the street corners, and as far as I could tell, they once held small mailboxes.

At the flashing red light, turn right onto Harrison Avenue. Half a mile later, at the grassy triangle, turn left onto Franklin Avenue. Half a mile beyond that, at the light, turn left onto Main Street.

Now, for the next three miles, you'll be retracing part of your route. Pass the Edison National Historic Site and Llewellyn Park, into the town of West Orange. Just after the large, old, lit free-standing public clock on your right, turn right at the light onto Northfield Avenue and then make an immediate left onto Valley Road. After crossing over Interstate 280, Valley Road bends right. For a little variety, go straight at the stop sign onto Quinby Place, and then turn left at the "T" intersection onto Rollinson Street. A quarter mile later, turn right at the next "T" intersection at the small strip mall onto South Valley Road, once again passing Gimmee Jimmy's (last call for cookies!).

Continue straight on Valley Road, which changes name to North Ridgefield Road as you enter the village of South Orange. You can tell you've crossed that border, because once again the streets are dotted with those wonderfully warm, glowing gas lights.

Pass the stone building or the Orange Lawn Tennis Club above you to your right, and coast past the park spread before you on your left. Also on your left, you'll pass the South Orange Junior High, where I've taught the spring and fall evening sessions of my class on introduction to bicycle touring. At the light, continue straight across the busy South Orange Avenue to stay on Ridgewood Road. (By the way, if you're in the mood for some of the best pizza I've had anywhere in creation, turn left instead down the steep and busy South Orange Avenue; in about a quarter mile, stop in front of the unprepossessing white store front of Reservoir Pizza and take your pick. Their red sauce is not to be outdone.)

After only a few hundred yards on Ridgefield Road, go straight at the yellow flasher onto Walton Avenue, past the tennis courts and playground of Farrell Field. At the "Y" intersection, bear left onto Maplewood Avenue, which then curves right. At the first intersection, which is Parker Avenue, look right up the hill up to number 41 Maplewood Avenue: from 1951 to 1957, this demure beige house with plain olive pillars and brick steps was the home of General "Stormin'" Norman Schwarzkopf, who gained fame for his skillful command of the Allied forces during the Persian Gulf War against Saddam Hussein in early 1991. As you continue pedaling along Maplewood Avenue, consider another of the town's claims to fame: it was the home of dentist William Lowell who in 1924 patented the first golf tee.

Now, refreshed from your journey of sustenance for the mind and body, turn left at the edge of Maplewood village into the New Jersey Transit railroad station for the train ride home.

A Pre-Breakfast Warm-Up

Sussex County, New Jersey

This short ride is a perfect opportunity for a strong rider to get in some serious hill-climbing before joining more languorous companions for breakfast and a gentler day-long two-wheeled exploration. It's ideally suited for cyclists bed-and-breakfasting at the Apple Valley Inn in Glenwood, New Jersey, although it could be added onto either or both of the two other rides with the inn on its route to make a longer and more challenging ride (see "Of Apples and Animals" and "From New Jersey to Florida" in the New York section). Like those other two rides, this is one of the minority in this book that cannot be reached by public transportation. See "From New Jersey to Florida" for driving directions from New York City.

This particular ride is dubbed "Little Green Arrows" in my mind, because it was inspired by seeing an anonymous chartreuse arrow demurely painted on the edge of the pavement, pointing in the starting direction. That arrow beckoned to me. The Apple Valley Inn hostess, Mitzi Durham, said it was for a Multiple Sclerosis Society fund-raising ride to High Point, even though it did not have the familiar initials MS characterizing such arrows in my neck of the woods. Whatever. I never saw another one on this route, and the actual destination of the little green arrows remains a mystery. But it did inspire this ride, which I did literally complete before one of

Ride Ratings

Length: 9 miles
Configuration: loop
Difficulty: rolling to hilly; traffic is light to moderately light
Surface: good pavement throughout

—Highlights: This workout features some spectacular forest and valley views and thrilling downhills.

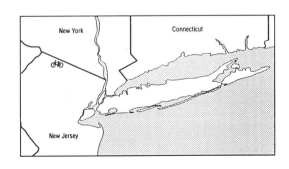

Mitzi's delectable break-fasts. It was a marvelous way to begin the day, not least of all because the late July weekend had been beastly hot, and I love riding by a summer dawn's first rosy light, and coming inside all aerobi-cally exercised and glow-ing to sit down before fresh orange juice and steaming blueberry pancakes.

The ride starts out with several miles of climbing—you may even want to drop into your granny gear—and then gives you the reward of descents, ending with an easy rolling cool-down straightaway return. The triangular loop is also easy to remember if you don't want to carry this whole book, as it involves only three roads: right out of the Apple Valley Inn onto Route 565 South for 3.5 miles, left onto Route 641 for 1.5 miles, and left onto Route 517 North for the 4 miles back.

Turn right out of the driveway of the Apple Valley Inn and make that imme-diate right onto Sussex County Route 565 South, which parallels the creek next to the Inn. Pass the gazebo and the footbridge, of which the Durhams are so proud, and you'll immediately start a climb to get the old ticker pumped up. There is much to look at on this ride; scarcely a quarter mile into it is the three-story clapboard Glenwood Mills on the left, dated 1805-1888. Keep pedaling upward past shaded, tree-hung yards and gardens, curving right past the Vernon Township High School. Eventually, a long, narrow valley will open up to your right, paralleled by a farther wooded ridge. As you breathe hard and keep ped-aling, take advantage of the slow pace to enjoy the purple periwinkle and the delicate white filigree of the Queen Anne's lace and the other wildflowers adorn-ing the roadside.

After fully a mile and a half of climbing, you'll reach the crest. And what a view! Don't pass it by. The road swoops in an S through Everett Martin's Horse Farm nestled in that long, narrow valley. The farmhouse buildings are spar-kling white, the fields green and marked by a border of split-rail fences—a per-fect picture for easel or film.

When you've caught your breath and a swig of water, then enjoy the curv-ing downhill, which flattens out as you ride along the floor of the long, shallow valley between two forested ridges. Climb once again, past the white cabins and kitchen building of Camp Sussex on your left, a camp for girls and boys, up to The Summit—a new development of large homes on your right. But the name lies. The real summit is yet half a mile ahead.

After cresting, on your downhill coast don't miss your next turn, but a quarter mile ahead—left at the first major intersection onto Sussex County Route 641, also known as Drew Mountain Road. Now, after all your climbing, you have the reward of a mile-long descent, past the Pochuck Volunteer Ambulance Corps and various houses. The downhill is steep with sharp curves, so resist the temptation to let 'er loose until the road opens up. As you soar past a pond on your right, you'll build enough momentum to carry you up the next rise.

Turn left at the first stop sign onto Sussex County Route 517 North: a Mobil gas station marks the corner where you turn. (I actually wrote "service station" first, but in this age of self-pumping, window-cleaning, and oil-checking while the proprietor holds your credit card hostage, that's a long-gone relic and a sign of my age!)

Since Route 517 has some moderate traffic, keep your ears alert. You'll pedal past Saint Francis de Sales Roman Catholic Church nearly hidden on your right, and then see the brick Walnut Ridge School commanding the rise on your left. Shortly past it, on the side of a red barn on your right, are painted the words MISTY MEADOWS—and behind the barn, the pond and the meadows in the hollow are indeed floating in mist at dawn, and I almost expected to see faeries (with an "e") flitting through the humid shadows.

Bear right to follow the road past the schools to your left; here you can really open up to 30 miles per hour. At the "T" intersection half a mile beyond, turn left to stay on Route 517 North (Sandhill Road goes to the right).

At the intersection with Route 644, keep cycling straight ahead, past Someplace Special, a gourmet deli where you might want to stop for picnic lunch fixings. (If you have tacked this ride onto the beginning of "From New Jersey to Florida," however, you can turn right here onto Route 644 and then follow the directions to Florida.)

On this straightaway back to the Apple Valley Inn, don't miss the remarkable rock outcropping forming miniature white and gray cliffs behind the houses on your right. Pass Glenwood Cemetery and the Pochuck Farm Market, and turn left into the Apple Valley Inn. Bon appetit!

NEW YORK

MANHATTAN'S OTHER ISLAND

New York County, New York

Manhattan, the island considered the heart of New York City, is surrounded by other islands. Staten Island, of course, is one of the five boroughs of New York City (think of it: New York is a city composed of five counties . . .). But a lesser-known island of the city is Roosevelt Island.

Originally called Welfare Island, Roosevelt Island in the 19th century was a place of confinement for criminals and the insane. On its southern tip there are still window-gaping ruins of the stone buildings dating from that era. But in the mid-1970s, during a major push for urban renewal, attractive apartment buildings were constructed, and Roosevelt Island became a desirable residential middle-class neighborhood just a stone's throw away from Manhattan's posh Upper East Side, at attractively lower rents. In fact, in late 1983, when my West Side apartment building was going co-op, I briefly looked on Roosevelt Island as a possible place to live.

Long and slender, the island is about a quarter of a mile wide and two miles long, paralleling Manhattan from East 48th to East 86th Streets. The only way to drive to it by car is across the Island Bridge from Queens. For years, the only way to get yourself and your bike to it from Manhattan was via a most engaging aerial tramway over the East River—the way this ride takes you. Now there is also a subway stop there (the Roosevelt Island stop of the Q train on the IND Sixth Avenue line), but that's no fun.

Ride Ratings

Length: 13 miles
Configuration: long and skinny loop
Difficulty: easy, mostly flat, though some stair climbing is required; traffic is light to moderately light, especially on weekends
Surface: pavement as good as New York City ever has

—Highlights: This ride tours some of the city's best-known attractions, including Zabar's, the American Museum of Natural History & the Hayden Planetarium, the John Lennon memorial, and Roosevelt Island.

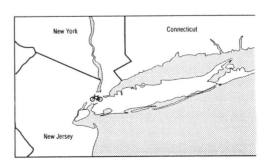

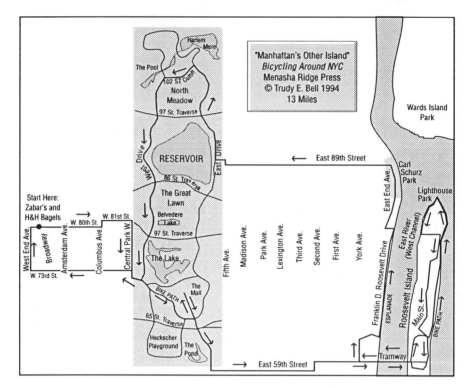

Because of its relative isolation from public transportation and automobile traffic, Roosevelt Island is a surprisingly quiet interlude after the horn-honking, red light-jumping clamor of Manhattan. The streets of the "downtown" area are paved with red terra-cotta tile, and on weekends the wheeled vehicles you're most likely to see are bicycles and wheelchairs. Yes, wheelchairs. On the northern end of the island is the Coler Memorial Hospital, dedicated to the convalescing or permanently disabled. In fact, Roosevelt Island with its ramps and walks and elevators is exemplary in showing how a city can be designed to be accessible to the handicapped.

This ride starts on Manhattan's Upper West Side (my old stomping ground) at the corner of West 80th Street and Broadway. You can get there easily from the IRT (Broadway) subway line, taking the local #1 or #9 train to the West 79th Street stop at Broadway; alternatively you can take IND (Eighth Avenue) line to Columbus Circle (West 59th Street) and ride north up Broadway to the starting point.

No matter how you get there, come hungry. The first stop is H&H Bagels, baker of those round, heavy, doughnut-shaped Jewish breads that cry out for cream cheese and lox (smoked salmon). As the fragrant, hip-high paper bags stacked around the store testify, H&H is also supplier to many of the delis in the city. Bagels fresh out of the oven are like hot dumplings, steaming and soft. But like the manna of Exodus, they last but a day, turning into veritable rocks unless frozen. Long-time residents of New York City will hotly defend the bagel baker they like best, arguing on the basis of taste, topping (sesame v. poppy v.

salt v. onion), and texture (the traditional dense that is boiled before baking as H&H makes v. the newer fluffy). For a really heated debate, get into a discussion whether or not a cinnamon-raisin bagel is a legitimate bagel (some bakers still don't make them). Well, for my money, H&H is the best baker in town, and I'll quietly fuel up for my ride and just listen while others thrash out the deep and heavy culinary philosophy.

H&H is across 80th Street from another long-standing New York City landmark: Zabar's, the ultimate delicatessen. Two decades ago, it was just one single-story shop; now it's several adjoining two-story buildings taking up half the block. Don't go in if you suffer from claustrophobia, as Zabar's is always a grab-a-number-and-wait noisy crush, especially on Saturday and Sunday mornings. But if you have time and you want some of the best gourmet food around at some of the best prices—plus the mad scene thrown in for entertainment—lock up your bike and push your way inside.

Copper bowls, sieves, garlic presses, and unidentifiable implements dangle within reach from every possible square inch from the ceiling. The smell of fresh-ground coffee wafts through the air, leading you to scores of beans from around the world; for many years Zabar's was one of only two suppliers in the nation selling the precious and rare Jamaican Blue Mountain (the other was in San Francisco). Cheeses are also a bewildering international array of rounds and blocks, some of them cut and open with samples, and little signs describing the flavor, uses, and origins of each kind. Fresh pasta, the most delicious assortment of bacons (Canadian, Irish, and other), dozens of loose and bagged teas, spices, and breads beg to be bought and eaten. And there are excellent bargains on cooking implements and appliances (in the 1970s when the Cuisinart food processor became the darling of television chefs, Zabar's waged a well-publicized price war with Bloomingdale's and Macy's Cellar).

If you're an impulse buyer (as I am) and a lover of fine foods (ditto), you'll never walk out without dropping less than $50. Come to think of it, Zabar's is best saved for the end of the trip, when you can schlepp (such a wonderfully descriptive Yiddish word) your booty home on the subway instead of on your bike. When you've sated your senses and your appetite, wend your way back out into the sunshine and onto the bike, and ride west on one-way West 80th Street.

After two long blocks, the street will end at a "T" intersection at Columbus Avenue; cross and walk your bike left on the sidewalk, against traffic, one block up. In the late 1970s, Columbus Avenue turned from a boarded-up district of single-room occupancy welfare hotels into one of New York City's best-known restaurant rows, famous especially for nouvelle cuisine and its experimental, rather yuppie tone. You might want to consider your choices for dinner at the ride's end.

At the first corner, turn right onto two-way West 81st Street. On a summer weekend you may see booths of local craftspeople selling their wares, as during the warm months this is a popular area for street fairs—a function as common as block parties in residential New York City neighborhoods. Ride another long block, slowing, noting on your right the green-patina copper dome of the Hayden Planetarium, with its constellations of night and its weekend laser light shows.

Cross the very busy Central Park West but do not follow the cars going straight. Instead, turn right (south) onto the hexagonal tiles of the walkway. To your left is a wall with the trees of Central Park. On your right, across Central Park West, are the majestic marble columns of the American Museum of Natural History, housing in its echoing corridors the skeletons of ancient dinosaurs and the sparking crystals of amethyst and jade in the Hall of Gems and Minerals. These are both worth a return trip some rainy weekend unsuitable for cycling, if only for the museum's and planetarium's fabulous gift shops.

Turn left into the first entrance into Central Park, at West 77th Street, across from the New-York Historical Society (which once had a brochure on its origins titled "The Importance of Being Hyphenated.") The historical society is also worth a visit, as it has nice exhibits of local interest that change several times a year.

In Central Park, ride right at the stop sign marking the "T" intersection to ride part of Park Drive, passing The Lake to your left. If you're riding on a weekend, or midday during the summer, chances are there are no automobiles other than park vehicles, for cars are blessedly prohibited certain hours.

Don't work up a head of steam, though, for at the next light you'll follow the road right, but turn left at the second light onto the paved bike path. Your landmark is a sign saying WEST 72ND STREET RIGHT; PARK DRIVE LEFT. For a short while I will now be guiding you on the route along which I used to cycle to work each morning for five years. It's about as pretty as a ride can be in one of the biggest cities in the world, so take your time to enjoy it.

Shortly after you get on the path, just past the brick snack bar building that is painted to look like stone, make a right at a "Y" intersection onto the path of fine gravel.

To your right, over the chain-link fence wound with morning glories, is the broad green of the Sheep Meadow with Manhattan's midtown spires in the distance. If the day is warm, you may see hundreds or even thousands of sunbathers with picnic baskets, guitars, strollers, bikes keeled over onto the grass, and wide-eyed one-year-olds toddling unsteadily in the unaccustomed outdoor freedom.

Head straight at the end of the fence, cross the asphalt, and head up a dirt path for 50 feet; at the iron fence turn right onto another paved bike path (when you get there, you'll see this is more obvious than it sounds). On warm weekends that asphalt area you just crossed is likely to be crowded with volleyball players, roller-skaters, expert trick jump-ropers, boom-box radios, and hundreds of spectators. Sometimes you may see some piece of weirdness unique to New York City. Once, for about a month in the early 1980s, there was a guy constructing elaborate miniature Stonehenge-like structures out of the fist-sized rocks in the dirt—until, unfortunately, he was discouraged by park authorities. For a number of years, off and on, one might see a sinewy man practicing T'ai Chi with dirty city pigeons perched on his oiled arms and head. Don't ask me . . .

In just a few yards, the path will split at a "Y." Take the left fork, then make another immediate left to ride up the beautiful, tree-shaded wide promenade lined with benches. Here you can practice freewheeling no hands. At the end of the promenade, stop at the courtyard to admire the Central Park band shell, site of many free summer concerts. Turn around and retrace your path through the promenade, until you emerge between the statues of Robert Burns and Walter Scott. Head right around the circle past the statue of Christopher Columbus, and cross Park Drive at the light.

Coast straight down the paved path designated for pedestrians, not the one for carriages—otherwise you may regret the reeking horse droppings on your tires. (Hint from the experienced: do not ride through puddles in horsey Central Park; the rainwater dissolves the droppings into a smelly slurry that splashes all over your frame, with an odor that persists until you give your bike a complete shower.) On your right, down in a ravine, in winter you may catch a glimpse of ice skaters on Wollman Rink, reconditioned in the late 1980s by the famous multimillionaire Donald Trump. There you can rent skates at a reasonable fee and join the adults and children outside on the ice. On your left is the entrance to the Central Park Zoo, also renovated in the 1980s to show animals in environments ranging from the equatorial rain forest to the polar ice caps. The zoo is open every day of the year from 10 A.M.-5 P.M..

The end of the path will emerge onto an extension of East 60th Street, so watch for traffic. Head straight for one short block, then turn left (east) at the light onto West 59th Street. You are now at Manhattan's Grand Army Plaza (as opposed to one by the same name in Queens), and the grand stone building fronting the plaza is the richly world-renowned Plaza Hotel. It's also the site of a number of famous movies, including *Plaza Suite* and the very funny introduction-to-civilization scene in *Crocodile Dundee*. If you want a taste of elegance, lock your bike and walk up the wide stone steps to peek inside at the magnificent atrium, where you'll hear the gentle clink of crystal and sterling as discreet waiters serve truffle omelets and chardonnay for brunch.

Continue east on 59th Street, crossing New York City's most famous street, Fifth Avenue. At the corner of the G.M. Building opposite the Plaza is the world's largest toy store F.A.O. Schwarz. Fifth Avenue also divides the city in half lengthwise, into east and west, with all the address numbers on the cross streets starting low here and ending up high at either the East River (toward which you are heading) or the Hudson River (behind you). So once you cross Fifth Avenue, you'll be riding on East 59th Street.

Now you'll ride five long blocks, a bit less than a mile. A handy rule of thumb for calculating distances in New York City is that 20 uptown blocks or six crosstown blocks make a mile. You'll cross Madison Avenue (headquarters of most of the country's major advertising agencies that warp your mind on television) and Park Avenue (home of the city's richest, including the fictional investment banker Sherman McCoy in Tom Wolfe's *Bonfire of the Vanities*). Park Avenue is actually useful for a cyclist to remember, for north of East 45th Street its lanes are wider than those on most avenues and buses are not allowed—thus I favor it for uptown-downtown commuting.

Continue your ride east on East 59th Street. At the corner of Lexington Avenue is chic Bloomingdale's. Between Third Avenue and Second Avenue, on your left, watch for Forbidden Planet, one of several major science fiction shops in the city. Here you can find books of your favorite authors, including those not so famous as Isaac Asimov, Robert A. Heinlein, or Arthur C. Clarke, plus videos, toys, masks, games, and who knows what all. You can probably also find company, for many of the aficionados who hang out among the racks also crave a good conversation with someone who groks why the shorthand for the genre is always sf and never sci-fi.

At Second Avenue, dismount and head left onto the sidewalk, toward the Manhattan terminus of the tramway to Roosevelt Island. Two stories above your head are the brightly painted girders strung with cables, along which you may see one of the trams moving to or fro. On a windy day, the springing of the wire cables sounds like a plucked metallic rubber band. With luck, the elevator will be working; otherwise, hoist your bike up the stairs to the second level, pay your fare (slightly higher than whatever is the going rate for a subway token), and enjoy the scenery from this height for few minutes while waiting for the next tram.

Trams leave every 15 minutes; no reservations are required. Each tram is one large open car surrounded by windows and is more like a scenic ski lift ride than public transportation. Two wide doors slide apart with plenty of time allowed for loading all passengers, packages, and bicycles. Passengers are often in a festive, wide-eyed spirit, for even veteran subway riders seldom take the tram unless they've made a specific point of it. The ride itself is all of four minutes, so have your camera at the ready as the ground falls away. Note below you the one intriguing mansion with its impeccable grounds nestled at an unusual angle among all the surrounding skyscrapers.

Watch the container ships and barges chugging up and down the East River, and take note of long, skinny Roosevelt Island fast approaching. The little pointed hut you'll see near the island's southern tip once spurted an impressive fountain drawn from the East River, until sometime in the 1980s it was discovered that the brackish spray from the river—which is actually a tidal estuary of the Atlantic Ocean—was killing the vegetation and corroding useful metal on the island's southern end.

When the tram docks and opens its doors, walk your bike down the ramp, then ride left away from the station to begin your tour of the island. The whole circuit of Roosevelt Island is about four miles; if you like the place, feel free to explore some of the cross streets along the way—the place is so small, it's impossible to get really lost.

Head right at the "T" intersection and follow the one-way signs along the western branch of East River, enjoying the sight of Manhattan's skyscrapers less than a quarter of a mile away across the river. (New York City definitely looks best when seen from a distance.) Cycle past the Roosevelt Island subway station. At the stop sign, follow the one-way signs to the right. In less than a minute, you'll find yourself on the east side of Roosevelt Island. There a children's playground has as its backdrop a giant three-stack factory in Queens, which has its own industrial-architecture charm.

At the children's playground, enter the bike path to the right, heading north along the raised path paralleling the East River (this eastern branch is on your right). When I was riding here on a warm Indian-summer Columbus Day weekend, there were so few people that the predominant sound was the lapping of the water below to my right. The path wanders under some apartment buildings and becomes a fitness circuit, past basketball courts, and under the 59th Street Bridge to Queens. This bridge is the inspiration for Simon and Garfunkle's 1966 hit "The 59th Street Bridge Song (Feelin' Groovy)," which, come to think of it, gives touring cyclists some excellent advice.

Turn right at the next stop sign, at every succeeding choice of paths bearing right to keep the river on your right. Shortly you'll approach the Coler Memorial Hospital on your left. Head through the gate, which is closed to cars on weekends, to continue your circuit of Roosevelt Island.

Shortly thereafter—a bit over a mile after leaving the tram—you'll enter Lighthouse Park, the park at the northern tip of the island. This attractive park is named, not surprisingly, after a small abandoned lighthouse at its northern tip. Below the lighthouse is a plaque in memory of one Vicki Holland (1931-79), who worked with the disabled. Stop for a moment to note the rhythmic swells of the water, where the East River divides into its two branches around the island. And if you're already feeling hungry after the four miles you've ridden since leaving Zabar's and H&H Bagels, you can grill yourself a hotdog on one of the public barbecue grills dotted over the grass. Lighthouse Park also has some special memories for me, because it was there—while I was scouting out this ride for this book—that I chanced to meet a Florida cyclist named Jim Arth temporarily working in the New York City area. He took such an interest in this book project that over the next year was a great help in mapping out about a third of the rides. So, this is a charmed ride; have a Pepsi with a cyclist you may meet—it may lead to many nice outings together.

Leave Lighthouse Park on the side opposite to which you entered, by riding along the paved bike path on the side facing Manhattan, this time keeping the East River's west branch on your right. You'll know you're doing it right because when you look across to Manhattan, you'll see the white columns of Gracie Mansion (home of New York City's mayor) and the trees of Carl Schurz Park— where you'll be riding in an hour or so.

In a quarter mile the path will end, but continue riding straight toward the tennis courts, heading right around the courts to join a road. At this "T" intersection there is a huge-boled maple that, when I was there, sported a sign that read PEOPLE ENJOYED THE SHADE OF THIS TREE WHEN LINCOLN GAVE THE GETTYSBURG ADDRESS.

Follow the road's one-way signs around to the right. Eventually it becomes Roosevelt Island's Main Street, leading past the town square into town. Here you will pass shops on your left and a coffee shop on your right, in the base of apartment buildings with small plazas in between. Automobile traffic is very light, bike racks abound, and pedestrians stroll at a pace so leisurely you'll hardly believe you're in part of New York City.

At the triangle at the end of Main Street, make a right around the circle. Turn left at the DO NOT ENTER sign (so as not to ride the wrong way on a one-way street); turn right at the next "T" intersection to ride as far south on the island as the roads permit. At the next "T" intersection turn right, noting that the very southern tip of the island is still undeveloped; the ruins of the former smallpox infirmary and prison hospital are blocked off with cyclone fencing topped with barbed wire.

At the next "T" intersection, turn right, passing Goldwater Memorial Hospital. When you pass under the tramway, turn right onto the road to the tram, and in less than 50 yards you can enter the tram station to return to Manhattan.

Take the five-minute, gently swaying tram ride back over the East River to Manhattan. Ride the elevator or hoist your bike down the stairs to street level, onto the busy one-way East 60th Street heading east. Cross Second Avenue and First Avenue, and turn left onto the busy two-way York Avenue to head uptown. Ride slowly though, for you're in this traffic for only three blocks.

At East 63rd Street, cross to the sidewalk on the north side, turn right, and ride on the sidewalk up a ramp, over the fast-moving FDR (Franklin D. Roosevelt) Drive, and left down the ramp on the opposite side. At the base of the ramp, make a sharp "U" turn to head north; if you've done it right, the East River will be on your right. You are now cycling on one of New York City's several esplanades—level, paved walkways along shorelines that remain the city's well-kept secrets from all but joggers and local residents.

Ride slowly for about a mile along the esplanade to enjoy your view of Roosevelt Island in the river to your right. Occasional brass markers in the pavement will inform you what cross-street you have reached in your northward travels. At East 80th Street, this section of the esplanade ends in a long set of stairs—three flights of 20 stairs each, with a landing in between. Hoist your bike up, resting in between, to the pedestrian bridge back over the FDR Drive—your reward is worth the effort. Make a right immediately after leaving the bridge to continue northward along the new esplanade beginning in front of you, walking your bike to obey the yellow stencils declaring NO BIKE RIDING.

In about a quarter of a mile, you'll enter Carl Schurz Park, even with the lighthouse at the northern tip of Roosevelt Island. You can relax here to enjoy the sun dappling on the East River, and to say farewell to your last view of Manhattan's other island. Then, walk your bike to continue north through the park.

Here, in very short distance, you'll head left onto the overpass, up a few broad stairs. Follow the path to the left, turn left at the "T" intersection in front of you to avoid the stairs to the right, and then walk down the little ramp curving around to your right to emerge at East End Avenue and East 88th Street. Actually, there are a lot of paths crisscrossing this park, so if you get confused, don't worry about it—you just want to get yourself down out of the park onto East End Avenue.

Head right (north) up East End Avenue, and make a left onto one-way East 89th Street to head west. At the corner of Second Avenue, take note of the restaurant Sala Thai—a wonderful find for delicious Thai cuisine. East 89th Street will end at Fifth Avenue, and ahead of you will be the wall surrounding Central Park. On the corner to your left is New York's famed cylindrical Guggenheim Museum, designed by Frank Lloyd Wright.

Pull your bike onto the sidewalk and walk one block north, against the downtown Fifth Avenue traffic, to enter Central Park at East 90th Street. Head right (north) on the Park Drive to follow the flow of joggers, cyclists, (or cars, if it's a weekday). Work your way to the left side of Park Drive. At the signs for the 102nd Street cutoff, head left; it's the most popular route for many joggers and some cyclists, and its level pavement cuts off the significant hills of the northernmost end of Central Park.

At the "T" intersection ending the cutoff, turn left to rejoin Park Drive, keeping a sharp eye out for cyclists speeding down the hill from your right. Now you can just meander up and down the rolling hillocks of Central Park (which is not flat), enjoying the sight of picnickers in the grassy hollows tossing Aerobies and Frisbees.

Head right up the ramp to exit at West 72nd Street. Turn right to head north on the busy Central Park West, but get off your bike. You are now at the entrance to Strawberry Fields, a contemplative garden created in Central Park by a donation of Yoko Ono as a memorial to her husband John Lennon, the member of the Beatles who wrote many of their most famous songs. Turn around and look across Central Park West at the imposing building on the northwest corner of 72nd Street. That is the Dakota, where Lennon and Ono lived, and outside of which Lennon was shot. The Dakota was also made famous as the central site of the action in the horror movie *Rosemary's Baby* (starring Mia Farrow); as a lesser claim to fame, it played a pivotal role in Jack Finney's time-travel science fiction novel *Time and Again*. Only in New York, eh?

Remount your bike and ride north for one block, turning left onto one-way westbound West 73rd Street. After three long blocks, look north along the southbound lane of Broadway; one block north is the green market Fairway, famed for its wide selection of superb vegetables at low prices, and quite holding its own against Zabar's for coffees and cheeses as well.

Ride one block farther and turn right to head north onto two-way West End Avenue. To your left is the 17-story Schwab House, one of the first luxury apartment complexes to be built after World War II, and my own home from 1975-1988; occupying an entire city block with 650 apartments, it is its own voting district with the voting machines rolled into the lobby at each election.

Continue north on West End Avenue, and turn right onto one-way eastbound East 80th Street for one block to Broadway. Here you are, back at your starting point between Zabar's and H&H Bagels, to provision up on gourmet delicacies for dinner.

CLAY PIT PONDS MEANDER
Richmond County, New York

Ride Ratings

Length: 10 or 14 miles
Configuration: figure 8
Difficulty: virtually flat; traffic on shorter ride is light, but on some stretches of longer ride it is moderately heavy
Surface: good pavement throughout

—Highlights: This easy family outing starts with a ride on the Staten Island Ferry, then a train ride; enjoy the Conference House Park and the nature trail in Clay Pit Ponds State Park Preserve.

Staten Island has the reputation for being rural, and compared to midtown Manhattan it is, especially at its southern tip. Its ruralness was threatened in the 1960s, when the Verrazano-Narrows Bridge provided the first ready auto link with Brooklyn, eliminating Staten Island's isolation as the island borough. Nonetheless, the southern tip has preserved some of its original character. While you won't see cows and sheep as in some of the rides of outlying New Jersey, you will get a reprieve from urban noise and crowds. It may even, at times, be hard to remember you're still in one of the five boroughs of New York City.

This trip is not a bike ride so much as a day-long excursion with some bicycling included. You'll tool along some pleasant, older suburban byways—suburbs so old and relatively forgotten, in fact, that only in 1990 did they convert from individual septic tanks to a central sewer system.

There are a lot of twists and turns, since most through roads in Staten Island are heavily traveled and side roads are limited in how far they will take you. The 9-mile ride is suitable for the whole family although there are some busy spots; the 13-mile ride probably has too much traffic for very young riders, but in many cases kids can ride on the sidewalks to the right of the street. Be wary of the Hagstrom map of Staten Island, for in this area it is full of errors, as I will note.

There are ocean views and

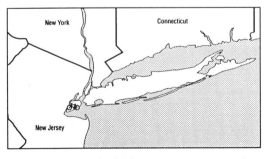

New York

Connecticut

New Jersey

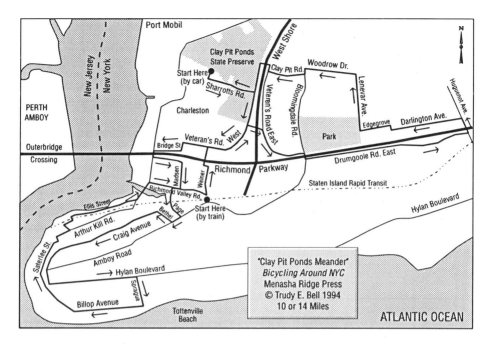

"Clay Pit Ponds Meander"
Bicycling Around NYC
Menasha Ridge Press
© Trudy E. Bell 1994
10 or 14 Miles

tucked-away roads almost like trails to enjoy on this route. There's also the fun of joining high-performance cyclists riding fast along some frontage roads alongside main highways. But the main attraction is Clay Pit Ponds State Park Preserve—a virtually unknown treasure in the southern part of the island. It's a relatively new park, being established in 1977, and has the distinction of being New York City's only State Park Preserve. It's small—260 acres—so can be seen in its entirety in an afternoon, and has a wonderful 1-1/2-mile walking trail, a 3-mile bridle trail, an herb garden, a drinking fountain, and a couple of picnic tables. Combined with the Staten Island ferry, which is always fun, and a ride on the above-ground Staten Island Rapid Transit Operating Authority train (see the preface for information about taking your bicycle on SIRTOA), the activities could easily fill a relaxing day. Don't bother to pack a picnic lunch, as there are services along the route.

If you want to drive from New York City, call Clay Pit Ponds park for specific directions from your location: (718) 967-1976. From New Jersey, get yourself to the Outerbridge Crossing to Route 440 northbound; take Exit 3 (Woodrow Road), follow the service road (Veterans Road) as it turns left twice under the overpass; turn right onto Sharrotts Road (the next stop sign), and half a mile later turn right onto Carlin Street and drive to the end. Park in the gravel lot of Clay Pit Ponds State Park Preserve, and pick up the description in the middle, starting your day with the bicycle ride and ending with the hike through the park. (*Note:* although the preserve itself is open dawn to dusk, its parking lot is open only from 9 A.M. to 5 P.M., and they really do close that big yellow gate at 5 P.M.. If you're planning to arrive earlier or stay later than those hours, park along Carlin Street outside the gate.)

If you take the SIRTOA, get off the train at the Richmond Valley stop. Hoist your bike up the western stairs onto the street; at this point you'll be on an overpass with bright green railings. That's Richmond Valley Road, and is where you begin this ride. After you come up the stairs, turn left onto Richmond Valley Road. At the first stop sign, turn left onto the busy Page Avenue, taking the overpass over the SIRTOA tracks. At the next light, turn right onto Amboy Road. Here, you may want to buy lunch fixings, for there are plenty of choices: an A&P grocery story, a deli, a bagel shop, a convenience store, a pharmacy, and a bank to finance all of the above.

At the next intersection, turn right onto Bethel Avenue. This is one turn you cannot miss; it is marked on the right by the white brick Bethel United Methodist Church in the middle of a cemetery. There are even gravestones in the church's front yard, a reminder of ashes to ashes and dust to dust.

Turn left onto Craig Avenue, on which you'll stay for the next mile or so. There is a stop sign at virtually every cross street, but take your time: this street is quiet and wooded, lined with old, unprepossessing Victorian-era houses fronted by large wraparound porches, the type for lazily moving porch swings.

At Main Street the traffic picks up a bit, but here's another chance to stop for snacks at a deli. Follow Craig Road as it bears left and crosses Amboy Road. At that corner, note the beautifully restored beige and grey Victorian House with a marvelous wraparound porch. Just beyond it, follow Craig Avenue as it bends left again at Shore Road.

Turn left at the "T" intersection onto the wide Hylan Boulevard, watching for the automobile traffic for the next half mile. In half a mile, turn right onto Sprague Avenue, almost to the end. At the dead-end sign, turn right onto Billop Avenue; soon you will be riding along a narrow, tree-shaded country lane that feels deliciously forgotten. Follow Billop Avenue as it bears right; now you are riding next to Conference House Park.

At Hylan Boulevard, continue straight on one-way Satterlee Street. Then make an immediate left between two wooden posts into the gravel drive of Conference House Park. At the end of the driveway is a fieldstone manor house, built in 1680 by Christopher Billop. Billop, a naval captain, is alleged to have won Staten Island for New York away from New Jersey by sailing around it in less than 24 hours.

Billop's house was also the site of a major conference during the Revolutionary War. In 1776, the British had won the Battle of Long Island, regaining control of New York. That September the British commander Lord Howe met here with representatives of the American rebels—John Adams, Benjamin Franklin, and Edmund Rutledge. Howe offered amnesty to all American rebels who returned to British allegiance. But Adams, Franklin, and Rutledge refused to surrender. And you know the rest.

Today the Conference House can be reserved by organizations wanting to hold a retreat. Nonconference visitors may explore its 18th-century furnishings on tours Tuesday through Sunday from 1-5 P.M., with admission free on Tuesdays and Thursdays. The grounds are open from dawn to dusk. A manicured lawn dotted with magnificent shade trees slopes down to command a view of sailboats on the entrance to the Arthur Kill, the narrow waterway between Staten Island and New Jersey.

Unfortunately, this body of water, lined with precious wetlands, has been the site of hundreds of oil spills from tankers en route to New York or New Jersey. In the early 1970s, the Arthur Kill had been considered almost dead. But in an odd twist of fate, the widespread collapse of industry in the New York area over the last couple of decades has actually helped the environment as the wetlands return to nature. Now the Arthur Kill has maybe 150 species of fish and 125 species of birds. It's doubtful you'll see any signs of muck or mire in the placid marina with its lighthouse, so sit on the grass and enjoy the view. The Conference House grounds also offer an outdoor drinking fountain, plus "His" and "Hers" public outhouses. (Hey, they're better than trying to find a facility bush . . .)

Leave Conference House Park by turning left to stay on the one-way Satterlee Street, which narrows briefly to a mysterious, winding single lane, and then opens to a quiet residential area. Turn left at the "T" intersection onto Amboy Street and make an immediate right onto Hopping Avenue, where you'll pass bigger, more gracious houses with larger lawns.

The next few turns come very quickly but are easier to follow than they may sound. Turn left at the next "T" intersection onto Bentley Street and make an immediate right onto Arthur Kill Avenue. Take the first left onto Main Street, turn right at the end onto Utah Street, and left at the "T" intersection onto Johnson Street, over the bridge over the SIRTOA tracks. To your left, reachable if you had taken Bentley Street to its end, is the Tottenville station, marking the end of the train line.

At the end of this overpass, turn right to coast down Ellis Street, handling your bike with care over the very bumpy old-time cobbles. The not-very-pretty Tottenville Marina with its dry-docked boats is spread out to your left, but beyond is a great panorama of the Outerbridge Crossing. The pavement smooths out in a quarter mile, and you'll ride past several patio, pool, and carpet factory outlets.

Turn left at the "T" intersection onto busy Arthur Kill Road, catching another brief—and better—glimpse of the Outerbridge Crossing to the left, reflected in the water of the plant. Turn right onto Richmond Valley Road. As you near Page Avenue, you'll pedal past hundreds of gigantic flat-sided spools of cable at the AT&T Nassau Metals plant. Some apartment-dwellers in New York City use various sized spools—when they can spirit them off a construction site - as end tables or even dining room tables, especially if their interior decorating scheme is of the era Contemporary Orangecrate or Early Matrimonial.

Cross Page Avenue, and in a few tenths of a mile—just before you reach the overpass and the stairway back down to the Richmond Valley station of the SIRTOA—make a left turn left onto Weiner Street, up a hill through a quiet residential neighborhood. For a scenic detour through a development of unexpectedly new and gracious homes, take the first right onto Butler Street, which becomes the Meade Street Loop. Follow the road as it bends left. At the "T" intersection with Weiner Street, turn right to continue your path.

Make a left at the next "T" intersection onto Boscombe Avenue, and an immediate right onto Tyrellian Street onto the overpass over Richmond Parkway, where the cars whiz noisily below. This overpass reminds me of one in San Jose, California, where a girlfriend and I used to go when we were in junior high. We'd stand and wave vigorously at the traffic below, delighting in an occasional honk or answering wave. The trucks were the best; we'd make a steam-whistle pulling motion, and the observant, grinning drivers would blast their horns in reply. Try it here—see what happens.

Turn right at the "T" intersection on the other side of the overpass onto Veterans Road West, a gently curving downhill frontage road paralleling the West Shore Expressway. Make another right at the DO NOT ENTER signs where the road bends right onto Englewood Avenue and crosses another overpass over West Shore Expressway.

At the other end of the overpass, at the "T" intersection with Veterans Road East, you have a choice. If you want the 10-mile ride, turn left onto Veterans Road East, make the next left onto Sharrotts Road, and coast half a mile down the gentle hill to Carlin Street, where you turn right and enter Clay Pit Ponds State Park Preserve. Now, skip down a page to the double asterisks (**).

If you want the 14-mile ride, turn right onto Veterans Road East for a long, swooping left-hand curve. At the first intersection, less than half a mile later, turn right onto Bloomingdale Road and cross over the busy Richmond Parkway. At the "T" intersection, turn right onto one-way Drumgoole Road East, a wide, smooth, one-way frontage road paralleling the Richmond Parkway.

This early part of Drumgoole Road East has very little traffic, but the cars and trucks pick up as you ride along. If you like it, stay on it for another mile. If you'd prefer something quieter, in a few tenths of a mile turn right onto Minturn Avenue, hang the first left onto Bradford Avenue, and continue straight for about half a mile, even past the dead-end sign and right through the driveway of the garden center that appears to be the end of the line. You'll end up back on Drumgoole Road East. Follow the left fork of the "Y" intersection where Drumgoole Road East veers left, and turn left at the next major intersection onto Huguenot Avenue.

You'll cross over the Richmond Parkway, but instead of essentially retracing your route on Drumgoole Road West, pedal another block north and turn left on Darlington Avenue into a quiet suburban neighborhood. In spite of what the Hagstrom map shows, this road does not go through. So, turn right onto Foster Road and take an immediate left onto Edgegrove Avenue. Turn right at the end onto unmarked Lenevar Street, riding along a field to your left. On the Hagstrom map, the field is designated as a proposed park, but it hasn't been "developed" yet (think about it—developing a park!), and retains its own charm as a rather wild and large vacant lot.

Stay on Lenevar Street until the end, turning left at the "T" intersection onto the moderately busy Woodrow Road. In half a mile, turn left at the next "T" intersection onto Bloomingdale Road. These couple of streets show the contrast between the older Staten Island and the aggressive development of newer housing tracts. Ride slowly, because you want to take the first right onto Clay Pit Road—a road that clearly has remained untouched throughout all the flurry of condo-building. Savor this short stretch, as it is shady and beautiful, reminiscent of an earlier time. And in spite of what the map shows, it is a through road.

Turn right at the "T" intersection onto Veterans Road East, which is one-way in this section, with no traffic. Follow the road as it makes a quick left under West Shore Expressway, and another left to parallel the expressway in the opposite direction. As you come out of this second left, look to your right: you'll see a yellow gate barring an extension of Clay Pit Road, now closed and rutted, heading off into the woods to your right. Although the map shows it as a wide through road (before the expressway was built it may have been), it is now little more than a hiking path into Clay Pit Ponds State Park Preserve, beckoning in its mysterious undergrowth.

Turn right at the first stop sign onto Sharrotts Road and coast down the gentle incline to Carlin Street. Turn right and ride into the gravel parking lot of the preserve.

(**) In the park, there's a bike rack where you can lock up your steed next to the park office, and a drinking fountain to relieve your thirst.

Why the unromantic name of Clay Pit Ponds, for heaven's sake? Well, starting back in the Cretaceous period nearly 70 million years ago and continuing up to about 12,000 years ago, glaciers deposited all kinds of sands and clays in this area of the southern shore of Staten Island. Leni Lenape Indians also made this area their home. Fast-forward to the 19th century: the area was intensely mined for clay for fire bricks, terra-cotta ornaments, urns, plaques, medallions, and other objets d'art. The clay mining left many small pockets and deep pits in the ground, which filled with water and became ponds. Then more recently, a young collector of reptiles and amphibians discovered the richness of wildlife in this region. And in 1977 the 260 acres was made a state park preserve.

The small area of the preserve includes many different habitats easily visible to the untrained eye (and believe me, mine is untrained): ponds, bogs, sandy barrens, mature woodlands, streams, freshwater wetlands, and fields. There are two trails that will take you through these habitats, with the longest one taking less than an hour. But don't rush it. The descriptive trail guide, available at the park office, indicates stops along the trail by identifying changes in the landscape and vegetation rather than by numbers. This method really does heighten your awareness of your surroundings by getting you to look for changes rather than numbers. And the changes can be remarkable, such as emerging from a wood into an open sandy area similar to the pine barrens of Long Island and New Jersey. Look carefully even for things not mentioned in the guide; when I was hiking there, I saw a large white mushroom, 5 inches tall by 3 inches wide, with a star-shaped split on top like the crust on a loaf of peasant bread.

Before you go hiking, first visit the wildflower garden outside the park office. In a small plot there are labeled growing specimens of the most common plants to be seen, which you (and children, of course) will later enjoy identifying in the wild along the walk. The best times to view the flowers are either the spring or the late summer. The preserve also offers guided tours, nature related arts and crafts, programs on gardening and beekeeping, evening campfires, and seasonal festivals. For information and a seasonal calendar, call (718) 967-1876, or write to Clay Pit Ponds State Park Preserve, 83 Nielsen Avenue, Staten Island, NY 10309.

When you complete the trail's loop, enjoy your picnic lunch at the shady tables next to the park office. When you're ready to resume your ride, head back out Carlin Street, and turn left at the "T" intersection onto Sharrotts Road—you may catch the smell of horses from the bridle trail on your left. Half a mile later, turn right onto Veterans Road West, which parallels the West Shore Expressway. This wide, smooth road gives you plenty of room to share with the moderate traffic, as well as the other cyclists and joggers exercising along this route. The road will bend to the right so that now it's paralleling Richmond Parkway.

Now pay close attention. Turn left onto West Shore Expressway, which looks like an on-ramp. It is. But while the cars will bear right, you will go straight so as not to take Route 440 to the Outerbridge crossing. In a few hundred yards, the bumpy road will become North Bridge Street. You will know you've done it correctly when you pass the blue and white Richmond Ceramic Tile on your right. The blue bridge of the Outerbridge Crossing towers above you, stretching out ahead.

North Bridge Street bends to the right and will carry you alongside the bridge. Turn left at the "T" intersection for a brief ride under the bridge on Arthur Kill Road, and make an immediate left onto South Bridge Street. Yes, I know this section of the ride is industrial ugly, but it gets better; meanwhile, be philosophical about the Poseidon Pools factory showroom and the smell of old oil that lingers outside the truck repair yard.

South Bridge Street bends right and ends at a "T" intersection with the very busy, wide, divided Boscombe Street. Turn left, being very careful of the fast cars, and make an immediate right onto Madsen Avenue. The payoff is the lovely contrast of the quiet residential street.

Turn left at the "T" intersection onto Richmond Valley Road. In a quarter mile you'll recognize the overpass above the Richmond Valley station of the SIRTOA. Descend the stairs with your bike, and reboard the train heading back to the Staten Island Ferry.

OLD CROTON AQUEDUCT TRAIL

Westchester County, New York

Even though this book is supposed to be about on-road tours, this ride up the Old Croton Aqueduct trail along the east bank of the Hudson River is so beautiful and accessible even to those without mountain bikes that it would be a shame to leave it out for lack of pavement. The ride is perfect for riders of all abilities, since the lovely wooded aqueduct portion is completely free from automobile traffic. It's also great for history buffs steeped in Americana. Best of all, this foray into lower Westchester County is only a subway token away from the heart of Manhattan.

The Old Croton Aqueduct, built in 1842, was the first to supply water to New York City from the Croton Reservoir 40 miles north. The aqueduct itself is buried underground, but certain portions of it are traced out by a hard-packed dirt trail that runs for miles as a public easement through forest and back yards.

The aqueduct trail passes from Yonkers to Irvington just south of the Tappan Zee Bridge. It runs between some of Westchester County's most spectacular mansions, across the grounds of Mercy College, Sunnyside (Washington Irving's former home), and Lyndhurst (the former estate of 19th-century American financier Jay Gould). Between the leaves of the trees, there are wonderful views of sunlight glinting off the Hudson River and the New Jersey palisades on the far shore. The trail itself is essentially flat and gener-

Ride Ratings

Length: 12, 21 or 26 miles
Configuration: a long, skinny figure 8
Difficulty: flat on the aqueduct trail, gently rolling on-road; traffic ranges from nonexistent to moderately heavy; route requires some stair climbing
Surface: hard-packed dirt for 5 miles of aqueduct trail, good pavement elsewhere

—Highlights: This day ride within subway distance of New York City takes a little-known trail to Tarrytown, New York; see Van Cortlandt Park, 18th and 19th century manors, a flea market, and vistas of the Hudson River.

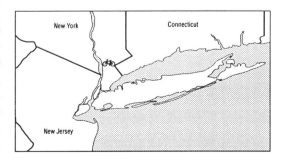

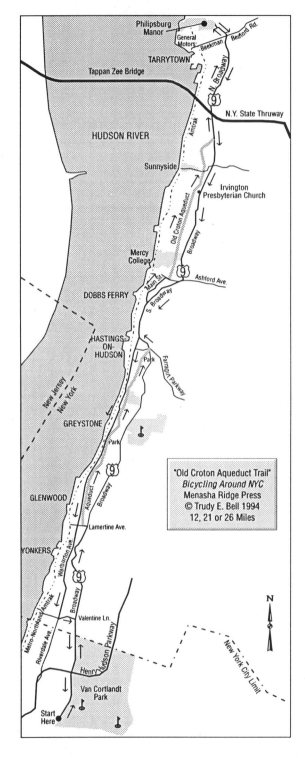

"Old Croton Aqueduct Trail"
Bicycling Around NYC
Menasha Ridge Press
© Trudy E. Bell 1994
12, 21 or 26 Miles

ally straight; the only "traffic" along it is an occasional jogger, dog-walker, or neighborhood bicyclist.

Like the Rahway River ride elsewhere in this book, this Croton Aqueduct ride is one I happened on completely by accident: some years ago fellow cyclist Mark Edelman and I wandered out for a day's jaunt toward Tarrytown and wondered about the dashed lines marking the aqueduct on Hagstrom's map of Lower Westchester County. When we went see what it looked like, *voilá!*, the wonderful trail opened before our eyes. I've never seen it mentioned in rides scheduled by the New York Cycle Club, American Youth Hostels, or any other group and as far as I can tell, this is the first time it's been featured in any printed guide.

This ride has pleased cyclists on at least two occasions: when my coworker and fellow cyclist Karen Fitzgerald and I led informal rides for people from my office, and when I brought the students of my bicycle touring class offered through New York's continuing education school, The Learning Annex. Moral of the story: always check out curious features on maps. You never know when you'll get lucky.

There are two cautions to this ride. First, although the aqueduct trail is suitable for thin-tire road bikes as well as mountain bikes, you'll enjoy it best if you don't ride it right after a rain

—give it a day or two to dry out. Second, the nonaqueduct portion of the two longer rides requires pedaling on some main streets (mostly U.S. Route 9) with traffic that can be moderately heavy at times. Be alert, wear a helmet, and use your ears. To encounter a minimum of traffic, the best time to ride is extremely early on a Sunday morning.

If you wish to minimize the portions of cycling on city streets—such as if you are on an outing with children—you can start the ride by driving to the parking lot on Lamartine Avenue in Yonkers. Alternatively, you can take the Metro-North Commuter Railroad to the Yonkers station and ride up Main Street, turn left onto Warburton Avenue, and then right up the steep grade of Lamartine Avenue to the beginning of the aqueduct trail. (See the preface to this book for information on obtaining a pass to take your bicycle on Metro-North trains). In either case, simply go both up and back along the aqueduct trail, a round trip of about 12 miles.

For those doing the longest version from Manhattan including the city streets, start at the 72nd Street subway station of the IRT Broadway line. Although there are a couple of places to buy food on the ride, on the subway ride itself— which will last the better part of an hour—you might feel like relaxing with *The New York Times*, a second cup of coffee, or some breakfast.

This main intersection of West 72nd Street and Broadway has plenty of places that will gladly exchange your hard-earned cash for food. Since this was my old stomping ground for 13 years, I can vouch for the breads and rugalach (piecrust-like pastry wrapped around a filling) at the Royale Bakery on the north side of West 72nd Street halfway between Broadway and West End Avenue. In addition, the cheese strudel at the Famous Dairy Restaurant on the south side of West 72nd Street between Broadway and Amsterdam Avenue is amazing, if you don't mind how it weighs on your stomach, cholesterol, and conscience.

When you've stocked up on breakfast-to-go for the subway ride, hoist your bike over the turnstiles (or ask the token seller if you can wheel it through the exit doors). Go downstairs to the uptown platform and take the #1 local train to the very end of the line: the Van Cortlandt Park stop in the Bronx. Although there's no way to cut the subway portion short by taking an express, don't despair of spending a sunny morning all underground: for the last half of the trip the subway becomes an elevated line, giving you an overhead tour of the northernmost Inwood section of Manhattan and then of the Bronx.

At the Van Cortlandt stop, carry your bike down the stairs. There are a couple of fast-food places and delis here, as well as a few public parking spaces in case you drove.

Cross divided Broadway (U.S. Route 9) so you can ride north, with the green playing fields of Van Cortlandt Park on your right. You may fill your water bottles at the public restrooms in the stone Van Cortlandt Park visitor's center just north of the subway station. With 1146 acres of fields, forests, and trails, Van Cortlandt Park is New York City's third-largest park (after Pelham Bay Park and Flushing Meadows Corona Park). Among other treasures, the park is home to 50 horses, two golf courses, a swimming pool, and a mansion where George Washington really did sleep. It is also home to a host of deer, rabbits, raccoons, horned owls, wood ducks, swans, and other wildlife (including picnickers), which you may spot as you pedal along its western edge.

This Broadway, along which you'll be cycling for just under four miles, is an extension of the same Broadway running from the southern tip of Manhattan and famous for its midtown theatre district (they're not called Broadway shows for nothing). In colonial times it was called Broad Way, because it was indeed a broad and well-traveled road all the way from New York City to Albany. To this day, it still goes the whole way as U.S. Route 9, and some intrepid cyclists undisturbed by the traffic and tenements of Spanish Harlem will ride out of New York City via Broadway instead of shortcutting the 10 miles or so on the #1 train.

A quarter of a mile up from the subway station on your left is the tiny hole-in-the-wall specialty shop called Lloyd's Carrot Cake. And that spicy confection is indeed what they have, in several varieties, with or without nuts. It's right next to a Chinese takeout restaurant, the combination worth remembering for your return.

A mile and a half north—a bit after leaving the northwestern corner of Van Cortlandt Park—look to your left: there's the Yonkers Bicycle Center, a good place to stop if you have some question about the operation of your bike. A mile beyond that, bear left at the "Y" intersection to continue on South Broadway (follow the signs for Routes 9 and 9A). A quarter mile later, note the old stone church whose belfry sports a magnificent antique clock—along with a satellite earth-station antenna! You're now riding through urban Yonkers. Keep following the signs for Route 9, which will eventually lead you onto one-way North Broadway heading north.

When you've ridden perhaps 20 or 30 minutes (just under four miles) from the Van Cortlandt Park subway stop, keep your eyes out for the High School of Commerce and the Yonkers Christian Assembly church on your left. A hundred feet beyond those landmarks, turn left onto Lamartine Avenue, an obscure little street that descends sharply down toward the Hudson River.

Ride your brakes to go slowly only halfway down the short block, and turn right into what appears to be a parking lot. A parking lot it is, where you can leave your car if you've cut off the southern portion of this ride. But if you look at the northern end of the lot, you'll see a dirt path receding into the forest. This is the entrance to the Old Croton Aqueduct trail.

Ride carefully onto the aqueduct trail, watching for the occasional bits of broken glass that, for sociological reasons that escape me, seem to decorate every East Coast parking lot. In a few hundred yards, you'll lose the pavement and encounter a tall, cylindrical, chimneylike structure. This is the first of a series of ventilators you will see for the old aqueduct, and are also convenient mileage markers. This one has a black numeral "21" painted high up on its sides, meaning that from this point on the aqueduct it is 21 miles north to the New Croton Reservoir.

Until the time of the Croton project there were only nine public water supply systems in the United States, most of them little more than large, centrally located cisterns. In the 1840s, a 40-mile aqueduct was an engineering feat of almost unprecedented size and complexity, exceeded only by two famous great aqueducts of ancient Rome nearly 2000 years earlier.

When the Croton Aqueduct was completed in 1842, its 3-foot conduits supplied about 80 million gallons of fresh water each day under the path you are riding, south to an Egyptian-style Murray Hill reservoir in Manhattan on the site where the main building of the New York Public Library is today (42nd Street and Fifth Avenue). The aqueduct was engineered by John B. Jervis (for whom Port Jervis, New York is named). Jervis' professional reputation reached its zenith with the official opening of the aqueduct on October 14, 1842: that day all the church bells in New York City rang from dawn until dusk. (For comparison, today the city pumps 1.5 billion gallons a day from a dozen reservoirs in the Croton system plus half a dozen more reservoirs in the Catskill system west of the Hudson.)

As you ride up the trail, enjoy your peeps of the Hudson River to your left through the trees. You're riding on what seems like a ledge or terrace on the hillside; to your left, you look down on the roofs and backyards of the houses, while to the right you look up at foundations. Actually, on this northward course you're riding up a very gentle hill, but you wouldn't know it: the net gain in grade is only 13.25 inches per mile—enough for the flow of the water to be assisted by gravity.

The trail is quiet except for the twittering of birds and squirrels; the noise of cars is satisfyingly remote. The riding is easiest in the spring and fall; in the humid summer, the lush underbrush reaches out over the trail to snag your legs. But as compensation, even on the hottest summer day, this shady trail is cool and breezy.

About half a mile north of the first chimney ventilator, you'll ride through someone's junk-filled backyard. Relax, it gets nicer further north, I promise. You'll emerge from the junk heap onto the intersection of three quiet streets; continue straight on Philipse Place (where the aqueduct itself parallels your course under the level sidewalk to your right) and then ride up the hill onto the unmarked Shonnard Terrace. Turn left to rejoin the trail where the level section marking the aqueduct crosses the road and emerges to your left.

From here on north, the riding is easier and prettier. Just after passing ventilator 20 (20 miles to the Croton Dam), note the miniature gorge to your right. You may even hear the plashing of a small waterfall. This little stretch is one of the few where you become keenly aware that you're riding on an artificial structure.

A quarter mile later, you'll pass a stone building that looks like a multistory pumping station. Inside are all kinds of black-painted gears, but resist the temptation to climb around on it or to let kids do so: you never know when something might move and crush a leg.

A bit north of the pumping station is my absolutely favorite secret place on the aqueduct: the ruins of some magnificent old stone estate on the rise to the right. The overgrown entrance is flanked by two stone lions, mouths stretched wide in eternal silent roars. If you climb up the tumbled stone-block stairs, you can stand in the remains of the foundation and walls of a house that seems puzzlingly small for the stately entrance. Trails wind off to the left along the stone walls. Many mysteries cling to this spot: what was it? why is it in such disrepair? was the aqueduct approach once its main entrance? Someday, I want to know.

After passing ventilator 19, the aqueduct trail is now wide and flat enough to be a full-fledged road. Half a mile later, note the abandoned stone stairway that once gave access to the roads paralleling the aqueduct above and below. After passing by another small gorge with a creek, you'll emerge onto Pinecrest Road. Ride straight across a small parking lot and between two wooden logs to the right to resume your travel on the aqueduct trail. You'll know you've done it right when you pass ventilator 18.

In half a mile you'll emerge in another parking lot at William Street. Continue straight on the unmarked Aqueduct Lane, cross Washington Avenue, and resume the aqueduct trail. Look down into the yards at your left, for soon you'll pass a tiny family graveyard with half a dozen large stones.

Abruptly, and without warning, the aqueduct trail will lead you out of the woods. The trail bends right at the traffic light at the intersection of Route 9 (Broadway) and Farragut Parkway. Watching for traffic, turn left onto Route 9 and follow it for about a mile.

At the "Y" intersection, take the left branch onto Livingston Avenue, coasting down to Main Street. You are now riding through the village of Dobbs Ferry, a small, quaint town with plenty of delicatessens, pizza parlors, and markets— a few conveniently open seven days a week. As this is the last convenient spot to pick up lunch for a picnic and to top off your water bottle, take advantage of this bit of civilization.

Continue north up Main Street to the "T" intersection with Cedar Street. But instead of turning, head straight ahead toward the little plaza with stone benches, and lift your bike over the curb onto the sidewalk. Now, if you're hungry, you could enjoy lunch here at one of the stone tables, perhaps trying your hand at a game of checkers on the inlaid checkerboard. Or, if you prefer to dine in grassy comfort, hoist your bike down the sandy path at your right to rejoin the aqueduct trail, which crosses over a creek.

In less than half a mile, cross the entrance road onto the manicured grounds of Mercy College. Here the aqueduct trail becomes a narrow, deeply grooved dirt track that heads behind the main building and straight across the campus. Follow its unambiguous lead, eventually passing ventilator 17. After crossing Ardsley Avenue (the Hagstrom map writes it "Arsley"), go straight for 50 yards along the private road of Columbia University Press to resume the aqueduct trail.

Now you're passing the backs of gracious mansions in Irvington, named after the 19th-century American author Washington Irving, famous for his stories "Rip Van Winkle" and "The Legend of Sleepy Hollow." Another famous Irvington resident was Louis Comfort Tiffany, creator of Tiffany glass, who apparently got his artistic inspiration as a boy in the 1860s by sitting on the bank of the Hudson River sketching the swirling patterns of leaves and flower petals.

After crossing another gravel road slow down, for here spectacular specimens of certain trees are labeled. Note especially the towering greenish purple copper beech that dates back to 1853.

As you continue riding, you'll pass on your left one of the few octagonal houses left in the United States: the pink-and-white Octagon House with its octagonal gazebo, built in 1860 for banker Paul Armour. Now on the National Register of Historic Places, in the late 1980s the house, its cupola, wraparound porch, gazebo, and grounds, were lovingly restored by its current owner.

Continue riding, past Memorial Park with its softball diamond, bike rack, picnic table, wading pool, playground equipment, and three lighted tennis courts. Then the aqueduct passes high over Station Road, perhaps the clearest example on this ride that you are riding on a manmade structure, and an impressive one at that. Although you're still riding on a dirt trail wide enough for vegetation on both sides, well below you a two-lane highway carries traffic.

In a quarter mile, the trail emerges into a parking lot and seems to abandon you. Have no fear. Continue straight through the lot, cross the busy Main Street into the school parking lot straight ahead (ignore the DO NOT ENTER signs), ride to the back, and continue on the dirt track of the aqueduct trail.

One of the several paved roads you'll cross is Sunnyside Lane, distinguished by a double yellow line. If you follow this road to the left, you'll end up at the home of the early 19th-century writer Washington Irving. Stroll down the winding path to Sunnyside, the small Dutch farmhouse Irving bought in 1835 and transformed into the one-of-a-kind cottage he called his "snuggery." Ladies in hoopskirts will greet you at the door of the cottage while the cook prepares Irving's favorite dishes on the iron stove. Now the house is filled with his furnishings and memorabilia. There is also a gift shop, picnic grounds, and free parking.

When you've explored your fill, retrace your path back up Sunnyside Lane and turn left to continue riding on the aqueduct trail. You will cycle past a creek and past a stone wall with some abandoned greenhouses. Shortly after passing ventilator 15, you'll enter the wide grassy lawns of Lyndhurst, the Gothic Revival estate of 19th-century "robber baron" railroad magnate Jay Gould. This is the end of this ride's travels on the dirt aqueduct trail (unless you've chosen to return by the same route).

At Lyndhurst, you can take a tour through Gould's stone mansion (which is open Tuesday through Sunday 10 A.M. to 5 P.M., with guided tours May through October; for information call 914-631-0046). Explore the ruins of the greenhouses, where there are also public restrooms. You can also poke around the flea market that is set up in the parking lot there many summer weekends. And you can lie on the grass and bask in the sun and enjoy a picnic lunch; the inspired might bring a Frisbee or ball for playing catch.

When you're refreshed, continue north briefly on the aqueduct trail, which remains a faint dirt track traversing the vast greens. The trail will soon dump you back out onto Route 9 (Broadway).

Here you have a choice. If you wish to return south to New York City, turn right onto Highway 9 and skip down to the double asterisks (**) for further directions, making for a total round trip of about 21 miles.

If instead you'd like to continue your historical tour for a total length of 26 miles, turn left onto Route 9 to head for Tarrytown and the Philipsburg Manor, Upper Mills. Watch traffic carefully: you are now approaching the on-ramps to the Tappan Zee Bridge across the Hudson River and the New York State Thruway (Interstate 87), and on summer weekends the traffic can be quite heavy. Ride on the wide sidewalk to the left (against traffic), if that makes you feel more secure. You'll pass a diner on your right. North of the Tappan Zee Bridge traffic will abate somewhat and you can continue on the road itself straight into downtown Tarrytown.

Philipsburg Manor's Upper Mills will come up rather suddenly on your left. With its gristmill, stone manor house, and New World Dutch barn, it was the northern headquarters of the mighty Dutch-American trading center of Frederick Philipse in the 17th and 18th centuries. Now reduced from its original 52,500 acres to a mere 20, the main buildings have been restored to their appearance at their most prosperous time (1720-1750). Kept up as a working farm with the techniques of the time, there are tours through the various buildings conducted by guides in period costumes. (For admission information, call 914-631-8200.) I particularly like the waterwheel-driven gristmill with its heavy grindstone, still milling corn and wheat into flour as in the olden days.

You can buy this wonderful flour in the Philipsburg Manor gift shop for a couple of dollars per two-pound bag—and you definitely should. It is the best whole-grain flour I have ever found anywhere, utterly free of the bitterness that seems to plague many commercial whole-grain flours. The whole-wheat flour is wonderfully sweet and light, and can be substituted for half the all-purpose flour in most recipes. The corn flour is has a finer texture and sweeter taste than commercial cornmeal. Just make sure that, once home, you pour it into airtight containers and store it in the refrigerator, to prevent the natural oils in the germ from going rancid. And don't sift it, or you'll sift out the bran. The gift shop also has restrooms and the usual assortment of trinkets, plus giveaways such as recipes for 18th-century baked goods.

When you leave Philipsburg Manor, turn right out of the parking lot to head south on South Broadway (Route 9) back toward New York City. You'll stay on Highway 9 for nearly five miles, passing the main entrances to Lyndhurst (**), the Belvedere Estate, Sunnyside, and the beautiful stone building of St. Barnabas Church. Where Route 9 intersects Main Street heading right into Irvington, you might want to duck into the Irvington Presbyterian Church: its pale blue-and-green stained-glass windows were donated by Tiffany in 1912. Further down Main Street, peek into the library at the small amber stained-glass Tiffany lamps hanging from the bookshelves.

On this ride down Route 9, you'll also pass the front entrances of Columbia University Press and Mercy College. Look up: this stretch of Route 9 is flanked by truly majestic maples, some with trunks a full three feet in diameter.

About three miles south of Philipsburg Manor, turn right at the "T" intersection to continue on Route 9, making a short, steep climb followed by a long descent. Bypass Dobbs Ferry and continue south on Route 9 more than a mile more until you reach a "Y" intersection. Bear right onto Warburton Avenue to ride closer to the Hudson River.

You'll ride through the village of Hastings-on-Hudson with its many shops, including the unprepossessing Hastings Prime Meats. Started as a butcher shop in the early 1950s, the place has grown into a full-fledged gourmet grocery store with the reputation of being the Zabar's of Westchester County. And like that famous mecca in New York City's upper west side (see "Manhattan's Other Island"), Hastings' narrow aisles are crowded elbow-to-elbow with locals who come to gossip among the double Devon creams and crimini mushrooms.

Back on the road again, look to your right: you'll begin to catch glimpses of the Hudson River with the cliffs of the New Jersey palisades on the opposite shore. Stop for a moment at the small shady park with benches on your right, to gaze up at the statues of Robert Fulton and Henry Hudson, anachronistically robed in Greek togas, shading their eyes as they gaze across the river. What with the East Coast climate and standards of modesty in the past centuries, I can't imagine either Hudson or Fulton appearing in public wrapped in large bath towels, but probably the sculptors of 1924 intended their subjects' dress (or undress) to symbolize their scholastic foresight.

As you continue south on Warburton Avenue, note the popularity of elegant five-globed lamps in people's yards—undoubtedly a holdover of a more gracious era. Eventually you'll pass the Hudson River Museum, a quite nice, small science museum complete with a planetarium for projecting the wonders of the night sky missed by city-dwellers, such as, say, the stars and the moon. (Yup, the moon. Here's a quiz, city-dweller: what is the phase of the moon right now? Full? Crescent? Nine out of ten New Yorkers can't answer the question correctly, because a) the high buildings obstruct the view, b) the city lights scatter so much light into the sky that even a full moon pales, and/or c) who trusts other New Yorkers enough to go outside at night and stare up at the sky? End of personal tirade about urban disconnectedness with the universe.)

As you continue to approach New York City, the streets get more urban and congested, so watch for the automobile traffic. Near the Yonkers Metro-North train station, Warburton Avenue changes name to Riverdale Avenue. Now begin watching carefully, for in about a mile you'll turn left at a light onto Valentine Lane.

Ride to the end, then turn right at the "T" intersection onto South Broadway. Now you're back on Route 9. In about a quarter mile, you'll recognize the trees of the northern edge of Van Cortlandt Park to your left. Eventually you'll pass the Chinese takeout restaurant and Lloyd's Carrot Cake (seconds, or dinner anyone?). And ahead of you is the superstructure of the IRT subway line. Climb the stairs and relax on the #1 local back into the city.

For some fascinating details on the construction of the Old Croton aqueduct system, read the preface to *The Reminiscences of John B. Jervis: Engineer of the Old Croton*, edited by Neal FitzSimons, Syracuse University Press, 1971.

OF APPLES AND ANIMALS

Sussex County, New Jersey & Orange County, New York

Ride Ratings

Length: 17, 32 or 37 miles
Configuration: figure 8
Difficulty: rolling hills, little traffic
Surface: good pavement throughout

—Highlights: This ride may be combined with "A Pre-Breakfast Warm-Up" to total 46 miles, or with "From New Jersey to Florida" for more than 70 miles; it features pick-your-own strawberries (June) or apples (September), exotic animals, and the longer rides explore an artist' retreat.

The inspiration for this ride was what I first took for a hallucination. One June afternoon I was scouting out suitable roads on my bike—which is the hard way, I found, but my old car had a cantankerous fuel pump—and rounded a corner onto a narrow, quiet lane. The hills were dotted with horses and sheep. Oh, how nice and pastoral for the bike book, I thought. As I passed one of the typical farmhouses in this area, I looked to my left and saw two elephants quietly munching on a bale of hay.

Yes, elephants. In an open field. In upstate New York. Not in a zoo.

I stopped my bike dead in the middle of the quiet country lane, and literally shook my head, disbelieving my eyes. Sure enough, two large Dumbos, unsurprised by my presence, were standing behind an electrified fence enjoying their midafternoon snack. I snapped a photo, regretting that all I'd brought was one of those disposable cameras, and that the exposure was the last on the roll. When my astonishment wore off, I started to remount my bike and glanced to my right. A couple of horses and a zebra were watching the proceedings.

Yes, a regulation black-and-white-striped zebra. No, this was not Hearst Castle at San Simeon, California. As I stood there, I swore I heard the chattering and screaming of monkeys from a nearby barn. What could this be? The farmhouse yielded no clue—there was no

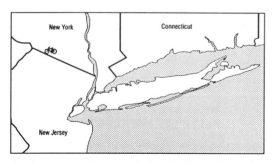

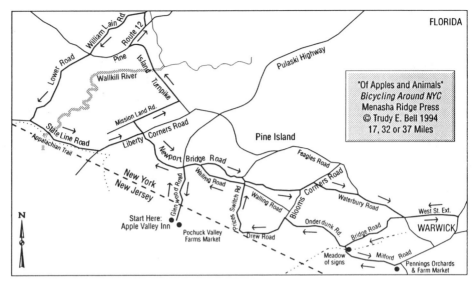

name, no sign, nothing. The only indication I wasn't totally out of my tree was a van in the driveway whose side bore the name DAWN ANIMAL AGENCY, with a West 46th Street address in New York City. At least if I were hallucinating, I thought, someone else was having the same hallucination.

A year later, on a hot day in late July, I passed by the farm again. This time the van and, regrettably, the elephants were gone. The zebra was still there, at home in a little stable near the fence, although try as I might I could not persuade the creature to show me anything but its rear end. This time a curious llama watched me making a fool of myself in my antics with the camera-shy zebra. I think there was also a peacock.

There is obviously a revolving show—and something of a mystery here. I did not go up and knock on the door to ask the occupants about their remarkable hobby. I prefer all the question marks popping in my mind. You may feel differently. In any event you're in for a treat.

This ride is one of a threesome in this area, all centered on the bed-and-breakfast Apple Valley Inn in Glenwood, New Jersey and ideal for a weekend getaway. You can make this excursion as short as 17 miles by doing either half of the figure 8 (the eastern half of the figure 8 features the apples; the western half features the exotic animals). Adding the detours to the town of Warwick and to Pennings Orchards will give you the maximum distance. You can make it 46 miles long by tacking the 9 hilly miles of the "Pre-Breakfast Warm-Up" ride onto its beginning. And gonzo cyclists can top 70 miles in a day by integrating it with the "From New Jersey to Florida" ride. Something for everyone.

Driving directions to this area are in "From New Jersey to Florida," along with the particulars for the enticing inn. This "Of Apples and Animals" route, by the way, has few services—virtually none if you don't take the detours into Warwick or to Pennings Farm. So you might choose to enjoy one treat offered by the inn's proprietress Mitzi Durham: a picnic lunch she'll pack for you (at a modest charge) with 24 hours' notice.

The ride begins by turning left out of the Apple Valley Inn onto Sussex

County Route 517 North (Glenwood Road). However, if you want to pick up a snack for the trip, first turn right and take Route 517 only a few hundred feet south to the Pochuck Valley Farms market, which will be the first complex of buildings on your left. Here you can stock up on home-baked bagels and vine-ripened tomatoes pregnant with juice. By the way, Pochuck Farms is one of the places in this area where you can pick strawberries, apples, or other goodies in season. When you're ready, retrace your route to head north on Route 517, this time passing the inn on your left.

Less than half a mile north of the inn, you'll pass under some of the tallest, most majestic willows I've ever seen bending their tresses to earth. Shortly thereafter, you'll cross over the border into New York State, where the Glenwood Road changes to Orange County Route 26. Stay on it for another mile and a quarter.

Turn right at the first intersection onto Newport Bridge Road. After an initial descent into farmland and across the placid Pochuck Creek with its ducks, stands of trees, and a waterfall under the bridge, the road begins a steady climb. In about a mile and a half, bear right at the "Y" intersection with Prices Switch Road to stay on Newport Bridge Road. The few gracious buildings around you are the hamlet of Amity.

Don't miss the overgrown cemetery ahead 50 yards and to your left, marked by a tall monument towering out of the weeds. And enjoy your gaze at the neatly kept Amity Presbyterian Church to your right, established in 1796, which still holds services and commands a view of a farm valley and distant hills.

Just after the church, where Prices Switch Road heads right at the green house with a remarkable assortment of junk in its front yard, continue straight to stay on Newport Bridge Road. Now you're coasting generally downhill.

After a bit more than a mile, turn left at the stop sign onto Blooms Corners Road. As you climb, look to your right for bushes of wild raspberries and blackberries—sweet and ripe in July. In less than half a mile, take the first right onto Waterbury Road, continuing the climb up to a plateau dotted with large houses. Then, enjoy the winding descent past homes nestled among the trees.

A mile later, you'll stop short at a "T" intersection with two roads heading off to the right. Pass the first (DeKay Road) and turn right onto the second, watching for cars on this rather busy Orange County Route 1A. After an initial climb, you'll coast down to a farm stand at the base of the hill where you'll be pedaling through open cornfields. On the shortest route, that farm stand may be your only source of sustenance.

Stop at the light that marks the crossroads with West Street Extension. You cannot miss this intersection: it is across from a barn with five (5) huge silos! There's also an open field growing squash, although with crop rotation I'm sure that's subject to change. Now you have a decision: if you'd like to continue with rural riding, turn right onto West Street Extension and continue the description at the double asterisks (**).

If you'd like to explore the town of Warwick, turn left onto West Street Extension—this detour will add approximately two miles to your ride. In a few minutes the houses will become more suburban as you approach the original West Street; you'll soon reach the intersection with Oakland Avenue (New York

State Route 94), the main road through town. Turn right (south), cross the railroad tracks, and in one block is Jackie's Deli, open seven days a week from 7 A.M. to 11 P.M.—just what a cyclist needs to know.

The tracks are disappointing to those interested in public transportation: no passenger train comes through this town anymore, and these days the railroad station is the offices of the local newspaper, the *Advertiser* (no pretended separation of church and state there!). If you'd driven here instead, you could park your car in the municipal parking lot at McEwen and Spring Streets just north of West Street. When I was there, Warwick also had a bare-bones bicycle repair shop—emphasis on repair, not on bikes, for the makeshift shop had no stock—open Tuesday through Friday 10 A.M.-5 P.M. and Saturday 10 A.M.-1 P.M., but I'd call first to make an appointment: (914) 986-7233.

When you've toured the sights to your satisfaction, return the way you came, west on West Street (gee, I wonder why it was given that name?). In scarcely more than a mile, you'll be passing farms once again. At the familiar five silos, cross Orange County Route 1A.

(**) Continue west on West Street Extension, passing a cluster of three schools: elementary, middle, and high. All were obviously built in the early 1960s when, I swear, every school in the country followed the same architectural scheme of one-story open breezeways and blue-and-brick color plan. Did they get a group discount on plans and paint?

Turn left at the "T" intersection onto Sanfordville Road, coasting down past farms and nouveau farms; where the main road bends right, its name changes to Covered Bridge Road, but don't get your hopes up at seeing a covered bridge. It has long disappeared into the mists of time. Still, this road is very pretty, with its farmhouses and split-rail fences. And there's a surprise waiting at the bottom, so don't go screaming down too fast.

Where the railroad tracks parallel the road slow down, turn left to stay on Covered Bridge Road, and dismount immediately. What to the casual glance looks like a fallen-down shed built above the Wawayanda Creek is upon closer examination actually the two-peaked roof of a museum in excellent condition, thank you: a strange but affecting haven for local artists and musicians called Pacem in Terris, Latin for Peace on Earth.

A small calligraphy sign explains that Pacem in Terris is "an oasis of quiet, a sign of hope and trust in what is human in human beings in a mechanized world. It is above all an integrated work of art in which nature, design, sculptures, mosaics are one man's artistic credo." It also features occasional concerts, advertised by fliers in local establishments. Open Saturdays and Sundays between 11 A.M. and 6 P.M. from May to October, there is no admission charge.

Although it is avowed not to be a church or connected with any religion or cult, a quiet spirit imbuing the place urges tiptoing and whispers. In the tiny plaza, stepping stones are embedded with symbols for the sun, earth, and moon as well as faces, spirals, fish, and a star of David. I was trespassing on a weekday, so I didn't get to step inside.

As I headed back up Covered Bridge Road the way I came—which I urge you to do while walking your bike—I spied a trace of a footpath heading off into the brush to the right. A black post riddled with railroad stakes, an undeniable reminder of the crucifixion, held a little piece of wood carved to read MEADOW OF SIGNS.

I wheeled my bike under the tangle of leaves and branches, and indeed, the path did open up into a meadow, but not before taking me past silent steel sculptures of a human face burned out with a blow torch. The sculptures evoked the silhouettes of Hiroshima burned in a concrete wall. Why steel? "Straightforward and unadorned, in steel for neither wood nor stone are the stuff of our age, and it is steel that threatens our survival," a legend explains. A larger version of that sculpture is at Nanzan University in Nagoya, Japan, with replicas in Cathedral of Saint John the Divine in New York City, Pennsylvania State University, and Church of the Savior in Washington, D.C. The meadow also has other truly wonderful outdoor sculptures, plus a large wood-frame house that is apparently an artists' workshop. As I rolled my bike out back onto the road, I marveled at what the chance exploration of the trace of a footpath can reveal.

At Pacem in Terris, you have the decision of another detour. If you want to continue rural riding, recross the railroad tracks and turn left at the "T" intersection to start climbing Onderdunk Road, and skip down to the quadruple asterisks (****).

If you'd like to visit a pick-your-own orchard (and add about three miles to the ride), cross the bridge over Wawayanda Creek and hang an immediate left onto the unmarked Fancher Road. At the end, turn left onto the busy New York State Route 94 and ride for a rolling mile and a quarter, past a Christmas tree farm and the Warwick Conference Center.

Turn right into the gravel drive of Pennings Orchards and Farm Market. Attached to the farm market is a little custard stand, and I knew immediately what I wanted for lunch when I saw a sign offering a cantaloupe sundae. Vanilla and raspberry yogurt topped with chunks of fresh melon, raspberries, strawberries, blueberries, and granola, it was a delightful change from those fake-tasting syrups. Cradling the cold confection, I wandered through the farm market, admiring the veggies, spices, and homemade jams (think about birthdays and Christmas!), ending up with freshly-picked white corn for dinner.

Pennings is a 150-acre farm that grows 15 varieties of yellow and yes! white peaches, available from July 1 to September 20. The farm also grows more than a dozen varieties of apples ranging from the traditional red and golden delicious to the tartly sweet Cortlandt and Northern Spy. You can pick your own from August 15 to October 1. Moreover, every September and October you can press your own hand-selected applies into cider. (*Hint:* You absolutely must treat yourself to Northern Spy; the apple does not keep or travel well, so you never find it in New York City, but its strong perfume makes locally-pressed cider exotic.)

To resume the ride, turn left out of Pennings onto Route 94, taking the first paved right onto Fancher Road. At the end, turn right at the "T" intersection over the creek, past Pacem in Terris, and over the railroad tracks. Turn left at the "T" intersection onto Onderdunk Road.

(****) You'll be climbing once again, past greenhouses with enormous fans, past Bell Acres (no relation, I wish!), past a model windmill, over a crest with a lovely wooded view, and down to a "T" intersection. Turn left onto Blooms

Corners Road and continue your descent, taking the first right at the green-and-white farmhouses onto Drew Road. (If you want to head to Florida, turn right onto Blooms Corners Road instead and pick up the directions in "From New Jersey to Florida.") You'll continue a steep descent on a country lane with vegetable gardens on both sides, past a few houses, and some cattails. Unfortunately, there is a bottom and then a steep ascent, but hang in there, it's short.

Where Drew Road joins Prices Switch Road, go straight, following the sign toward Pine Island. Watch out for patches of sand and gravel. As you head down again, you'll see farm fields on both sides and a lovely prospect of the far hills to your left.

After a bit longer than a mile, make the first left onto Walling Road. After a brief climb, you'll get the downhill payoff. In a mile, turn left at the yield sign onto Newport Bridge Road, in time to cross what is presumably the Newport Bridge over the talkative, burbling Pochuck Bridge. Notice the ruined pillars of an old bridge to your right.

Now you're in cattle country. It was here that I was startled into stopping and staring at seven cows, all of which were identically black with a white band encircling their middle. I couldn't believe seeing seven cows with the same markings, so whipped out my camera, feeling as if I were taking a photo for the "Far Side" cartoonist Gary Larson. A few minutes later I passed a sign noting that they were Belted Galloways and fine beef cattle.

At the intersection with Glenwood Road (Orange County Route 26), you will have completed the first loop of the figure 8-17 miles if you did not go to either Warwick or Pennings Orchards and 22 miles if you visited both. The Apple Valley Inn is a mile and a half to your left.

If you're up for continuing the second half of the figure 8, cross Glenwood Road to continue on Newport Bridge Road. Now you're circumnavigating a valley of coalblack dirt with wispy green stocks of onions stretching as far as the eye can see. According to Mitzi, this area is the onion capital of the world, where the yellow onions packaged into red net bags or sold loose at A&P and other grocery chains are grown. On your right you'll pass a house with solar panels on its roof, and a little shrine of Saint Francis.

At the intersection with Liberty Corners Road (Orange County Route 88), turn right, then make an immediate left onto Rudinski Road, past a farm with black-and-white cows lazing in the field and alongside another flat valley. Here the road may be covered with clods left by harrows and other farm machinery. Turn right at the end onto unmarked Mission Land Road. The onion fields spread dead flat all around you, their black rows receding to the vanishing point; purple thistles are at the roadside next to corn fields at your right. Pedal slowly through the onion-scented air for the next mile or so.

The interlude ends at the busy Pine Island Turnpike (Orange County Route 1). Watch for trucks and other traffic as you turn left. After about a mile, you'll cross over the Wallkill River. In another mile, make the first right onto unmarked Orange County Route 12, where the Pine Island Turnpike bends left. Watch for gravel. Admire the archway to a stone-walled vegetable garden. Half a mile along Route 12, make the first left onto Orange County Route 62, watching for gravel on the roadside here as well.

In another half mile, again hang the first left onto unmarked William Lain

Road. Here is where you want to ride slowly, keeping your eyes and ears alert for whatever exotic animals may be around. Note the stone lion in the drive and the black wrought-iron doorway on the right. And after the farmhouse, out in the field on the right where I saw the zebra, there is a compelling life-size statue of a running pure-white horse, mane and tail flying in the wind.

This quiet country lane begins climbing, so pause often to enjoy the vistas of the corn planted on the hill to your right, or the horses in the valley over your left shoulder—and in June, the fragrance of the wild rose. Cross busy Pine Island Turnpike (Route 1) to continue on Lower Road. The lane winds and rolls, and the soil is now not coal black but brown and stony; surely there is some fascinating geological tale here in the very earth. You'll ride past the small, well-kept Loree Cemetery on the left with its many markers dating from the 19th century. And then you may see a small green valley on your right with black-and-white cattle lying beneath spreading maples in the heat of mid-day.

Turn left at the yield sign onto State Line Road, which is indeed parallel to the New Jersey border and scarcely a quarter mile north. After a brief climb, you're in for a wonderful rollercoaster descent through sod farms down to the Wallkill River. Somewhere along here the road changes name to Oil City Road; the brief stretch on either side of the river is also an official part of the Appalachian Trail, and I saw a lone and lean young man walking under a huge backpack that was much more worn and beat-up than my panniers.

Turn left at the "T" intersection onto unmarked Liberty Corners Road (Orange County Route 88), past the farm selling fresh eggs. A mile later, turn right onto the first paved road into the cool woods; you're now retracing your path out on Newport Bridge Road alongside the onion fields. A mile and a half later, turn right onto unmarked Glenwood Road (Orange County Route 26), which becomes Sussex County Route 517 as you cross the border back into New Jersey. A mile south of the border, turn right into the Apple Valley Inn.

FROM NEW JERSEY TO FLORIDA

Sussex County, New Jersey & Orange County, New York

Head north from New Jersey to Florida? Yup, that's exactly what you do here—to Florida, New York, that is.

This ride is one of three at the New Jersey/New York border, all with the focus of the Apple Valley Inn in Glenwood, New Jersey, (the other two rides are "A Pre-Breakfast Warm-Up" and "Of Apples and Animals"). One reason for the trio is that the area and the B&B are so perfect for cycling, they will seduce you into staying longer than a one-day blitz trip. In addition, this area is not readily accessible to public transportation from New York City, so if you've taken the trouble to get a car and drive here, you deserve to relax and enjoy a full weekend of rides!

This ride features a choice of where to spend the night. For those wanting to "rough it" in the great outdoors, there is the Black Bear Campground, which is complete with swimming pool and camp store and is rather posh as campgrounds go. For those wanting to pamper themselves, there is, of course, the rambling Apple Valley Inn, which also has a swimming pool. In either case, treat yourself to a stay both Friday and Saturday night to give yourself a chance to unwind and to start your ride as early as the dawn and the fragrance of coffee inspire you.

The directions for driving to Apple Valley Inn from New York City sound involved, but following them is straightforward; the trip will take about an hour and a half in average traffic. Exit the Lincoln Tunnel and follow the signs for Route 3

Ride Ratings

Length: 24 or 34 miles
Configuration: loop
Difficulty: shorter ride is flat; longer ride adds 10 hilly miles; trafic moderate to nonexistent
Surface: fair to good pavement throughout

—Highlights: This ride can be combined with "A Pre-Breakfast Warm-Up" for a total of 43 miles, and with "Of Apples and Animals" for more than 70 miles; it features secluded woods, a wonderful toy store, onion fields, a craftbarn, wild raspberries and blackberries; the Appalachian Trail ; the longer ride visits Sugar Loaf, the famed artists' colony.

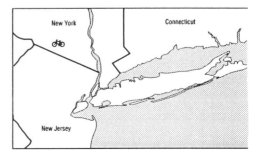

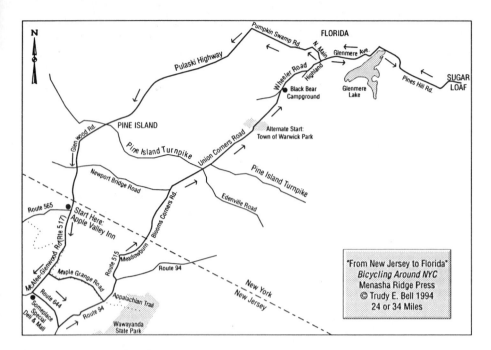

West. Take Route 3 all the way to Route 46 West (only a mile after you pass the Garden State Parkway). After 4 miles, turn right onto Route 23 North. After 21.5 miles, take the Vernon Highlands Lakes exit onto Route 515 North. Drive 9 miles more into the town of Vernon (you'll know you're there because it's at the base of a steep hill). One block after the first stoplight turn left onto Route 644. 1.5 miles later, at the "T" intersection, turn right onto Route 517 North. In 2.8 miles, on your left, will be the Apple Valley Inn, just past Pochuck Valley Farms store.

If you've come up for just the day with no intention of staying over, you can start and end the ride at the Warwick Town Park on Orange County Route 41 (also called Union Corners Road), about three miles south of Florida (see the map). In this case, take the New York State Thruway (Interstate 87) to Exit 16. Take Routes 6/17 west to Exit 126. Take Routes 94/17A south into downtown Florida. Turn left at the light onto North Main Street and then turn right at the next light onto Highland Avenue (Route 41), which becomes Wheeler Road and then Union Corners Road. Turn left into the Warwick Town Park. The park is open daily from 9 a.m. to sunset, and has a parking lot, restrooms, and running water. If you start here, follow the directions beginning at the double asterisks (**) three pages down.

The first half of the ride (beginning from the Apple Valley Inn) is rolling to moderately hilly, but remarkably enough, even with the climbs you still seem to be coasting more than grinding. The second half of the ride flattens out through the cultivated black earth of the onion fields. Alan Wolf, my occasional cycling companion from Morristown, New Jersey, must be credited for scouting out the first half of this very lovely ride for this book, and for discovering the fantastic toy store.

The longer 34-mile option adds 10 miles of pretty but heart-pounding hills as you continue northeast from Florida over the ridge and down into the village of Sugar Loaf, a community of craftsmen founded in 1749. It's still a place where leatherworkers, woodcarvers, potters, and others create and offer their wares. Although it's been somewhat yuppified by rich New Yorkers, it's still less cutesy than Woodstock, New York, or Chester, New Jersey. Even if you don't feel like so much exertion, don't despair of being deprived of local handicrafts; the basic 24-mile ride also passes the fascinating and surprisingly reasonable Craft Barn.

To begin the ride from Apple Valley Inn, turn right out of the inn's driveway onto Sussex County Route 517 South. A few hundred yards south is the Pochuck Valley Farms market, open early enough even for the dawn-rising cyclist, with fragrant fresh-brewed coffee and prices about half those in the city. Even if you're a Pritikin freak or a cholesterol-watcher, sin just a little for one of Pochuck's still-warm, morning-baked, old-fashioned doughnuts, a 25-cent nutmeg-flavored treasure that is not at all greasy or heavy. Plain or dusted with cinnamon, your choice. And don't pass up a chance to pocket a few of the fuzzy peaches from their own trees—and to note which freshly-picked veggies you may want to buy to take home with you at the end of your stay!

Thus laden, continue south along the narrow shoulder, watching for the cars that will occasionally whiz by even at 6 A.M. In less than half a mile, you'll pass the Glenwood Post Office in a trailer, and then the silent gravestones of the Glenwood Cemetery on your left. Keep looking to your left, for in another quarter mile you'll pass a remarkable rock formation—a startling miniature cliff—behind some houses. What a great place for adventurous children to play! On humid summer mornings, just past Carol Drive, you may see mists rising over the grasses to your left. And three-quarters of a mile later on your right are some cooling trees and inviting rafts on Vernon Valley Lake—but alas! the park is open to members only.

Two miles from the inn, at the first major intersection, turn left onto Maple Grange Road. (When I was here there was a sign proclaiming that the road was closed to through traffic. But it lied; the perfectly fine road went right on through to Route 94. One thing I've discovered is that disgusted residents sometimes post such signs to discourage nonlocal traffic. Alternatively, sometimes a road may indeed be closed to cars but perfectly accessible to cyclists. Give it a try; the worst you can do is turn around. Or, if you're in a no-risk mood, go on another three-quarters mile south, turn left onto Route 644 past the gourmet deli, Someplace Special, and then left onto Routes 515/94 North to resume this ride.)

Maple Grange Road—and its counterpart heading off to the right, Lounsberry Road—is part of the legendary Appalachian Trail, so keep your eyes alert for backpackers, who abound. It is also a wonderful swooping downhill, passing unpretentious working farms. As you soar down this quiet road, through cornfields and the wafting smell of fertilizing manure enriching the earth, lift your eyes to the spectacular forested ridge directly in front of you. Hope you're warmed up, because that's your next climb. No, just kidding! (A little Dave Barry-style humor here.)

The few buildings around the railroad tracks are the center of Maple Grange. A third of a mile beyond, turn left at the "T" intersection onto joint Routes 515/94 North. Yes, this road is busy, but you have to bear with it only three-quarters of a mile. You'll pass a fruit and vegetable stand, where you can pick up another fresh snack. At the next intersection, which is marked by a huge white house, bear left at the fork to follow Route 515 (Prices Switch Road) as it splits off from Route 94. A sign at the intersection might direct you to Amity and Pine Island.

Ride slowly here, if you brake for toys. Only a hundred yards after the turn, in the woods to your left, is The Toy Chest, a seriously wonderful toy store open Tuesday through Friday 9:30 A.M.-5 P.M. and Saturday from 10 A.M.-5 P.M. (201) 764-7477. Step inside and surprise! enjoy hearing the classical music. This is not one of those tired outlets for video games bought by unimaginative parents to appease their TV-addict offspring (ooh, personal prejudices here). Here you'll find dolls and trains and puzzles and books and giant Legos and blocks and sturdy nursery furniture and all sorts of goodies that will sorely tempt even you to build and throw. The problem, of course, is getting it all bungeed onto the bike.

Ah, well. Back outside again, stick those streamers into your bicycle handlebar grips and pedal away left to continue on Route 515 North. Walk your bike across the railroad tracks that cross the road diagonally, then take your time to enjoy this country lane as you coast gently down over a creek. When I was there in late July, it was lined with the white filigree of Queen Anne's lace, purple thistles, and other wildflowers. In fact, purple was a dominant color for all kinds of flowers: beebalm, cornflower, aster, wild phlox, and even the tall, lovely but cursed loosestrife, which is taking over the wetlands from the cattails.

Just after a large white house on your left whose drive is marked by white brick pillars topped with stone lions, turn right onto Meadowburn Road. Now you'll plunge down and down, under the shade of a magnificent oak whose trunk is at least four to five feet across. Continue coasting down, passing on your left an estate's wooden gate that has within it a smaller wooden gate! You'll cross from New Jersey into New York at the spot where the double yellow line in the road ends and a demure sign informs you that you're entering town of Warwick. A few tenths of a mile later, atop the next rise, an ancient family plot's gravestones are visible behind a stone wall on your right.

Bear right at the next intersection; the barn spiked with so many lightning rods reminded me of Ray Bradbury's rapt and haunting novel *Something Wicked This Way Comes*. Here, where Drew Road heads off to the left, your road changes name to Blooms Corners Road. On the way up the following hill, enjoy the profusion of brilliant vermilion trumpet flowers on the bushes to your left.

Now the terrain becomes rolling—up and down, up and down—eventually settling into a long and steady, but gentle, upgrade. Bear right at the triangle with Newport Road to stay on Blooms Corners Road, still climbing. But in late July, if you keep your eyes alert, the reward for the slow travel is espying the sweet wild raspberries in the brambles on your right. I stuffed my mouth and stained my fingers with their juice, feeling smug to be living off the land. (The ripest berries practically fall off the stems into your hands, offering no resistance to a gentle tug.)

Head straight where Waterbury Road climbs to your right, riding past a modern frame house on your left whose walls are practically all windows. Now you can rest on a well-deserved downhill, past a house with solar panels on its roof, a grass airstrip, grazing horses, and a pond. You'll also pass the Edenville Inn, which is reputed to offer fine dinners but no lodging.

At the first stop sign, cross busy Highway 1. You're now on the Pine Island Turnpike. The buildings ahead are the small town of Edenville, which was settled in the early 1760s, and was named for the idyllic slopes of Mount Adam and Mount Eve. The day I was riding was so hot I stopped at the Country Market for a Gatorade and a bit of shade; the market is open 7 A.M.-5 P.M. Tuesday through Friday, 8 A.M.-5 P.M. on Saturday, and 8 A.M.-2 P.M. on Sunday.

Continue straight through the town, and continue straight onto Union Corners Road (County Route 41) where Pine Island Turnpike veers right. Now the going is relatively flat, and you're in dairy farm country. A mile and half north of Edenville, you can turn right into the Warwick Town Park for a picnic snack, restrooms, and water for your bottles. Here the shade of the tall trees is cool and breezy even on a July scorcher. There are also picnic shelters and barbecue grills.

(**) Warwick Town Park is also the starting place for this ride if you're doing it as a day trip instead of as an overnighter. In that case, you can park your car here; but pick it up by sunset, because the park's gates do indeed close at dusk.

Turn right out of the park to continue north on Route 41 (Union Corners Road), past Saint Joseph's Cemetery and fields with hay rolled in huge cylindrical bales. Again, you're on a long climb—but the climb also gives you plenty of time to look into the bushes and brambles on the right side of the road, this time for wild blackberries! Although in the hot July of the drought year I was there, the blackberries happened to be hard and sour for lack of water, the raspberries were always good. Maybe you'll be lucky with both.

Eventually, after such a long climb, there's the welcome sight of a yellow sign showing a truck on a downgrade. And cyclists, test your brakes—the road (which changes its name to Wheeler Road) is indeed steep for the next mile. Also, don't ride too fast, for the Black Bear Campground is only half a mile ahead on the right. Its air-conditioned camp store is open limited hours: 10 A.M.-1 P.M. on weekdays, 10 A.M.-8 P.M. on Saturday, and 10 A.M.-2 P.M. on Sunday. In addition to tent sites separated from the recreational vehicle sites, there are hot showers, ice machines, firewood, a laundry room, a swimming pool, playing fields, hiking, and fishing. For all these amenities, the campground seemed rather pricey as campgrounds go. For further information, call (914) 651-7717, or write: Black Bear Campground, Wheeler Road, Florida, NY 10921.

Half a mile further down the hill past the campground, look to your left: The Craft Barn is marked with a grouping of stone Buddhas and other figurines in a rock garden. If it's between 10 A.M. and 6 P.M. Tuesday through Sunday, don't pass this by. Park your steed under the apple trees (in July, small green summer apples were lying in the grass).

True to its name, The Craft Barn occupies a barn: a lofty 200-year-old structure of hand-hewn chestnut beams. Step inside; it is as much a museum as a store. Indeed, the proprietors travel the world to seek items not found anywhere in the United States. They are also proud of their reasonable prices—which, indeed, are reasonable. Japanese quilts, one-of-a-kind handmade dresses, painted glass bracelets from India, early American wooden puzzles for children, Rajasthan and Kashmir wool rugs, carved semiprecious stones, Russian painted eggs, Asian musical instruments, and metal wall sculptures will tempt your pocketbook and your bungee cords. I bought some straw coasters and trivets for a gift, and the Japanese-style gift wrapping alone was worth the stop.

There are also occasional free performances of an unusual nature: when I was there, a flyer announced Indonesian gamelan music along with shadow puppets doing a rendition of an Eskimo tale. A perfect break for an hour's rest. For more information about performances and wares, write to The Craft Barn, 30 Wheeler Road, Florida, NY 10921 or call (914) 651-7949.

Leaving The Craft Barn, turn left to continue downhill on Wheeler Road. A third of a mile later, where the road levels and bends left, it becomes Highland Road; continue to follow it into downtown Florida. At the first light, which is North Main Street (Routes 17A and 94), you have a choice. If you want to ride the basic 24-mile route, turn left here and skip down a page to the four asterisks (****).

If you want to add the 10 hilly miles to and from Sugar Loaf, cross North Main Street and continue straight ahead on Glenmere Avenue. (You may want to buy some snacks and fill your water bottle at the Gulf station as you pass, for ahead of you are five miles of hills and no services until you reach Sugar Loaf.) Pedal up the hill, past Saint Joseph's School, through the outlying homes, cresting in half a mile. Now you're coasting downhill. After you pass the Jansen Nursery on your left, you're in the country again. Three quarters of a mile later, the road—now called the Glenmere Avenue Extension—bends left to circle the northern top of Glenmere Lake, along whose shore cluster Queen Anne's lace and loosestrife.

At the "T" intersection, turn right up Pines Hill Road (Hillside Road goes to the left); after a brief stiff climb, you'll be coasting down, past a brick wall, into a little valley filled with the beautiful purple loosestrife. Soon you're climbing again through the woods, cresting, riding through a small community of homes, through the intersection of Black Meadow Road. Once again, begin climbing to a ridge with a wonderful view and a big stone farmhouse. Now you begin descending steeply (yup, you do have to pedal up this one on the way back). At the "T" intersection at the bottom, turn right onto King's Highway (Orange County Route 13). Less than a quarter mile later, you're riding through the artisan's village of Sugar Loaf.

Sugar Loaf is the year-round home for about 50 independent artisans, who live and work in the original barns dating back to the 18th century. Even in colonial times it was known as a craft and provision center for farmers and a horse trading area. Patriotic Sugar Loaf residents fought in the French and Indian War of the 1750s and the American Revolution in the 1770s. The Methodist Church, built in 1810, and the post office, built in 1829, are still community meeting places. During the Civil War the parsonage on Main Street—now the home of Cheshire Glass—was a critical link in the Underground Railroad, helping many runaway slaves on the road to freedom. Sugar Loaf is also the birthplace of Hambletonian (1849-1876), the father of the American trotting horse. Although in the 20th century the discontinuation of a passenger railroad and the mechanization of farming made it harder for local farmers and businesses to survive, the craft revival of the 1960s attracted artists and artisans and now the village prospers.

There's plenty to eat and look at and buy in all the rough-hewn log shoppes: Shaker furniture, stained glass, pottery, pewterware, woodcarvings, leather goods, photographs, drawings, Egyptian ceramic jewelry, Japanese flower arrangements, handblown glass, wooden toys, rag dolls, metal sculptures—there's even a shop specializing in kaleidoscopes. For this trip, you would be well advised to carry empty panniers and to load up on potential Christmas presents. (Of course, you also have to lug those presents back over the ridge . . .) At least take time to enjoy a well-deserved, leisurely lunch in one of the open-air cafes. The entire village is only a quarter mile long, and with the weekend car and pedestrian traffic, you might find it more pleasant to lock your bike at one end and then just stroll down and back.

To return to Florida and rejoin the basic route, retrace the way you came. Head north out of Sugar Loaf on King's Highway, make the first left onto Pines Hill Road for that hefty climb. Three miles later over hill and dale, turn left onto Glenmere Avenue Extension, riding briefly along the northern tip of Glenmere Lake before the road bends right and eventually heads downhill into the center of Florida. At the first stop light, turn right onto North Main Street (Routes 17A and 94) to resume the basic ride.

(****) Florida's North Main Street is surprisingly busy for such a modest town, so you may feel more comfortable walking your bike north on the sidewalk to your left. That will also give you the chance to dip in as you choose into a pharmacy, hardware store, delicatessen, Chinese takeout, or ice cream store. On my sweaty, red-faced, hot ride I stopped in for another Gatorade at Coleman's Deli. When the older proprietor asked conversationally why I wanted a receipt and I replied I was writing this bike book, he joked: "You going to write about Coleman's Deli with the tables and the patio?" "And us, Patty and Terry?" grinned a long-haired young waitress, throwing her arm around the older man's shoulders. "Sure!" I promised, taking a verbal snapshot.

Continue north less than half a mile, turning left at the next light onto Meadow Street (Orange County Route 25). This road is dead flat, but it has no shoulder and there is enough traffic from cars and farm trucks that you should ride with care. Very soon you'll leave the last buildings of Florida, and the road's name changes to Pumpkin Swamp Road. You'll be riding between furrowed coalblack fields with the green foot-high spiked tops of onions. The air is aromatic with the essence of onions, and the cattails and loosestrife vie for the water in the irrigation ditches dropping five feet down to your right.

Ride to the end of the road, an even two miles, and turn left at the "T" intersection onto Orange County Route 6 West (the Pulaski Highway). Here the shoulder is moderately wide, but watch for the gravel and occasional passing trucks. Now the road becomes gently rolling, and will stay that way for the next 5-1/2 miles. Watch for the crops in the surrounding fields; not only are there the familiar onions, but also squash, cucumbers, and grassy sod.

On the sun-beating day I was riding through this open territory, the hot headwind heated my water bottles to the point where I could have brewed tea or taken a bath, and there was precious little shade. Nonetheless, there are enough opportunities to raise a tall cold one at what look like small roadhouses with names like the Triple J Inn. There are also a number of small grocery stores and Granny's Garden Vegetables (where you can buy brown eggs). And even the occasional modest rise in the road brings with it a beautiful prospect of the cultivated valley and the surrounding hills. Take pleasure in the simple gifts.

The first stop sign is the crossroads marking the center of Pine Island, with an Exxon gas station, pizza parlor, and the Jolly Onion restaurant across the street - a place I never had the chance to try, but that is reputed to have good food. At this intersection, head straight ahead (south) onto Orange County Route 26 (Glenwood Road) for another couple of miles. On this rolling road you'll pass the Maplelyn Farms on your left, where racehorses are bred. A quarter mile south you'll cross into New Jersey (where the road becomes Sussex County Route 517), and then ride under some huge, majestic willows. Less than a third of a mile later turn right into the drive of the Apple Valley Inn.

The inn is actually a rambling white clapboard house built in 1831, with the remains of an apple orchard on the hills behind it. A creek gurgles along one edge of the property, over which proprietors John and Mitzi Durham (and their white Sealyham Alabama—Bama for short—named after Mitzi's home state) have built an arched bridge of which they are very proud. The bridge leads to a flower garden with a gazebo and gently swaying porch swing—a blissful place to relax your road-weary muscles with a glass of iced tea or sherry. A few flagstone steps up from the garden is the good-sized swimming pool, so bring your water wings.

The Durhams, only the fourth set of owners in its long history, fell in love with the house in 1974, turning it into a bed and breakfast in 1987 when most of their children had grown up and moved away. Now there are six bedrooms for guests on the second and third floor, with shared or private baths.

True to the inn's name, the apple theme runs everywhere: from the miniature bushel basket of cherry-sized apples on a nightstand to the apple-scented shampoo in the bath. Green and red apples are hand-stenciled on the sides of the white beams on the third floor, a labor of love that took Mitzi and a friend two years to complete. Copies of *Country Living, Country Homes*, and *Victoria* are stacked next to each bed while collections of antique dolls, quilts, and Persian rugs are scattered in the nooks and sitting areas on all three floors.

The hearty breakfast on the long plank table in the dining room is exactly what cyclists need to fuel up for the day; Mitzi will also pack a picnic lunch for you if she has 24 hours notice. If you get back by 4 or 5 P.M., you'll be just in time for tea in the skylighted sunroom or out by the brook or pool.

If you like hiking, bring your boots. The inn is close to the Appalachian Trail and so many backpackers also find their way there. When I was there in late July, guests included Glenda and Don Sutherland, a couple of health-care workers who were hiking all the way from Georgia to Maine. They told hilarious stories about hikers with such trail names as Bad Bob, Me and My Shadow, and the Pregnant Rhinos. They found the inn so congenial they took up John's offer to spend another two nights and he would "slack-pack" them (drive them to certain portions of the trail that they would then hike without their back-packs, so they would indeed walk the whole route) to Harriman.

Maybe the power failure had something to do with it. A violent lightning storm knocked out the electricity for six hours. Mitzi had invited the guests to stay for a summer family feast of buttery corn on the cob, scarlet vine-ripened tomatoes slippery in their sweet juice, home-baked bread, and zucchini sautéed in garlic and onions. By candlelight we laughed, and Mitzi later gave me a recipe so bizarre I absolutely had to go home and try it: jelly from the common wildflower Queen Anne's lace. It is so delicious—with a spicy berry richness that on toast is reminiscent of honey—that I made a dozen jars of it for Christmas presents, and I hereby immortalize it for you.

QUEEN ANNE'S LACE JELLY
40 blossoms (heads) of Queen Anne's lace, washed
3-1/2 cups water
4 cups sugar
1 package Surejell powdered pectin (supposedly only Surejell works)
Heat water to boiling and turn off heat. Cover and steep the heads of Queen Anne's lace in the hot water for 10 minutes. Remove flowers and strain the resulting "tea" through cheesecloth in a colander. Reheat the tea to boiling and add the Surejell. Reheat to boiling and boil hard for 1 minute, stirring constantly. Add the sugar all at once, reheat to boiling, and boil hard for 1 minute, stirring constantly. Skim. Pour into hot, sterilized half-pint canning jars, and seal with sterilized lids and rings. Turn the jars upside down for 5 minutes (to kill any microscopic beasties on the lids). Turn right side up, cool 12 hours, label, and store in a dark place. Makes five half-pints.

The original recipe, which Mitzi credits to Frances Dellow in Marathon, New York, in the mid-1970s, called for only 30 heads of Queen Anne's Lace, a few drops of yellow food coloring, and boiling the final batch for 15 minutes. I like the stronger-flavored jelly; the food coloring is completely unnecessary as the natural jelly is a lovely transparent golden honey; and I followed the Surejell directions for a final boil of only 1 minute. Try both Dellow's original and my alterations, and see which you prefer.

In either case, well into winter, you can still taste sweet memories of your weekend in New Jersey and Florida.

EAST TO THE ORIENT
Suffolk County, New York

Ride Ratings

Length: 23 miles
Configuration: line
Difficulty: flat; headwinds when outbound; traffic ranges from moderate to very light
Surface: adequate to fair pavement

—*Highlights: This ride can be combined with "Wine Country Wanderer" or "Shelter Island Vacation" for a total of up to 91 miles; this ride features wetlands, views of the Atlantic Ocean and Long Island Sound, historic sites, and swimming, hiking, and picnicking at Orient Beach State Park.*

Orient Point, at the very tip of Long Island's north fork, like Montauk Point at the tip of the South Fork, is a favorite destination of bicyclists in the tri-state area. Each June the American Youth Hostels sponsors the Strawberry Festival ride to Orient Point from Mattituck. On the proper Saturday you too can link this ride to Orient Point with a visit to Mattituck for the privilege of standing in line in huge circus tents for a heaping bowl of outstanding strawberry shortcake. (See the "Wine Country Wanderer" ride.)

Even without the red-and-white calories, Orient Point with the Orient Beach State Park is wonderful. Since it does not have the resort history of Montauk, the area is less built up, making for true rural riding. The roads are flat, the traffic moderate to nonexistent, with abundant wetlands and bird life, and villages dating back to the 18th century and before. On any day but Tuesday, you can hike two miles in Orient Beach State Park to a bird sanctuary or swim in the quiet saltwater and lounge with a picnic lunch.

At a hundredsomething miles from New York City, Orient Point is best explored as part of a long weekend holiday. For that reason I've designed this ride to link with others out here on the end of Long Island. In addition to the Mattituck ride, you can join it to the Shelter Island ride for a total of 46 miles. Overnight options, in fact, include staying at one of the

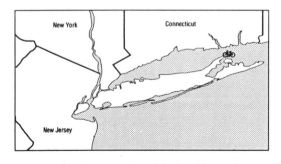

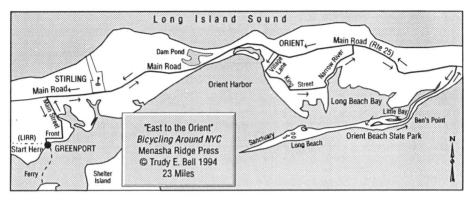

many inns on Shelter Island (see the "Shelter Island Retreat"). Strong cyclists preferring even longer distances can create their own multiday itinerary by linking this expedition to Orient Point with the other Long Island rides of their choice.

No matter what you do, take a hint from experience: for the least traffic and the most options of places to stay overnight, take time off work to create your own long weekend—don't vacation with the masses on Memorial Day, July 4, or Labor Day weekends. Also, on Long Island, the weather stays warm well into the fall—but remains quite chilly and rainy even late into the spring.

Your expedition to Orient Point starts from Greenport, New York—the very last stop on the Long Island Rail Road, 2-1/2 hours from the city (see the preface for information on obtaining a pass for your bicycle on the train). It so happens that the Greenport Station of the LIRR is right next to the dock of the ferry to Shelter Island—wonderfully convenient if you have decided to vacation without a car and are going to stay on Shelter Island.

From either the train station or ferry dock, downtown Greenport is just a block north, where you'll turn right (east) at the light onto Front Street (New York State Route 25E). The town is both quaint and busy; here you can stop at a sport shop, drugstore, or fuel up at a deli, grocery store, or any one of a number of restaurants. (I vote for the Chowder Pot Pub.) Make sure to fill your water bottles and tuck some raisins into your pockets, for there will be stretches without services on the ride.

Follow Route 25E where it turns left (north) at the flashing red light, riding past more stores. Watch for automobile traffic: Greenport is busy in the summer. Also, take care on the bumpy, ancient concrete road, which can sport sand and gravel. The road bends left at the competing "holy Trinity" of a Baptist, Methodist, and Catholic churches (I bet traffic is fun on Sundays), past a little triangular park where an American flag commemorates the veterans of World War II and the Korean War.

At the "T" intersection about a mile north of Greenport, turn right at the flashing red light to head out to Orient Point. Again, watch for traffic. But most important, watch your own riding on the shoulder. The good news is, the shoulder is three or four feet wide, tempting you to ride two abreast. Don't do it. The bad news is, the shoulder is old and rather chewed-up concrete half an inch below the level of the main road. When my cycling companion Jim Arth and I were mapping out this route, we were riding side by side, and the left edge of my front tire wandered too close to the road's raised lip. Headfirst I pitched over the handlebars, landing with my full weight on my left hand, spraining the muscle below my thumb and tearing the rotator cuff in my shoulder. That popular "pitching injury" restricted my activities for more than half a year. You don't need it. Take your time and attend to your riding, and you'll enjoy the whole trip.

Houses will give way to flat, open land. In a couple miles you'll pass over a bridge, and a mile and a half later you'll pass Latham's Farm Stand on your right. This is a huge stand, so make a note to pick up some strawberries, tomatoes, or other local produce on the return. Or what about provisions for lunch today?

A quarter of a mile later, after The Candyman (I brake for fresh homemade chocolates), turn right onto Village Lane. The intersection is unmistakable, for there is a small triangle marked with a miniature Washington Monument. You are now entering the village of Orient, a quiet hamlet dating back more than two centuries, where many of the buildings have historical markers.

Perhaps the most interesting is the Shaw House a bit farther down on the right, built in 1730 by Richard Shaw. On the night of August 1, 1777, James Griffith, pursued by British soldiers during the Revolutionary War, leaped from the upper windows and escaped into the forest. At one point his widow was taken for dead and was placed in a receiving vault, only to revive and return home, much to the consternation of her neighbors.

Even if you're not a history buff, the ocean views these people have are spectacular. Follow Village Lane as it bends left. A bit later, as it bears left again, it becomes King Street. A quarter of a mile later, bear right at the "Y" intersection to stay on King Street. Now you're surrounded by wide open spaces; a pillared farmhouse on your left commands a wonderful view across an open field out to the ocean. Shelter Island is in the distance beyond Orient Point.

Turn left at the "T" intersection onto Narrow River Road. Don't rush. When Jim and I were here, it was a perfect suspended moment of cycling. We let the tailwind carry us at 8 miles per hour past swaying marsh grass seven or eight feet high. The sun was warm on our shoulders, puffy clouds dotted the washed blue sky, gulls floated on thermals above . . . cycling seldom gets better than this.

The road bends several times, passing the red and white buildings of the small Narrow River Marina. A mile beyond, the interlude ends. Refreshed by the magic, turn right at the "T" intersection to resume your eastward travel on Route 25E. You'll pass a small orchard on your right. A third of a mile later, a striking yellow and white modern windmill turns in the farm field on your left, across from a small graveyard enclosed by stone walls. Here's another opportunity to pick up some farm-fresh fruits and vegetables at Terry's Farm Stand on your right.

A couple of miles after rejoining Route 25E, you've reached your destination: Orient Beach State Park. (Route 25E actually continues for another quarter mile at a dock for a ferry to Connecticut—the first leg of a bike-and-ferry trip I once plotted out all the way to Labrador, but have not yet taken. But that's another story.) Turn right, through the gates into the park.

This park is wonderful. It posts signs reading CAUTION: BICYCLE RIDERS AHEAD and limits cars to 25 miles per hour. It's open from 8 A.M. to 4:30 P.M. all year, except Tuesdays. As luck would have it, Jim and I arrived on a Tuesday, and were sitting outside the closed gates glumly eating our peanut butter sandwiches when a ranger came by. Once we explained our mission, the kind gentleman allowed us to enter.

The two-mile-long park road takes you on a narrow neck of land between the Atlantic Ocean and the gleaming water of Little Bay on your right. Here and there, on 20-foot-high platforms built for the purpose, ospreys build their huge nests of haphazard sticks and feed their peeping young. All but wiped out by the pesticide DDT in the 1970s, this large hawk with brown-and-white wings is making a significant recovery along the marshes and bays of eastern Long Island.

Eventually the road ends by circling right around a one-way loop. You have arrived. Here, for your enjoyment, are picnic tables (including some under shelters), barbecue grills, restrooms, sports equipment to be borrowed free of charge, a refreshment stand, and volleyball nets. Rick's Seafood Cafe serves real meals, as opposed to the refreshment stand's hotdogs and other snacks.

A sand-filled playground, in addition to the expected swings and jungle gyms, also had play houses, ship's rigging for climbing, and—best of all—serious metal backhoes for making mountains and molehills out of the sand. Jim and I immediately ran to climb aboard and swivel them around and pull on the levers to scoop up sand and deposit it elsewhere. Tested and approved.

Rest your bones on benches overlooking the pebbly beach and out over the water to Gardiners Island, Plum Island, and Montauk Point (the farthest tip of Long Island's south fork). Also, if you have the time and the hiking shoes, you might try the two-mile-long trail to a bird sanctuary at the very tip of Orient Point.

To return, retrace your route out the park road, avoiding the glass-sharp white shells on the road dropped by gulls cracking open oysters, clams, and other shellfish. At the "T" intersection at the park entrance, turn left onto Route 25 West.

A mile later, for sheer variety, turn right onto Old Main Road, which passes the Charles Rose Airport to your right. Never fear, this is a small-time grass strip where private planes are almost lost behind the tall grasses. In less than a quarter mile, Old Main Road rejoins Route 25W; bear right to continue west.

A quarter of a mile later, you'll pass Peaken's Tavern on your right. Built in 1656, this large shake house is the last of seven houses remaining on Long Island that were built in the mid-17th century. Nearly two miles later, on your right is the Orient Congregational Church, the oldest church of that denomination in the state of New York. A first meeting house was built there before 1718; it adopted the Congregational form of worship in 1735; the present building was built in 1843. In colonial times, it was also the site of this community's stocks and whipping post.

A mile later, you'll pass an undistinguished bramble-filled lot called Truman's Beach, known as Hard Beach by the first settlers. During the War of 1812, the American Naval officer Commodore Stephen Decatur lay at anchor off this sand spit with three ships—the *United States*, the *Macedonian*, and the

Hornet. Eight times in the last two centuries, storms tore through there and cut the oyster ponds off from the mainland.

A mile and a half later, don't miss the small, white East Marion chapel tucked away on your left; it was built in 1886. Half a mile later, on your right, is a huge farm stand—last call for fresh fruits and vegetables. Half a mile beyond is Island's End Golf and Country Club on your right. A mile beyond that, at the flashing yellow light, turn left to follow Route 25 back to Greenport.

SHELTER ISLAND VACATION
Suffolk County, New York

Shelter Island is good for what ails you—and what ails most New York City residents is stress. So take a week, or at least a long weekend, and run so far away from your problems that you can't do anything about them even if you want to!

Nestled between the two forks that form the tip of Long Island, Shelter Island is 100 miles from the hustle and hassle of New York City. The island is still isolated enough that it is accessible only by ferry—but reachable by public transportation if you don't care to drive. A 2-1/2-hour ride on the Long Island Rail Road will drop you at Greenport, the very end of the line on Long Island's north fork. See the preface for information on obtaining a bicycle permit on the LIRR—or, if you don't feel like going to the bother of manhandling your bike on the train, call Picozzi's Bike Shop on Route 114 in Shelter Island Heights to reserve a rental (516-749-0045).

A few steps away from the Greenport train station is the dock where you and your bicycle can catch the ferry to Shelter Island; the fare for the ride, which lasts literally only 3 minutes, is a couple of dollars, with a discount given for a round trip. The ferry runs for about 18 hours a day all year, and during the summer functions as a continuous shuttle: as soon as it is filled, it leaves. The wait is never longer than 10 or 15 minutes, and the ferry is fun to watch.

There are a lot of vacation-type relaxing things to do on Shelter Is-

Ride Ratings

Length: 10, 18 or 26 miles
Configuration: 2 adjoining loops
Difficulty: rolling; traffic ranges from moderate to very light
Surface: good pavement throughout

—Highlights: This ride can be combined with "Wine Country Wanderer" and/or "East to the Orient" for a total of up to 91 miles; it offers all the choices of a resort area: romantic bed-and-breakfast inns, fine dining, beaches, sailing, deep sea fishing, golf, tennis, and a 2000-acre nature preserve.

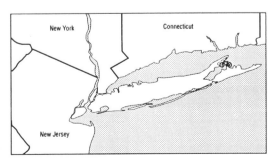

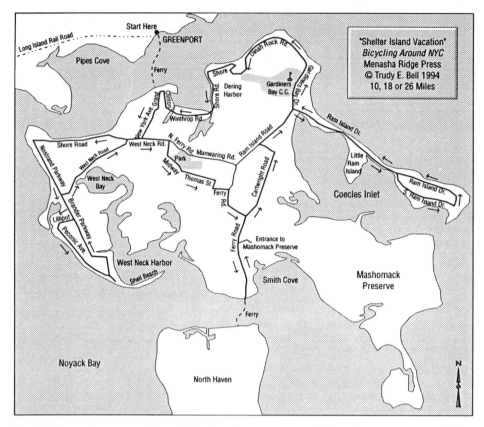

"Shelter Island Vacation"
Bicycling Around NYC
Menasha Ridge Press
© Trudy E. Bell 1994
10, 18 or 26 Miles

land. Bring a long novel and plenty of sunscreen and stretch out on one of the white sand beaches, or walk along the water's edge collecting shells. Try your hand at catching flounder, bluefish, sea bass, or other deep sea fishes in the gentle surf (because the island is so sheltered in the bay between Long Island's forks, the saltwater laps at your toes so tamely even a toddler can wade). Or plan to swing your clubs at the two golf courses (one with 9 holes and one with 18). Lovers can be pampered or left alone at their pick of a dozen or so of the luxurious inns or bed-and-breakfasts—some of which will not even disturb you with a phone or television. You can obtain a complete list of accommodations, which is updated each year, along with a superb map by writing to the Shelter Island Chamber of Commerce. Box 598, Shelter Island, NY 11964 or calling (516) 749-0399.

The athletic may register in the annual Shelter Island 10-kilometer race, which each June attracts some 10,000 spectators and runners. Bring hiking boots for some serious exploring of the salt marshes and forests of the Mashomack Preserve, an undeveloped wildlife preserve that occupies fully a third of the island; the marked trails range from 1.5 to 11 miles long.

Best of all, Shelter Island offers cycling opportunities for those of all strengths and inclinations, and that means happiness for everyone regardless of how much or little time each person spends on a bike. Casual riders who simply want to tool around have their pick of quiet roads and intriguing scenery right on the island itself. This ride will give you but an introduction; please enjoy striking off on your own. The island is big enough to have variety but small enough so it's impossible to get really lost—particularly nice if one idea is that adults and kids split up for a day on their own.

Avid cyclists can, as my cycling companion Jim Arth and I did two April nights, treat Shelter Island as a central base of operations with a reliable hot shower, good bed, and great food for four other rides in this book. Taking the north ferry to Greenport will allow even casual cyclists to enjoy a day ride to Orient Point (23 miles) or to the Mattituck vineyards (35 or 42 miles). Particularly athletic riders might also enjoy taking the south ferry to Sag Harbor to combine the Cedar Point Park ride with the trip to Montauk Point—a round trip of up to 80 miles. (For details, see "East to the Orient," "Wine Country Wanderer," "Cedar Point Park Pilgrimage," and "Montauk Point Explorer.")

A word about Long Island weather: if you have a choice, plan your rides for later in the season rather than earlier, or be prepared for some wet and chilly days. The eastern tip of the island—including Shelter Island—is the last place in the tri-state area to be rid of winter; by the same token, summer lingers well into traditional autumn months. In both cases, the weather lags that of New York City proper by a good month. The April day Jim Arth and I were exploring it, classic April showers were soaking our clothes and shoes to a squishy chill and slowly dissolving our map and notes. Yet on a solo mapping trip around the July 4 holiday, the sun was warm on my back and the air delightfully cool— cool enough even for long sleeves some days and for an energetic cyclist to remain refreshed for many miles. By September, the Gulf Stream has heated the Atlantic waters to a bathwater warmth, yet most of the summer crowds are gone.

The Shelter Island ride begins at the dock for the ferry you have taken from Greenport. Follow the one-way Grand Avenue (New York State Route 114 South) as it climbs up from the ferry dock and winds left, past the ivory and white Victorian gingerbread house with the tilted tower. Bear left at the "Y" intersection to stay on Route 114 South. Directly in front of you, up on a rise, is the gracious veranda and wraparound porch of a three-story white and green clapboard mansion: that is the Chequit Inn (Grand Avenue, Shelter Island, NY 11965, 516-749-0018).

Opened as an inn in 1871, the 44-room Chequit is like your greatgrandmother's closet. In the dining room is a mantelpiece that once belonged to William Randolph Hearst; in the lobby a brass chandelier from the old Montauk Yacht Club. The Chequit was built around a spreading maple, whose enormous branches now shade the terrace out front. Rooms are available either in the rambling house itself, or in a separate and somewhat more modern lodge annex called The Cottage, which overlooks Dering Harbor and the Shelter Island Yacht Club. Bicycles can be locked under the cover of the wraparound porch.

In years past, I've weekended there with two of my semiregular cycling companions, Karen Fitzgerald from New York City and Alan Wolf from Morristown, New Jersey, and what stands out in my mind was the scrumptious cucumber salad dressing. Be forewarned: The Chequit rates are fairly stiff, comparable to those of midtown-Manhattan hotels, with rooms in The Cottage being a bit cheaper. Special packages, which include a continental breakfast for two, are available for stays of three weekday nights and longer.

Past the Chequit, where Route 114 South heads left down Chase Avenue, you continue straight on Grand Avenue, which curves right. At the grassy triangle, bear left onto New York Avenue, passing the lake of Ice Pond Park and the grassy greens of a country club. At the stop sign, turn right onto the busy West Neck Road (the North Fork Bank is on the far left corner).

Less than a quarter mile later, continue straight onto Shore Road (West Neck heads off to the left). Shore Road will crest, and then carry you downhill and to the left. Now you are pedaling along the wide public Crescent Beach that I have never seen crowded; even when Karen and I were there on a hot Memorial Day weekend, there was plenty of room for relaxing with privacy on the white sand. Let its magic stop you for at least a few moments of watching the sailboats and gazing at the shore of the north fork only a few hundred yards across the water.

Continue west on Shore Road, past the Shelter Island Resort overlooking the beach (for reservations, call 516-729-2001). The road bends left, away from the water, and then right, changing its name to Rocky Point Road and climbing through the woods. At the dead-end sign, turn left onto Nostrand Parkway, continuing past Belvedere Estates. Now, just relax—you're pedaling along a wonderfully quiet and beautiful wooded stretch of fine old houses.

After a mile and a half of leisurely riding, maybe you're in the mood for some variety. Turn right onto Lilliput Lane, turning left at the end onto Peconic Avenue, past more quiet and quaint stone houses. Peconic Avenue will curve left; at the first full four-way intersection, turn right to stay on Peconic Avenue. At the very tip, where the street makes a sharp left, turn right onto the unmarked Oak Tree Lane, where the sign warns NARROW LANE, 20 MPH.

This little road will soon peter out into sand, and the chance to walk out the narrow West Neck to a lighthouse a quarter of a mile out in West Neck Harbor. The spacious sand of Shell Beach curves around to your left—another uncrowded treasure. As you hike out, look back over your right shoulder. Due west, you'll see several peninsulas from Long Island's north and south forks jutting into the bay. On a clear day, due west, in the distance behind the farthest spit of land, you may catch a glimpse of Robins Island: a forested 445-acre island out in the Great Peconic Bay that has never seen a developer's bulldozer.

Return the way you came, back to the end of Peconic Avenue. When you emerge from Oak Tree Lane, turn right onto East Brander Parkway. After the road bends left, turn right onto Brander Parkway, and ride for another quiet mile. At the yield sign, turn right onto West Neck Road. A mile later, at the "T" intersection, turn right to stay on the rather busy West Neck Road.

You have now completed the first of the ride's two loops, having pedaled about 9 miles so far. If you wish to return to the north ferry dock, take the second left onto State Route 114 North and follow the signs to the ferry.

Otherwise, just short of the intersection with Route 114 take a right onto Midway Road, riding past the woods of a town park. Take the second left onto Thomas Street, past the post office. Cross Route 114, and take the next right onto Thomas Avenue. Halfway down the block on the right is the unprepossessing Azalea House Bed & Breakfast (1 Thomas Avenue, P.O. Box 943, Shelter Island, NY 11964, 516-749-4252).

The big brown house, which was built as a B&B by Anna Kaasik and her family, opened its doors in 1989. Somewhat unusual in these parts, it is open year-round; five bedrooms are available in the winter and eight in the summer (Memorial Day to Labor Day, since New Yorkers summer by the calendar and not by the solstice and equinox). Some of the rooms, in bright knotty pine with clean-line Scandinavian-style furniture, have queen-sized beds, others twins.

Azalea House has a "flexible two-night policy" on weekends. That means if someone wants to stay a Saturday night, they must stay two nights; but if on a particular weekend someone wants only a Friday night, for that weekend another lucky caller could get the Saturday night by itself. Bicycles can be stored under a wooden deck outside, which is "not totally rain-proof," Ms. Kaasik said. But then, maybe you will be luckier than Jim Arth and I and not stay during a multiday downpour, right?

The Azalea House's style of serving breakfast is unique, and to me absolutely delightful. In most B&Bs the guests gather at a prearranged time for a family-style breakfast. This means being sociable first thing in the morning and being flexible about other strangers' schedules. Well, in Azalea House, as early as 6 A.M. a cart is quietly wheeled into a common sitting room where it remains for the next four hours. Guests can come and go as they please, helping themselves to coffee, hot pastries, juices, cereals, fruit, and condiments. So if you want to sleep in—or if you accidentally oversleep—no problem! If you want to get on the road as soon as it's light, great! If you want simply to slip out in the lightest robe and bring breakfast back to bed, by all means, enjoy! And, of course, if you do like company for breakfast, well, you can sit on the sofa in the common room and invite other guests to join you for some conversation.

Continuing the trip, at the next block turn left onto the main Route 114 South (Bateman Ferry Road). At this intersection directly ahead of you is the elegant Cogan's Country Restaurant, particularly convenient to Azalea House if you've visited by public transportation and don't feel like getting back onto the bike after a soaking hot shower at the end of the day. Across from Cogan's, the white Presbyterian church and its little graveyard are built on the site of the first meeting house in Shelter Island, which was built in 1743. Imagine how remote the place must have been then . . .

Follow Route 114 South as it makes a sharp turn right at the next "T" intersection, then left at the Shelter Island Historical Society and a cluster of small cottage shops, then right at the next "T" intersection.

About a third of a mile later, turn left into the entrance of the Mashomack Preserve, 2039 acres of pristine woodlands and salt marshes protected by the Nature Conservancy, accounting for a full third of the Shelter Island's area. Shelter Island was originally settled in 1652, with much of it owned by Nathaniel Sylvester (1610-1680), a sugar merchant from Barbados. This section was never really settled and remained in the hands of just a few families until purchased by the Nature Conservancy. As a result, it still looks much as it must have centuries ago.

Open for hiking 9 A.M.-5 P.M. every day except Tuesday, walks led by nature guides can be reserved (516-749-1001). The visitors' center has a map of the trails, ranging from a gentle walking loop of 1-1/2 miles to a hilly 11-mile expedition for hardy hikers out to a swamp on the northeastern edge. A bird sanctuary at the southern tip of the preserve, however, is completely off-limits to visitors.

When leaving the preserve, you have the following two choices: If you are linking your stay in Shelter Island with the Cedar Point Park and/or Montauk rides on Long Island's south fork, turn left and head south on Route 114 to catch the south ferry to North Haven. Once on land again, continue south on Route 114 through Sag Harbor. About 5-1/2 miles south of the ferry dock, turn left on Swamp Road. In another two miles or so, turn left onto Old Northwest Road. A couple of miles later, you will reach the entrance to Cedar Point Park; refer to "Cedar Point Park Pilgrimage" for directions to Amagansett.

However, to continue your exploration of Shelter Island, turn right and return the way you came on Route 114 North. But before leaving the preserve, make sure your water bottles are filled: there are no reliable public services for the next 15 miles.

At the traffic circle a third of a mile north of the preserve where Route 114 bends left, head straight onto Cartright Road. Half a mile later, you'll pass the Fox Point wildlife sanctuary to your right, with cultivated farm fields to the left and the small planes of a private airport.

Follow Cartright as it winds to the left, turning right at the "T" intersection onto the unmarked Ram Island Drive (also called Ram Island Road on the Hagstrom maps). Ahead of you is the enticing distant prospect of a harbor filled with sailboats, while around you the trees are filled with the distinctive calls of bobwhites and other birds—you definitely feel out in the country. To your immediate right is the water of the Coecles Inlet.

In three-quarters of a mile, you have a choice. If you want the 19-mile option, continue straight onto Gardiner's Bay Drive and skip down a page and a half to the double asterisks (**).

If instead you want the 26-mile option with some of the best scenery of the trip, make your first right onto Ram Island Drive. You are now heading out onto a peninsula 3-1/2 miles long. For its size, though, the peninsula has some impressive hills—and some lovely, quiet, wooded dales. First you'll be riding out on a narrow neck; the flats to your left are dotted with scrub pine and (yes!) native cacti that in late June or early July bloom abundantly with large yellow flowers. (Not all cacti thrive in deserts!) The beach to the left is supposedly a great one for collecting all kinds of shells as the tide moves out, confided several women who made a practice of walking out there after every high tide.

After an initial dead flat ride, you'll begin climbing. Bear left at the "Y" intersection to stay on Ram Island Drive. A quarter mile later, you'll be riding above a beach of gravel and jumbled concrete blocks to your left that is pounded with the rhythmic surf. Avoid riding over the broken shells on the road, which can be as sharp as any glass.

A couple tenths of a mile later, stop at the restricted area sign and watch the ospreys in the nest of hodgepodge sticks ahead on a platform atop what looks like a telephone pole. A species of large hawk nearly wiped out in the 1970s by the pesticide DDT, the heavy bird is now making a comeback in eastern Long

Island in spite of the rather low survival rate of its chicks. At the end of June you may be lucky enough to see a mom with her babe.

In the inlet to the right, the delightfully warm water lapped against a stony beach carpeted with dry seaweed. To me, the water in the inlet seemed slightly higher than the water in the sea to the left. A shovel-wielding man wading up to his knees called to his small daughter, who was also industriously digging: "Bonnie, we're going to have baked stuffed clams with linguini tonight!'

Climb again, and at the "Y" intersection, bear right onto South Ram Island Drive. Immediately to your right is the Ram's Head Inn, perhaps the most out-of-the-way bed-and-breakfast in this book. It's also an avowed escape from the world, for there are no telephones, televisions, radios, or clocks to remind you of the outside world. For science history buffs, this inn was the site of the First Shelter Island Conference on the Foundations of Quantum Mechanics, where the likes of J. Robert Oppenheimer, Linus Pauling, and other physicists changed our views of conceptualizing matter and the universe.

A gracious center hall colonial surrounded by long sweeping lawns, all of the inn's 17 rooms overlook the large shading oaks, dogwoods, or rhododendrons. The dining area and lounge look out across the lawn down to Coecles Harbor—a perfect setting for watching the rosy sun dip down to the horizon at the end of a day's ride. Guests may play tennis on the inn's courts, or—for free—take out one of the inn's two 13-foot sloops. Prices are moderate by New York City standards, and include a continental breakfast. A 10-percent discount is available for Sunday through Thursday nights, with a two-night minimum on weekends and a three-night minimum on holiday weekends. Children are allowed. Breakfast and dinner are available every day except Tuesday; the inn is open from the beginning of May through the end of October. Write Ram's Head Inn, Shelter Island Heights, NY 11965 or call (516) 749-0811.

Pedal past the inn, following the quiet road another mile until it deadends at Reel Point. There you can turn right and walk out on a stony beach and sit with your water bottle and sandwiches to enjoy the lapping of the waves. A rambling wood-and-glass private residence—which looks rather like a small beach-front hotel—is perched on the bluff to your left; in late June, a contented older woman slowly swayed back and forth on a porch swing and gazed over the water.

When you've had your fill of solitude, return and head straight onto North Ram Island Drive. Be careful of sand and gravel on the downhill. Shortly thereafter, take note of the magnificent house on your left—and the more magnificent view it commands to the right over marsh grasses and the bay to Orient Point.

Half a mile later, near the crest of the next major hill, there is a large mulberry tree to the right with its lower branches within reach. If it's late June or so, look for berry debris on the pavement; then reach up and pick the succulent treats, whose dark juice will stain your fingers, lips, and shirt. Mulberries—which look like blackberries—are so sweet I've often wondered why you can never buy mulberry jam or preserves. But their inaccessibility in high branches may account for it, leaving them only as light lunches for birds and cyclists. Perhaps this tree is a relic of the surge toward colonial independence; around the time of the Revolutionary War, activists for independence wrote how-to essays in almanacs urging colonists to plant mulberry trees and encourage the silkworm caterpillars, so as to become independent of British imports for silk fabric.

Continue straight at the stop sign onto Ram Island Drive, waving farewell to the Ram's Head Inn, up and down the rollercoaster road until the final flats. At the "T" intersection, turn right onto Gardiner's Bay Drive.

(**) A quarter of a mile later, you'll pass the greens and sand pits of the Gardiner's Bay Country Club. Follow the road as it bends gently left around Hay Beach Point. Continue on Gardiner's Bay Drive. Or, if you wish, turn right onto Point Lane to enjoy riding close to the beach and gazing at the spacious, gray beach houses. Turn left at the "T" intersection onto the unmarked Highberry Lane, and right at the next "T" intersection back onto Gardiner's Bay Drive. The drive soon changes its name to Dinah Rock Road.

At the top of the rise, allow the momentum from the downhill to carry you over the next rise. At the "T" intersection (yield sign), turn right onto Country Club Drive, and follow it right. A quarter mile later, turn right at the next "T" intersection onto the unmarked Manhasset Road, into the village of Dering Harbor. With 16 residents, Dering Harbor has the distinction of being the smallest village in the state of New York. It also enjoys lovely views over the harbor to Greenport; note the 50 yards of well-tended flower gardens to your right along the fence.

Follow the road as it bends to the left, passing an unusual Spanish-style home with the red tile roof. Turn right at the "Y" intersection onto the unmarked and narrow Shore Road, where the sign for through traffic points left. Here you will pass beautiful large houses with their own names and immaculate lawns stretching right down to the water; you are riding almost at the water's edge.

Head left at the circle, following the one-way signs, past mansion after white mansion, as you pedal on the water's level—gives you a good feel how the other 0.1 percent lives, eh? Not too shabby. At the next stop sign, head straight onto the unmarked Winthrop Road, bending right over a bridge crossing the mouth of Gardiner's Creek. Pass the high-end Dering Harbor Inn, with its one- and two-bedroom suites overlooking the harbor (516) 749-0900.

Three-quarters of a mile later, turn right at the "T" intersection onto Route 114 North. Here you'll pass Picozzi's Bike Shop on your left, established in 1927. It still looks like the "Gasoline Alley" garage. Here you can not only buy a bike or accessories or get some repairs, but can also rent one for your stay on the island should you decide not to schlepp your own on LIRR. For information on rentals, call (516) 749-0045.

Immediately thereafter, Route 114 north will carry you into Shelter Island Heights, where I stopped at the Island Food Centre for some truly exceptional Manhattan clam chowder (that's the one with tomatoes), a chicken salad sandwich, and homemade iced tea.

Keep heading north on Route 114, crossing a small bridge and turning right at the "T" intersection, following the signs to the north ferry. After the tennis courts, the road winds left, returning you to the ferry back to Greenport.

CEDAR POINT PARK PILGRIMAGE

Suffolk County, New York

Most people go to the south fork of Long Island to visit the ritzy Hamptons or the lighthouse at Montauk Point. This ride heads in a direction unexpected by tourists: north, to the northern shore of the south fork to Cedar Point Park. Because it's somewhat off the tourist-beaten path, it's a good trip for simply unwinding and letting the hurry slip from your bones. Seafaring-history buffs will want to poke around the indoor and outdoor exhibits at Amagansett's Town Marine Museum. Beach bums can choose between the energetic pounding of the Atlantic Ocean at the Atlantic Avenue public beach or the gentle lapping of Gardiner's Bay on the soft sand of Cedar Point Park's crescent beach. Hikers and naturalists will enjoy taking a long sandy walk to the abandoned lighthouse on Cedar Point, passing the nesting areas of the endangered terns, plovers, and other seabirds.

The ride can be done as an easy day trip, with a picnic in Cedar Point Park. Or you can be a bit more outdoorsy and bring a tent and sleeping bags for a night under the stars. Most appealing of all would be to plan for a relaxing or romantic three-day weekend, since this part of Long Island is a good 100 miles from New York City. In that case, you could stay at one of the many bed and breakfast inns in Amagansett or even on Shelter Island (10 miles north and slightly west of Cedar Point Park), and link this ride with one or more of this

Ride Ratings

Length: 18 or 22 miles
Configuration: loop
Difficulty: flat to rolling; traffic is light to moderate
Surface: good pavement throughout

—Highlights: This ride can be combined with "Montauk Point Explorer" for a total of 55 or 65 miles; in addition to great cycling, it offers a public beach, a marine museum, and camping or picnicking at Cedar Point Park— where you may hike to a 19th century lighthouse.

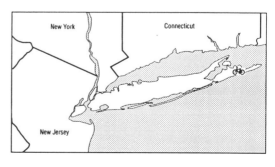

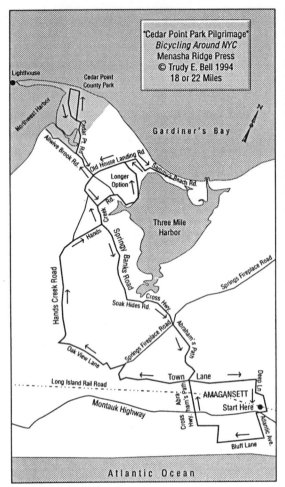

book's other explorations of eastern Suffolk County. Ambitious cyclists, for example, could combine this ride with the one from Amagansett to Montauk Point for a two-lighthouse roundtrip of 55 to 65 miles (depending on options taken). But don't race through it: there are too many neat little nooks and crannies you'd miss. For options and suggested linkages, see "Shelter Island Vacation" and "Montauk Point Explorer."

On this ride to Cedar Point Park, Cross Highway is a popular name. It occurs so frequently that I suspect it was originally a description rather than a name. If you look at a map of eastern Suffolk County, you will discover some other wonderful names indicative of their origin: Two Holes of Water, Stephen Hand's Path, Cattle Track, Abraham's Landing, and Soak Hides Road (the last of which you take on this ride). In fact, part of the fun of cycling is guessing about the terrain or history from topographic names, and you'll have plenty of opportunity here.

Whether you arrive by car or train, this ride begins at the Amagansett station of the Long Island Rail Road (the "Montauk Point Explorer" also starts from here). To get to Amagansett by public transportation, take the Montauk line of the Long Island Rail Road—a ride of more than two hours (see the preface for information on obtaining a pass for your bicycle on the train). If you drive, take the Long Island Expressway almost to its end; at Exit 71, take New York State Route 24 southeast (toward Flanders) until it ends at the Montauk Highway (New York State Route 80); turn left and follow the Montauk Highway for another half hour into Amagansett. The train station will be on your left.

Actually, "station" is too dignified a word: the place is more like a rude wooden bus shelter open on two sides. There also seem to be no restrictions on parking here—at least, no signs are visible. But you'd be well advised to call the town of Amagansett or the Long Island Rail Road to check for sure if you wish to leave your car overnight.

To make up for the lack of services at the station as well as to avoid the fast and heavy traffic on the Montauk Highway, the ride starts by circling around through local streets. Thus, within the first three miles you can buy lunch and visit some public restrooms before heading to Cedar Point Park.

Turn right out of the south end of the Amagansett railroad station onto the very busy Montauk Highway, then make a quick left onto Atlantic Avenue (which, true to its name, heads straight south to the Atlantic Ocean). The turn onto the avenue is at a triangular island marked with a light blue sign advertising the Town Marine Museum. If you pass the Amagansett Fire Station on your right, you've gone too far. On the other hand, if you've gone that far, you may as well continue another couple hundred yards to check out the Amagansett Farmer's Market for fresh fruits and veggies for lunch. Then double back for the turn onto Atlantic Avenue.

After half a mile, just before Atlantic Avenue drops off in a steep plunge, turn right onto Bluff Lane. True to its name, you'll be riding on the crest of a bluff falling away to your left, with its magnificent prospect of the Atlantic Ocean. (If you had continued straight at this intersection, you would have coasted down the steep hill and ended up at the Atlantic Avenue free public beach. Which may not be a bad idea . . .)

Just after your turn onto Bluff Lane, an American flag and two anchors on your left herald the Town Marine Museum. Open seven days a week between 10 A.M. and 5 P.M., there you can explore three floors of artifacts of the 19th century whaling industry, plus some ancient and not-so-ancient sailing craft. Dioramas and exhibits illustrate the history of whaling and fishing, as well as showing you present-day techniques, tools, and equipment of commercial fishermen.

As you leave the museum, turn left to continue along Bluff Lane. In a quarter mile to your left you'll find a monument to Donald Wingate Lamb (1897-1977), whose "guiding force and inspiration made possible the Atlantic coastal double dunes preserve" for the Nature Conservancy, the organization buying up undeveloped private lands to preserve this treasure. Indeed, as you look out toward the ocean, your eyes sweep two successive lines of dunes, protected to retain their wild and windswept aspect.

At the "T" intersection at the end of Bluff Lane, turn right onto Indian Well Plain Highway (the very appealing beach to your left is for town residents only, although you may be able to buy a popsicle or hotdog at the concession trucks). After a quarter mile, turn left onto Further Lane, cycling through the dappled shade of the majestic trees lining both sides of the street. At the "Y" intersection, take the right fork onto Skimhampton Road, and the next right onto Cross Highway.

When you come to the busy Montauk Highway, stop into the Amagansett General Store to your right to pick up snacks or a lunch. This is the only place to provision up until you get to Cedar Point Park halfway into this ride. Marvelously convenient, the general store is open Sunday through Thursday from 6:30 a.m. to midnight, and 24 hours on Friday and Saturday.

Cross the Montauk Highway. On the other side, Cross Highway changes its name to Abraham's Path. Continue straight for another half mile, and turn right into the town park. In addition to the basketball and tennis courts and a little playground, you'll find public restrooms. Fill your water bottles; this will be the last chance until Cedar Point Park.

Turn left at the next intersection onto Town Lane. A mile later, turn left at the end (at the diagonal "T" intersection) onto Accabonac Road, and make an immediate right onto Floyd Street. Now you'll make some quick turns, but the choices are more self-evident than the directions may sound. Follow the one-way signs right onto Cross Highway (number two), noting the tall, ivy-wound trees next to Calvary Church. Turn left at the "T" intersection onto the very busy Springs Fireplace Road. Have patience, you'll be off it shortly, as you will take the first right onto the quiet, short Jackson Street. At the end of Jackson, turn left as you cross the very busy Three Mile Harbor Road, jogging right to continue onto the quiet Oak View Lane.

Now, just ride until Oak View Lane ends. Shortly after you climb a small rise, note the house on your right with the red lintel over its gate. To me, the color and style was suggestive of the entrance to a Japanese rock garden—until I saw the Indian totem pole in the rear! You'll pass a complex of mobile homes on your left, as well as some stables, while pleasant woods remain on your right.

Turn right at the "T" intersection onto the unmarked Hands Creek Road. This road is wide and level, and you can really make some tracks, enjoying the view and the sounds of the forest on both sides. A couple of miles after the turn, note the hulking rock on the left, which some child has crudely painted to resemble a dinosaur.

At the first stop sign, bear left to stay on Hands Creek Road. You'll also begin a slight climb as the terrain becomes more rolling.

In another quarter mile, at the "Y" intersection, you have a choice. If you want to go directly onto Cedar Point Park only a couple of miles ahead, bear left here onto Allwive Brook Road, and skip ahead to the double asterisks (**). If you would like an optional four-mile rolling detour to explore a quiet, unassuming beach community, bear right to stay on the unmarked Hands Creek Road.

Hand's Creek Road passes pleasant homes nestled under the trees, eventually winding to the right and yielding a prospect of quiet, sheltered Three Mile Harbor, dead-ending at a boat landing. Just before the landing, however, is your turn, left onto Three Mile Harbor Drive. Don't be daunted by this initial steep climb. The road quickly turns into a rolling "rollercoaster" ride, up and down and around, and can be a lot of fun if you're energetic. In your enthusiasm, don't miss the stunning geometric house a quarter mile ahead on your right, surrounded by a well-groomed hedge and iron gates—the summer home of an architect from New Jersey.

Turn right at the "T" intersection onto Old House Landing Road, then take the first right onto Sammy's Beach Road, passing a small stone well on your right just after the turn. This road makes one turn to the left, then to the right, then emerges into the open on a neck scarcely a quarter mile wide. When I was there in early July, the water on both sides was a deep blue, dotted with occasional white boats; gulls wheeled and screeched in the sky above, and the sun was hot on my neck. Most precious of all, the dune vegetation was in colorful bloom.

The road eventually ends at a small parking area (permit needed for cars) and a private beach—Sammy's Beach, of course—overlooking the sailboat-dotted Gardiner's Bay. The peninsula of Cedar Point is immediately to your left, Shelter Island is in the middle distance, and Orient Point—the far tip of Long Island's north fork—is on the horizon. Behind you is Three Mile Harbor. On the sunny July day I visited, only two or three residents were reclining on the sand of Sammy's Beach in deck chairs, reading their newspapers or thick novels.

When you've enjoyed the view to your fill, retrace your route along Sammy's Beach Road. Turn left at the "T" intersection onto Old House Landing Road, and turn right onto Allwive Brook Road.

(**) After half a mile, turn right onto Cedar Point Road, and take the first left into Cedar Point Park, one of Suffolk County's parks with overnight camping. If you want a map, or want to register to stay overnight, stop in at the park office on your right.

The 608-acre family campground has a lot to offer: hot showers (of prime importance to cyclists), a camp store that sells the necessities plus some fast foods, a children's playground, and evening ranger programs. Between Memorial Day and Labor Day it is open seven days a week, and from the beginning of April through the end of October it is open Thursday through Saturday nights. When I was scouting these rides over a July 4th holiday weekend, I made the park my base of operations for four nights, and found it pleasant and cheerful to be among the parents and abundant children, who played in the sandy lanes.

The park also can be a godsend to a cyclist on a low budget: if bicyclists pedal in under their own steam with their camping gear, they can camp overnight for free. That's right, folks, absolutely free—a service also offered by other Suffolk County parks. The cyclists' sites do not have picnic tables. But they are away from the cars at the main campsites, and you have access to the showers and all the other park facilities. If you do bring your car, though, and you're not a Suffolk County resident, each night your campsite will cost you fully as much as a cheap motel.

For details about bike camping, especially during the off season, call the Suffolk County Parks Department at (516) 567-1700. The phone number specifically for Cedar Point Park is (516) 324-2195.

From the camp store, far out in the distance over the water, you can see the remains of an abandoned lighthouse. This lighthouse, built in 1839 to guide whaling ships into Sag Harbor, was originally on an island, but the hurricane of 1938 filled in the 200-yard expanse of water between it and Cedar Point. If you feel like a hike, you can pay the lighthouse a visit—a trek of at least 40 minutes each way. Walking straight out to the lighthouse by fording through the shifting dry sand is not an inconsiderable amount of work; I quickly found that the sand was firmer along the curve of the water's edge. It also gives you the chance to pick up seashells or examine the pebbles polished round and smooth by the tides. Take a water bottle, a snack, and some sunscreen; there are no facilities. If you bring your swimsuit and don't mind the fact that there is no life guard, you can also swim off the pebbly beach. But most important, bring binoculars to watch the shore birds, who lay their eggs in camouflaged nests in the dunes.

When you're ready to start the eight-mile return to the Amagansett train station, leave the park by its one entrance, and turn right onto Cedar Point

Road. At the "T" intersection, turn left onto unmarked Allwive Brook Road. Turn right at the stop sign to stay on Allwive Brook Road (Old House Landing Road goes to your left). In another three-quarters of a mile, bear right where the road joins unmarked Hands Creek Road. So far you have been retracing part of your route to Cedar Point Park. That will change.

At the next "Y" intersection, bear left at the fork onto Springy Banks Road, watching for the occasional traffic. Stay on this rolling road for a bit under two miles, enjoying its ups and downs.

Turn left onto Soak Hides Road, but don't go too fast. In a few hundred yards, almost obscured by the brush to your left, is a small marker erected during the 1976 United States Bicentennial explaining the odd name. Soak Hide Dreen, it turns out, was a stream once used to soften hides before turning them into leather goods. And indeed, the stream still babbles as it crosses under the road through a concrete culvert, passing from woodlands to tall grasses. Look carefully at the stream; its sandy bottom is bright orange. In midsummer, savor the fragrance of the miniature pink tea roses adorning the thorny vines climbing to the monument's left. Exactly the kind of treasures a motorist would never discover . . .

Continue along Soak Hides Road, turning left at the "T" intersection onto the very busy Three Mile Harbor Road. But never fear, in a few hundred yards you'll turn right onto Abraham's Path (the Hagstrom map calls it Cross Highway). A quarter mile after the turn, just before Morrell Street, a house on the right has seen fit to erect an official-looking traffic sign reading A--HOLE CROSSING. Takes all kinds . . .

Turn right at the "T" intersection onto the very busy Springs Fireplace Road, and then make an immediate left to continue on Abraham's Path. You may feel safer getting off the bike and running it across rather than pedaling through the turn.

After crossing Accabonac Road, Abraham's Path makes a wide, sweeping left turn to command a gorgeous panorama of open farmland. In the summer, magenta snapdragons and other wildflowers dot the grasses to your right. The July afternoon I beheld this surprise, the only disturbance to its pastoral beauty was two silver race cars without mufflers whose begoggled drivers repeatedly passed each other as if this were the Indy 500.

Turn left at the first stop sign onto Town Lane, which is absolutely level and will carry you through cornfields. Turn right onto Deep Lane, which—appropriate to its name—suddenly descends into a hollow, past orchards to your left and a stand of cattails to your right. Where the road makes a right-angle turn to your left, its name changes into Sidehill Road; follow it, and turn right at the "T" intersection onto Old Stone Highway. You'll soon pass the golf course of the South Fork Country Club.

Immediately after you cross the tracks of the Long Island Rail Road, turn right into the Amagansett train station—ready for the train or car ride back to New York City. Or perhaps you're warmed up enough in physique and enthusiasm to now head out to Montauk Point!

WINE COUNTRY WANDERER

Suffolk County, New York

This visit to Mattituck is one of those virtually ideal bike rides that can be tailored to any taste: short or long, with either straight riding or plenty of fascinating stops, with lots to delight the palate and the eye.

It's a favorite with the American Youth Hostels as its annual Strawberry Ride from Mattituck to Greenport, which I took several times in the early 1980s when I still preferred the security of a preplanned tour. Each June, hundreds of cyclists met shortly after breakfast at the Long Island Rail Road terminal in Penn Station to take the two-hour train ride out to Mattituck, their bicycles following in two huge rented Ryder trucks. In Mattituck they would be met by the long-distance animals, who had started from midtown Manhattan at sunrise to crank the 75 miles or so by noon.

All were in Mattituck around lunchtime, when the town's annual strawberry festival is in full swing in the fields of the high school. Live bands play under jolly red-and-white-striped tents while helium balloons dance on strings tied to the wrists of children in the crowd watching the antics of jugglers and clowns.

Best of all, adults and children line up to pay a dollar or two for a ticket that entitles them to a huge bowl of the best strawberry shortcake you're likely to find this side of a Platonic ideal. No store-bought sponge cake and Cool Whip, here. We are talking a full meal: thick, crusty home-baked

Ride Ratings

Length: 18, 35 or 42 miles
Configuration: loop
Difficulty: flat, though there are headwinds while outbound; traffic is light to moderate
Surface: good to bumpy pavement

—Highlights: This ride can be combined with "East to the Orient" and "Shelter Island Vacation" for a total of up to 91 miles; tour wineries and taste Long Island's famed merlot; pick strawberries and gaze at the heavens through a telescope in the only astronomical observatory on Long Island that is open to the public.

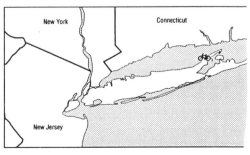

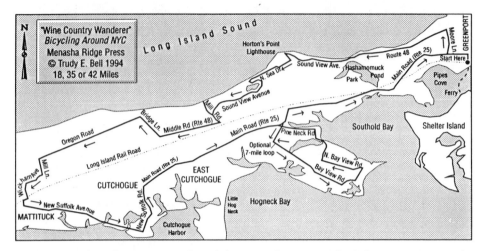

shortcake rich in butter topped with luscious berries picked that morning, and not-too-sweet whipped cream beaten from heavy cream. The real thing. It won't pass any Pritikin test, but if you allow yourself the calories when they're eminently worth it, here's an unforgettable lunch. To find out the particular June Saturday the festival will be held this year, call the Greenport-Southold Chamber of Commerce at (516) 477-1383; that office also distributes tourist information about most of Long Island's north fork, including lists of accommodations.

This ride also features several opportunities to tour local wineries and to sample some of the Long Island wines, including the superb merlot that has rapidly made Long Island the merlot capital of the world. There are also plenty of farms advertising pick-your-own strawberries. Once when I took the Strawberry Ride, one cyclist had bungeed an empty 5-gallon joint-compound container onto his rear rack, intending to pick enough to fill the entire white barrel and then take them home to make addictively wonderful strawberry preserves. Before you get ambitious, take heed from experience: I picked only one quart, and was glad when the box was full, as the constant bending over in the sun left my face streaming with salty sweat and my lower back aching. But by all means, *buy* 5 gallons from a local stand from folks who've done the hard work.

Because the eastern tip of Long Island is so far from New York City, this ride is best enjoyed in combination with others in the area as part of a whole weekend or multiday minivacation. For pedal-pushers wanting more time in the saddle over one or more days, the medium or long version of this Mattituck ride can be joined with the ride to Orient Point or the tour of Shelter Island. The total distance would then range from 45 miles (for the medium Mattituck ride plus the shortest Shelter Island ride) to 91 miles (for the longest combination of all three). See "East to the Orient" and "Shelter Island Vacation."

All three versions of the Mattituck ride starts from the Long Island Rail Road station in Greenport, New York, and heads west, following the course of the Strawberry Ride. The short option returns to New York City from Mattituck. By the way, if you do not wish to schlepp your bike on the train, you can take the train to Mattituck and rent a bike from Country Time Cycle on Main Road; for rental information, call the store at (516) 298-8700.

Greenport is the very last stop on the Long Island Rail Road, 2-1/2 hours from the city (see the preface for information on obtaining a pass for your bicycle on the train). It so happens that the Greenport station of the LIRR is right next to the dock of the ferry to Shelter Island—wonderfully convenient if you have decided make one of the bed-and-breakfast inns on Shelter Island your home base. (Greenport is also the origin of the ride out to Orient Point.)

From the train station, downtown Greenport is just a block north, where you'll turn left (west) at the light onto Front Street (New York State Route 25). If you want to fill your water bottles before starting out, turn right—east—on Route 25 instead; the quaint and busy town has a sport shop, drugstore, a deli, grocery store, and a number of restaurants. Enjoy some breakfast, but leave room for strawberries at lunchtime! Then head back west on Route 25.

Don't go too far, though—just a few tenths of a mile to the outskirts of town, and turn right after the high school onto Moore Lane. Just after you turn, note the turn-of-the-century brick powerhouse with its brick smokestack. Halfway up this road on your right is McCann's Trailer Park, where my bicycling companion Jim Arth and I stayed one April in my parents' truck camper during our own exploration of Orient Point and Mattituck for this book. Owned by the village and operated by the electric company, McCann's—which, for some reason, has an unlisted telephone number—is not high on the list for scenery. But it does have electricity and hot showers, and it has a longer season than the other campgrounds in this area.

Turn left at the "T" intersection onto Suffolk County Route 48. A mile west down the road, you'll pass a hotel, San Simeon by the Sound, overlooking the Long Island Sound. A quarter mile beyond is the Sound View Inn on the right, advertising a restaurant, pool, and private beach, where every room faces the beach and is right on the water. Jim and I later wished we had given one of these a try!

Soon you'll be entering the outskirts of Southold, marked by suburban homes and trees. Named after Southwold, East Suffolk in England, Southold is where the first Long Island settlers landed in 1640. In mid-April, the wispy wild-reaching golden stalks of forsythia brightened the whole area. Just after passing the pebbly Hashamomuck Beach with its parking lot on the right, keep alert; bear right onto Sound View Avenue where the main County Route 48 continues left.

Sound View Avenue is bumpy but beautiful. Between the houses on your right you can peek at the Long Island Sound and the distant Connecticut shore (contorted beach scrub is on your left). In half a mile you'll be riding through gently rolling fields, and then past houses with iron gates and brick columns.

At the "Y" intersection, bear right onto the Sound View Avenue Extension. In a quarter mile the road ends in a parking lot. You can lock your bike on the chain link fence if you wish to visit Horton's Point Lighthouse. Commissioned by George Washington in 1790, it wasn't built until nearly 60 years later (I'm sure there must be some fascinating stories about why it wasn't.) The lighthouse is now the site of the Southold Historical Society Marine Museum, which is open on the weekends in July and August beginning at 1 P.M. This town park also has a stairway leading down to the beach.

Leave the parking lot by riding straight out Lighthouse Road; in mid-April, the brilliant yellow forsythia hedge that lines the large yards to the right was practically aflame. Turn right at the stop sign to resume your westward journey on Sound View Avenue, crossing the bridge over Little Swampy Lake, over rolling hills and through more wooded residential areas.

Half a mile later, turn right at the four-way stop onto Horton Lane, following the road as it bends left and becomes North Sea Drive. The land flattens and opens up on the right to a pebbly beach overlooking the Long Island Sound; the beach sports a parking lot and bathhouses. Continue straight on North Sea Drive; you're now passing by true, unpretentious beach bungalows on the sand amid the scrub pines.

Now we're going for a sandy little scenic loop. Turn right at the "T" intersection onto Kenney Road, at The Elbow East—a restaurant that seems truly in the middle of nowhere. Make an immediate left at a second town park onto Leeton Drive, past more beach houses all facing the Sound to your right. Turn left at the end onto West Drive, which curves left and rolls up and down past sand dunes and more scrub pine trees. At the "T" intersection, turn right onto Kenney Road, then right again at the four-way stop onto Sound View Avenue. Through the forest on your right, you may catch glimpses of Great Pond and the Peconic Dunes County Park. Now just enjoy the gently rolling ride through the sandy forest.

Eventually you'll reach Goldsmith's Inlet Park, a Suffolk County Park. If you want to see the inlet, turn right onto Mill Road, which ends at a parking area with a beach at the inlet itself. Screeching gulls wheel overhead as you pick your way down to the water or find your way on the trails through the woods. When you're done exploring, retrace your way back on Mill Road to Sound View Avenue. Continue on Mill Road (or, if you bypassed the detour down Mill Road, turn left onto Mill Road) until it intersects Suffolk County Route 48 (Middle Road).

At this corner, a historical marker informs you that Mill Road was formerly Peconic's Old Mill Cartway, a road leading to a mill at Goldsmith's Inlet. Built in 1840 by money raised from 80 subscribers, the mill was one of New York's largest grain mills, powered by winds off the Sound. But the great whirling wings were torn off in a storm in 1898, and the rest of the mill was torn down in 1906.

Turn right onto the divided Route 48 heading west, enjoying your riding on the painted shoulder almost as wide as a traffic lane—one of the civilized amenities of many of Long Island's main roads. Now you can see vineyards on the flat land to your left, the grapevines crucified on horizontal wires. You're in Long Island's wine country.

Winemaking is relatively new for Long Island, starting in the early 1970s when the upstate New York wines were still regarded as something of a joke among snooty wine connoisseurs: the dry and semidry varietals were often poor sisters to French or California wines, while the sweet Concords tasted like Welch's grape juice (yes, that is the true flavor of the strong Concord grape). But Long Island's hearty, smooth, deep red merlot changed all that—and if you sample it, you'll understand why. And in a while you'll have your chance.

In a mile and a half, turn right onto Bridge Lane at the well-marked intersection. Now you're pedaling through flat, open farmland. Follow the road as it bends left and becomes Oregon Road, pedaling alongside the stretched-out grapevines. The flat, grassy swards of the sod farms make vast, green planes. The next four miles are some of the most pleasant riding you'll find in the tri-state area: a virtually traffic-free road through flat, beautiful farmland. It's hard to believe you're only 70 miles from one of this country's biggest megalopolises. For that reason, this section of road has also been part of the American Youth Hostels' Strawberry Ride, and you may well see other cyclists—quite a few, in fact, if you are out here on the weekend of Mattituck's strawberry festival.

Turn left onto Mill Lane; this is an old concrete road, not the more typical asphalt, so it stretches white in front of you. Half a mile later, take the first right onto Wickham Avenue (also concrete), following the one-way signs past a ramshackle farmhouse and a small, oblong, attractive lake in a miniature park. This is Wolf Pit Lake, where in colonial days marauding wolves used to be trapped. It was donated in 1967 to the Mattituck Park District by Mr. and Mrs. Ralph W. Tuthill and family, who subsequently (I guess) got half of the one-way part of Wickham Avenue named after them.

Continue to follow the road as it curves left through the suburbs of Mattituck, turning left at the triangle to stay on Wickham Avenue. Cross Route 48 at the light, ride over the railroad tracks, and turn right at Pike Street into the parking lot of the Mattituck "station" of the Long Island Rail Road. Now be alert here: there actually is no station building, just a flat concrete slab on either side of the tracks for getting on and off the train. For the shortest Mattituck ride of 18 miles, this is where you catch the train back to New York City.

Turn left just across from the train platform onto Love Lane (if you've just arrived here by train, turn right from the platform onto Love Lane), passing a laundromat, deli, bank, and other enterprises; you're now in the heart of Mattituck. If you're here for the Mattituck Strawberry Festival, turn left (east) at the blinker marking New York State Route 25 (Main Road) and ride less than half a mile to the Mattituck High School.

If you're here at any other time of year, at Route 25 turn right instead; in just a couple of blocks on your left there is an amazing bike shop that attracts serious buyers from far-away New York City. It's Country Time Cycle, open seven days a week in the summer.

When Jim Arth and I walked in, our first impulse was almost to start laughing: one side of the huge, immaculate showroom had all kinds of bicycles and the other side had sofas and reclining chairs! Yes, even though athletes and couch potatoes seem opposites, for historical reasons of family business, Country Time Cycle and Country Time Furniture share the same space. Even more amazing was the spacious downstairs, which is filled with hundreds of bikes on the floor and hanging on the walls and from the ceiling. The bikes were of a wide variety of brands (unlike the usual shop, which may specialize only in Schwinn, Raleigh, or some other line) ranging from Johnny's first bike up to Cannondale and Bianchi specialty models for racing or touring. It's the shop's ability to show discerning buyers many different models side by side "in the flesh" that attracts clientele from 75 miles away. By the way, Country Time also rents bicycles, so here's the place to pick up your steed if you went that route.

When you're ready to resume the ride, turn right out of Country Time Cycles to retrace your path on Route 25 east; take the first right at the Handy Pantry convenience store onto New Suffolk Avenue. This will spare you the traffic on Route 25, which can be unpleasantly heavy on summer weekends.

On New Suffolk Avenue, you'll be riding through older suburban residential districts. After you pass the round Marratooka Lake on your left, which is across from the small Mattituck Airport on your right, you'll be pedaling through gently rolling farm fields. Eventually the fields will give way to marshy inlets of the Great Peconic Bay, the body of water between the two forks of Long Island. Soon you're riding right along the water. To your right, the small nearby island is the privately owned Robins Island. Its 445 acres of beaches and steep bluffs are together one of the last undeveloped islands on the East Coast. The larger land mass beyond it is Shelter Island. At Jackson Avenue, look to your right down a private drive to see the twirling arms of a working windmill.

At the four-way flashing stop, continue straight on Main Street and ride a few blocks to the water's edge; this is the site of the Holland Torpedo Boat Station, where in 1900 the first submarine purchased by the U.S. Navy was tested. Retrace your route back up Main Street, turning right at the flashing light onto New Suffolk Road. Follow it as it winds through more farm fields and through orchards that in the middle of April are abloom in the pink lace finery of their blossoms.

At the light, turn right onto New York State Route 25, riding in the wide shoulders. Be careful! The shoulder is so wide that it will tempt you to ride two abreast. Don't do it! The shoulder is old and rather chewed-up concrete half an inch below the level of the main road. Give that lip wide berth, because if your front tire brushes against it, you could be pitched over the handlebars. Not a nice way to spend an afternoon.

Now, just stay on Route 25 east (Main Road). Here is where you'll be passing many of Long Island's wineries, one right after another: Peconic Bay Vineyards, Bedell Cellars, Pindar Vineyards, Lenz Winery, and half a dozen others. To me, seeing all the grapevines made it feel rather like cycling in my home state of California. Until the 1970s much of this area was potato farms (Long Island potatoes were almost as well known as Idaho spuds). Now sod farms and vineyards have taking their place.

Many of the wineries offer daily tours—the usual hours seem to be 11 A.M. to 6 P.M.—and some offer winetasting as well. (Go easy on the sampling; bicycling while intoxicated is as dumb as driving under the influence, with a greater risk of you being the one to get hurt.) Some of these wineries are on quiet side roads, clearly marked by signs and arrows; if you have the time, wander up and back some of these roads—they are marvelous for cycling.

By sheer luck, while wandering along some of those side roads not on the main route of this tour, Jim and I happened into the oldest vineyard on Long Island: the Hargrave Winery, established in 1972. On Route 48 (Middle Road) in Cutchogue, Hargrave Winery is a husband-and-wife operation; Alec Hargrave had originally majored in Chinese studies with Louisa studying wine chemistry. Jim and I broke the budget to sample a $20 bottle of their merlot, and could well understand why it's in a world class.

As you continue east on Main Road (Route 25), just past the little triangular cemetery with benches, you have a choice. If if you wish to return directly to Greenport for the 35-mile middle-length ride, just stay on Route 25 east (Main Road); skip down to the double asterisks (**).

For cyclists wishing to take the long 42-mile option, here you can take a seven-mile side tour here through the communities of Bayview and Cedar Beach. This is a mighty pleasant suburban loop with gently rolling open fields, homes, nurseries, and absolutely no traffic.

Make a right from Route 25 onto Corwin Lane and an immediate sharp right onto Bayview Road. In a quarter mile, you'll pass what sounds like a real contradiction in terms: an Indian museum across from the Custer Institute Observatory!

The Indian museum is run by the New York State Archaeological Association and is open on Sundays from 1:30-4:30 P.M. The brick astronomical observatory building offers the public the chance to look through the telescopes each Saturday night just after dark, the only astronomical observatory on Long Island to do so. It is run by the Custer Institute, a multidisciplinary educational society founded in 1927 that is, indeed, named after a niece of the famous General Custer; she later married Charles W. Elmer, a serious amateur astronomer who became one of the founders of the Perkin Elmer Optical Co.—a company noted for its construction of astronomical telescopes.

The observatory grounds are larger than may appear from the road. If you return here after dark on a clear Saturday night, you may have the chance to gaze at the planets, moon, or nebulae (colorful gas clouds in space) through as many as five different telescopes. One may be the observatory's 5-inch refractor (a telescope with a main lens 5 inches in diameter) made by the 19th century's famous team of American opticians, Alvan Clark and Sons; another may be a reflecting telescope with a main mirror 30 inches across—about as large as amateur instruments get. Most unusual for an amateur facility, the institute also operates a 3-meter radio telescope: a dish looking rather like a large version of the satellite antennas you may have seen for receiving television signals—only this one is 10 feet across and it listens to the gases and stars in the universe above. The observatory building also has an extensive library, a museum where you can gaze at a collection of meteorites (stones that fall onto the earth from outer space), and a gift shop.

For all you New Yorkers who have never even seen the Milky Way: time your bicycle trip for the proper weekend in October and attend the Custer Institute's Astronomy Jamboree, held annually since 1979. The jamboree is a three-day festival of workshops, guided nature walks, poetry readings and songs, and all-night "star parties" of gazing at the heavens. Past jamborees have even featured a moonlight cruise in Peconic Bay. Other times of the year, you may arrive in time for one of the public lectures or for a concert or art exhibit. For information, call the Custer Institute's recorded message at (516) 765-2626, or call Barbara Lebkuecher (who has been the institute's volunteer publicist since 1980) at (516) 722-3850.

Continue riding past a Christmas tree farm, enjoying the scenery. Eventually the road will bend left, becoming Cedar Beach Road. A house on the corner here is selling miniature cannons! presumably for your front lawn, as they are displayed here. Get one for your veteran friends, although lugging one of those cast-iron miniatures on the bike might be a problem!

Pass the Southold Community College Marine Technology Center. Now Shelter Island is directly ahead of you, looking very close across the water. If you brought your bathing suit, you might want to dismount and relax at the nearby Cedar Beach County Park. Follow the main road left as it becomes Paradise Point Road, then left again onto North Bayview Road. After about half a mile, follow North Bayview Road as it turns right (Jacobs Lane goes left), across a little concrete bridge, and left onto Pine Neck Road. That will bring you back to State Route 25, where you turn right to continue east on its wide painted shoulder to Greenport.

(**) In another five miles, State Route 25 will take you right to the Greenport railroad station and ferry dock to Shelter Island. You'll enter Southold, passing the historical museum and a number of stores, and soon passing some ships and the Seafood Barn Restaurant, which looks promising. A couple miles later you'll pass a spot advertising Greenport and Southold tourist information from the Greenport-Southold Chamber of Commerce. Less than a mile later, you'll enter Greenport. Follow the signs for the train station and the ferry, turning right onto Fifth Street and left at the next block onto Wiggins Street. Now you're back at the Long Island Rail Road station and the ferry dock to Shelter Island.

Barrier Island Contrasts

Suffolk County, New York

This long, relaxing bicycle ride is perfect for those endless summer days where the sun pinkens the sky at 5 A.M. and the day stays light until nearly 9 P.M., so you have time to do everything: exercise until you're glowing, picnic on the beach, wander through antiques shops, cast your line into the surf for bluefish, enjoy a superb seafood dinner, and snuggle into either a sleeping bag or the downy covers at a bed-and-breakfast inn.

My bicycling companion Jim Arth and I treated ourselves to both overnight contrasts: camping one night on the dunes at Smith Point County Park at the western end, and luxuriating the next night at the Grassmere Inn in Westhampton Beach on the eastern end.

Like most Long Island rides, the one big choice you have to make is between crowds and weather. Long Island is a favorite summering spot for New Yorkers because it is the coolest spot in the tri-state area in the dog days of summer. Thus it can be very crowded between Memorial Day and Labor Day. One way to enjoy the prime weather while avoiding the crowds (that is, car traffic) is to sneak your bicycling vacation midweek. Or, take a weekend off-season. While Long Island doesn't feel spring until May or June, the bathwater-warm Gulf Stream also prolongs the warmth of summer warm well into September or even early October.

When Jim and I were there in mid-April, we didn't know that.

Ride Ratings

Length: 30 or 59 miles

Configuration: 2 loops and a line

Difficulty: flat to gently rolling; traffic is light to moderate but can be heavy on long ride; headwinds may be strong in one direction

Surface: good pavement throughout

—Highlights: A sandbar barrier island offers dunes, the Atlantic Ocean, and wildlife refuges; taste superb seafood, luxuriate at a romantic bed-and-breakfast, or camp out—nude bathing is an option!

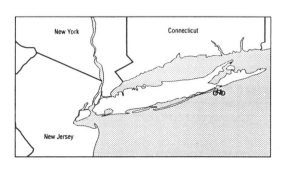

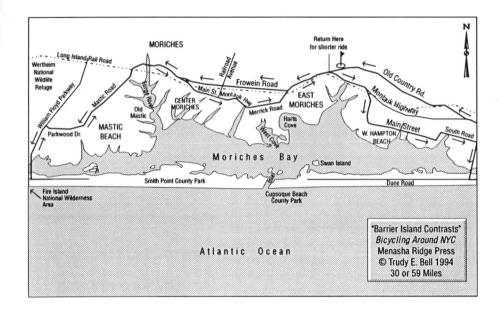

The air felt more like March and definitely nippy (highs in the 40s and low 50s) and we were grateful for our GoreTex's wind resistance. But we were also delighted at the sleepy nature—and lack of automobile traffic—of towns that in July weekends are crushed with Manhat-tanites vacationing as frantically as they work. We were also gratified by the off-season prices at the Grassmere Inn, which were literally half those charged during the peak summer months. (Even during the summer, midweek prices at B&Bs can be less than weekend rates, and reservations are easier to come by, even on the spur of the moment.)

The ride starts at Hampton Bays and heads west. The longer version takes you all the way to Smith Point County Park on Fire Island, where there is hiking, swimming, sunning yourself on the long beach, and overnight camping. Be aware, though, that the traffic is substantially heavier in the western portion. The shorter version of this ride turns around in Eastport, to concentrate on the more rustic eastern parts.

Both options allow you to spend a night at one of the bed-and-breakfast inns in Westhampton Beach or Quogue. If you want to take the shorter ride but still have your heart set on sleeping under the stars, you can camp at Sears Bellows Pond County Park just west of the ride's start. Experienced cyclists might enjoy joining this ride with the other Long Island rides in this book for a multiday trip exploring the entire eastern part of Suffolk County. See the introduction for some suggestions.

To get to Hampton Bays by public transportation, take the Montauk line of the Long Island Rail Road. (For information on obtaining a pass for taking your bicycle on the Long Island Rail Road, see the preface.) If you drive from New York City, take the Long Island Expressway almost to its end; at Exit 71, take New York State Route 24 southeast (toward Flanders) until it ends at the Montauk Highway (New York State Route 80); turn left into Hampton Bays. You can park your car at the railroad station, at Sears Bellows Pond County Park (which

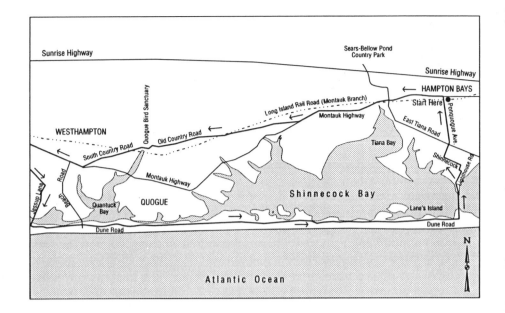

Route 24 passes), or—if you're a guest—at the B&B of your choice. Either way, the journey from midtown Manhattan is a minimum of two hours.

The Hampton Bays "station" of the LIRR has no building. Passengers step off the train onto wide concrete aprons on either side of the tracks, which go right through the center of the village. But don't despair of lack of food, water, or bathrooms. From the Hampton Bays station, which is on Ponquogue Avenue, ride a short block north, turning left at the light onto the main Montauk Highway to head west. Pedal carefully, for even during the off season this main stretch of road through Hampton Bays is a busy shopping district. You might prefer walking your bike on the sidewalk to examine your pick of delis, pizza parlors, bagel shops, diners, and other tempting stores.

After you pass the intersection with New York State Route 24 (with its signs to the Sunrise Highway, State Route 27), the first right-hand turn is Bellows Pond Road. If you're camping in Sears Bellows Pond County Park and want to register and stash your gear—or if you simply want to give the park a look-see—turn right (north). A quarter of a mile after you ride under the Sunrise Highway, turn left into the park.

The park, whose scrubby pines in sandy soil is typical of the Long Island pine barrens, has more than a dozen ponds and wetlands. Both the tent campsite and the trailer campsite overlook bodies of water. There is also a separate bicycle hostel area, where cyclists arriving under pedal power are entitled to stay for free. For details about bike camping, especially during the off season, call the Suffolk County Parks Department at (516) 567-1700. The number specifically for Sears Bellows Pond County Park is (516) 728-4480.

To return to the Montauk Highway, retrace your route: turn right out of the park onto Bellows Pond Road, under the Sunrise Highway, and make your first right onto the Montauk Highway.

Soon the Montauk Highway develops a wide painted shoulder—a feature blessedly common on many of Long Island's main roads. After the road passes under the train tracks of the LIRR, you are surrounded by wooded land. Watch for a yellow sign warning you of an upcoming "Y" intersection; bear right at the "Y" at the Lalanterna Italian Restaurant onto Old Country Road, which also has a wide painted shoulder. Eventually, the painted shoulder disappears, but no matter: the traffic is light, the road pretty and gently rolling through wooded land dotted with private homes.

At the first stop sign, turn right onto Lewis Road to cross the railroad tracks, and then make an immediate left to continue on Old Country Road. After about a mile, at the stop sign, you'll cross Suffolk County Route 104 (Quogue Riverhead Road), and Old Country Road becomes what its name advertises: an old country road only a lane and a half wide, through rural pastures and woods.

The road bends left and crosses the railroad tracks—a route you eventually want to take. But on the right Jim and I were intrigued by the small signs for the Quogue Wildlife Refuge and the Charles Banks Belt Nature Center of the New York State Department of Environmental Conservation. We pulled into the small gravel lot and picked up the literature in the little kiosk, which has a wooden gate admitting visitors to what is described as a "multisensory experience in nature."

Maybe it's just my prejudice against zoos, but I was taken aback to see the peacocks, turkeys, and crows in what seemed to me rather small chickenwire cages. "But they like it in concentration camps," Jim objected. "They're protected from their natural predators and get three meals a day." A more pleasant area was the Old Ice Pond, where Jim and I tempted the resident geese and swans to come up to our outstretched hands.

The 200-acre refuge, founded in 1934, is open every day from 9 A.M. to 5 P.M., with flat hiking trails available to people wearing comfortable walking shoes. The mile-long Main Trail passes through all the main habitats excepting one with dwarf pines. The quarter-mile trail through the Fairy Dell Tract leads you through wet woodland and a fresh-water swamp into a tidal brackish marsh with views of the Quantuck estuary. There is also a nature center building that is open Tuesdays and Thursdays from 1:30-4 P.M., but we were there at the wrong time to visit. Public restrooms, located near the deer pen, are open in the spring, summer, and fall.

Leaving the wildlife refuge, continue on your way along Old Country Road, which after crossing the railroad tracks changes its name to South Country Road. The road is flat and lightly wooded, with a few small buildings of light industries. This pleasant road soon dead-ends in a "T" intersection at the Montauk Highway, where you turn right (west) onto its wide painted shoulder.

Now you have another choice. If you've made reservations to stay in one of the bed-and-breakfast inns in Westhampton Beach and you want to lighten your bike of your overnight kit, in a few hundred yards take the first left-hand turn onto Aspatuck Road. If you want to continue the main ride, keep heading west on the Montauk highway and skip down to the double asterisks (**).

Aspatuck Road will take you to the heart of Westhampton Beach. A quarter of a mile after joining the road, be sure to bear right at the "Y" intersection to stay on it. Another quarter of a mile later, turn right at the "T" intersection onto

Main Street. To reach the Grassmere Inn, make the first left onto Beach Lane, and turn right at number 7 into the inn.

We ended up here by accident, having asked at a local bike shop where we might stay. There are a number of others, such as the Seafield House (516) 288-1559 one block east on Seafield Lane and The Inn at Quogue a mile farther east and passed by the ride's return loop. Both came highly recommended, although I was not able to visit.

The rambling Grassmere Inn, which has been a rooming house since 1900, is run year-round by Mrs. Barbara Caricola and her three daughters. We dumped our duffels upstairs in Room 3 and learned that the inn offers a choice of rooms, some with shared bath and some with private bath. Each of two cottages in the back has a living room and a kitchen as well as one or two bedrooms—perfect for a group. We liked the cozy, homey atmosphere of the open porch and sitting room.

Standard with the room price is a self-service extended continental breakfast (cereal and fruit along with home-baked pastries, juice, and coffee); early guests can enjoy tea in the late afternoon. In the making-life-easy department, the inn's proprietors will prepare a picnic lunch for you for your day's ride. Also, if you don't want to be bothered schlepping your bike on the LIRR, the inn has bicycles it loans to guests; you might want to call ahead to see if they have one your size.

The inn is just a few blocks from Westhampton Beach's beaches, so take your swimsuit, beach towel, and a long novel. It is also a few minutes' walk from shops, clubs, and several superb restaurants: in an exotic mood, we ordered sea skate at The Patio, a restaurant complete with flagstones and greenhouse atmosphere.

To return to the basic ride from Westhampton Beach, head straight north on Beach Road until it ends at the Montauk Highway, and then turn left to continue west, past a pizzeria and the other various small businesses on the outskirts of town.

(**) About a mile later, at the light, bear right onto another Old Country Road (Suffolk County Route 71); you'll know you've done it right if you pass Beaver Lake on your right. This road, too, has nice wide painted shoulders and is graced with woods on both sides. Don't accelerate too fast, though, for coming up is a major hazard: railroad tracks are laid diagonally across the road. Dismount and walk your bike across to avoid a major spill.

Now, you just stay on this pleasant road for another four miles, past Bide-a-Wee animal adoption center and the Cornell University Long Island Duck Research Center (the Long Island duck, by the way, is the one usually featured in menus as duck a l'orange). After the golf course of the Long Island Wyandanch Club, the road degenerates into potholes, but you'll be leaving it soon.

Go straight at the flashing yellow light, then turn left at the dead-end sign, and stop at the Montauk Highway. Now you have to make your decision whether to take the shorter or the longer ride. At this point, you've ridden nearly 13 miles; although that is less than half the length of the shorter ride, the return takes a longer route. If you opt for the shorter ride, turn left (east) onto the Montauk Highway and skip down two pages to the quadruple asterisks (****).

If you're heading all the way west to Smith Point County Park, turn right onto the Montauk Highway and continue with the directions below.

Of course, you want to get away from this traffic as soon as possible, so three-quarters of a mile father west, at the next flashing yellow light, turn right onto Frowein Road (Suffolk County Route 98 West). Frowein Road, also called the Moriches Bypass, has nice wide painted shoulders with a good surface, which along with the woods on both sides make up for the moderately heavy traffic.

If you brake for bakeries, keep a watch out for Railroad Avenue two miles ahead, which goes right past the Center Moriches railroad station of the Long Island Rail Road. If you hang a left on Railroad Avenue and go down half a block, you can refresh yourself with the impressive baked goods at the Hometown Bakery and Deli. Then resume your westward travel on Frowein Road.

At the next super-busy intersection, where Frowein Road joins several others, follow the signs for the Montauk Highway (Route 80) west, carefully watching the traffic. About a mile later, after the Montauk Highway crosses over the Forge River, take the first left onto the moderately busy Mastic Road. You'll stay on this main road until it ends about four miles later, though its name changes to Parkwood Drive as it eventually bears right.

At the "T" intersection, turn left onto the four-lane William Floyd Parkway, and ride that also to its end on Fire Island two-and-a-half miles south. The four lanes will funnel down to two to cross a narrow drawbridge. Ride carefully on the metal grates, which give remarkably little friction between your tires and the road. The bridge will take you over an inlet to the Great South Bay, which opens to your right.

The Smith Point for which Smith Point County Park is named is actually on the mainland jutting into the bay, visible as the point of land down and to your right. The park itself is on Fire Island, a sandbar barrier island paralleling Long Island's southern coast.

Fire Island is a good 35 miles long and only about a quarter-mile wide. In the early 1970s it had the reputation of being a swinging hot spot for cruising young singles both straight and gay, a steamy lifestyle inspiring at least one potboiler paperback (called, surprise, *Fire Island*). Most notable, perhaps, is Fire Island Pines, which every July 4 is the site for the annual Invasion of the Drag Queens, flocked by hundreds of men clad in negligees, ballroom gowns, spiked heels, or nuns' habits (a revelry started in 1975 initially as a protest against discrimination toward gay men). For better or worse, all the towns that were the center of that action—real or literary—are more than 10 miles west, separated from you by the nearly trackless sand dunes of Smith Point County Park land and the Fire Island National Wilderness Area—although about a mile west of the Smith Point park ranger station there is a "clothes optional" bathing beach.

Smith Point County Park is one of nine major Suffolk County Parks offering overnight camping. There are defined sites for RVs and tents near cinder-block buildings with flush toilets. If you meet very restrictive rules about self-contained water and waste—which I doubt most bike campers could—there is also overnight camping on the dunes. Unlike the Montauk or Cedar Point parks, there are no free camp sites designated specifically for cyclists. Since Jim and I were touring the area for this book in my parents' truck camper, that April we had our pick of the RV sites, and enjoyed the wind-whipped starry night and the washed-clean sunrise over the beach. Best of all was the sensation of being isolated out in the middle of nowhere—although, of course, we were only a couple of hours from what Frank Sinatra immortalized in song as "the city that never sleeps."

The road leaving Smith Point Park takes you past parking lots for tens of thousands of cars with under-the-road passageways to the beach, giving you some idea of the scale of the summer crowds for which the park is prepared. (Although one summer Saturday when John King and I were here years before I was writing this book, we were surprised at how few people were around . . .). The road bends right and carries you onto a two-lane drawbridge over the bay; watch your bicycle tires on the metal grates.

You are now riding on the William Floyd Parkway, named after one of the signers of the Declaration of Independence, whose estate about a mile east in Mastic has now been converted into a national park. Three-quarters of a mile past the bridge, the four-lane parkway develops a wide painted shoulder, perfect for cycling. There is also a 7-11 and a couple of other convenience stores along the way for refilling your water bottles and your gullet.

Two miles north of the drawbridge, turn right at a light onto Parkwood Drive. You're now riding through an unostentatious residential neighborhood. Follow the road as it bends left, turning right at the end onto Robinwood Drive and taking the next left onto the busy Mastic Road (here reality differs from what is shown on the Hagstrom map). Now you stay on this road for about three miles to the end, watching traffic carefully and not jumping the signals, some of which are delayed green. As compensation, you'll have plenty of temptation for deli sandwiches and ice cream. At the "Y" intersection with Herkimer Street, bear right to stay on Mastic Road.

Less than a quarter mile later, turn right at the "T" intersection onto the busy Montauk Highway (Route 80). Now, in terms of directions, your life is fairly easy: stay on the well-marked Montauk Highway for the next eight miles, through all its turns and name changes. First you'll ride past a shopping mall and the Aiello Nursery on your right, which in April was featuring the tiniest, cutest evergreens.

About a mile after joining the highway, bear right at the major "Y" intersection, following the signs to Center Moriches. When you get to Center Moriches, the highway briefly changes its name to Main Street; along with this stretch of stores there is also a bike shop on your left. Outside of town, when Jim and I were there, just before the East Moriches School, there was on the right a giant round boulder with a life-size painted sculpture of an eagle struggling to take off, and a fire-charred house behind it. By the time you take this ride, undoubtedly the burned-out house will have been razed, but I wonder if they'll preserve the eagle . . .

Half a mile later, the road bends left at the East Moriches Soldiers and Sailors Memorial. A mile and a half beyond that, you'll pass the small Spadaro Airport on your left. On a sunny mid-April day, the local sport seemed to be for small planes to take aloft jumpers, whose billowing parachutes opened into brilliant purple and magenta sections, gently drifting their passenger back to earth.

That airport is your warning landmark. The Montauk Highway bends right, past the blocked-off entrance to Old Country Road where you first made your decision to take the longer ride.

(****) The Montauk Highway crosses a couple of small bridges over Seatuck Creek and East River, both of which are small creeks. Now begin to watch carefully. At the white guardrail, where the Montauk Highway bears left, you go right onto South Country Road.

What a blessed relief from traffic! And the houses amid the woods are delightful. You'll coast down gently to the flood plain of the Speonk River, where in April the water from the Moriches Bay was gently lapping at the right-hand edge of the very road. The view of the bay opens on the right. The road turns into a country lane barely wide enough for two cars to pass.

A mile later, at the "T" intersection, turn left onto Apacuck Point Road, then right at the next "T" intersection onto South Road, over Beaverdam Creek and through the Westhampton Country Club.

A few tenths of a mile later, turn right at the stop sign onto Potunk Lane; you can see that this intersection is one block before road ends at a "T" intersection a grocery store just ahead. By the way, if you're riding any time but during the summer season and you need to stock up on water or snacks, this is the place to do it. Because of strict zoning laws, there are virtually no services for the next ten miles, and the few that do exist are closed off-season.

Follow Potunk Lane as it bends a couple of times and then becomes Jessup Lane. Jessup Lane will carry you over a small drawbridge over Moneybogue Bay; you can see the water through the grating below your bicycle tires. The road ends at a "T" intersection before the aqua and white structure of the Swordfish Beach Club.

Turn left onto Dune Road. You are now pedaling along the single road that runs along the spine of another sandbar barrier island, and for full scenic value you will stay on it until its end nine miles ahead.

One after another, you'll pass large, sleek beach homes, any one of which could be featured in *Architectural Digest* for its geometric lines and vast picture windows. Most of the houses are so large, in fact, that they take up most of their lot, and gave me the impression of shouldering each other for room. Some of them are rather extravagant; one with a cupola bears the whimsical name Taj Mama. Every now and then a more modest—and much older—true beach bungalow is tucked between its lavish neighbors, and the more open space around it made me sigh a little in relief at the contrast. The route is also dotted with several major private beach clubs: Quantuck Beach Club, Surf Club of Quogue, Quogue Beach Club. Between residences, you catch glimpses of the sun glinting off the water in the Quantuck Bay to your left, but either houses or the natural rise in the land usually obscures the Atlantic Ocean to your right.

This island is accessible to mainlandlubbers only through four bridges. The first one you reach, about a mile after the Jessup Lane bridge that brought you here, is at Beach Lane. By turning left here and riding just under a mile, you can return to the Grassmere Inn (number 7 Beach Lane) from this spot. The next bridge, at Post Lane, is a couple miles further ahead, just past the Surf Club of Quogue. (By the way, if you are staying at the Inn at Quogue, you can get there from here by turning left onto the Post Lane Bridge, then turning left at the "T" intersection onto Quogue Street and riding another block; the inn will be on your right.)

From my viewpoint, it is east of the Post Lane Bridge that this ride along the backbone of the barrier island turns truly wonderful. The area is virtually unpopulated, with salt marsh grass on the flood plane to your right bending before the wind. On your left is the Quogue Village Wetlands Preserve. There are boardwalks for bird-watchers to stroll through the marsh, but alas! they are barred by gates to all excepting Quogue town and village residents with permits. Keep your eyes skyward: the mid-April day I was there, I saw a small plane towing a sailplane that it then cut loose to glide and soar—but more exciting than that, I saw a mid-air refueling of a helicopter!

In the middle of this wildness, you'll pass the isolated private residences of Round Dunes to your right, where the small circular apartment buildings on stilts look exactly like flying saucers from a 1950s science fiction film.

East of Hampton Beach, the wetlands open wide to your left, with graceful-necked snowy egrets and other long-legged waterfowl stilting through the water and bending reeds. To your right rise classic sand dunes tufted with dune grass whose sparse roots keep the sand from disappearing before the wind. Dotting the dunes every quarter-mile or so are small, unpretentious beach bungalows that must date back at least half a century. Behind them, unseen, you hear the crashing of the Atlantic surf and smell the salt air. Ride slowly these few miles and savor this, how a barrier island should be.

Eventually, you'll pass the Hampton Beach Club, with its resort marina, parking, and signs that four-wheel-drive vehicles are allowed to drive along the beach in the early morning and later afternoon . . . Half a mile beyond is the Sand Bar Beach Club, east of which you'll start to see more houses and other beach clubs, including summer rentals. Ride through here in April when their shingles are out and put your dibs on where you'd like to spend your summer weekends. A few hundred yards later, you'll pass the huge parking lot of a town park. This town park lies at the westernmost border of the Shinnecock County Park West, which is obviously set up for the influx of tens of thousands of summer sun-worshippers.

Now ahead and to your left you can see the concrete arch of the Ponquogue Bridge. Its intersection with Dune Road is marked by a huge interchange with a traffic light—the only one on the entire island, as far as I could tell. In mid-April the emptiness and silence made this preparation for heavy traffic seem strange, but I wager the feeling is very different in August. Eventually you'll cross this bridge, the fourth and easternmost one joining the mainland to this sandbar. But for the moment, you may as well continue to the far eastern end, past the Shinnecock Commercial Dock with its fishing boats, past the couple of waterfront restaurants and cocktail lounges.

The road ends at a rather small Coast Guard lighthouse with an automated rotating and flashing beacon, warning small boats that they are approaching the choppy waters of the exceedingly narrow inlet to the Shinnecock Bay. Here you can rest a moment on a bench or open your lunch at one of the picnic tables overlooking the jumbled boulders, enjoying the occasional salt spray from a breaking ocean wave or a maneuvering fishing boat. Here you can gaze at the western end of another barrier island just a few hundred feet in front of you. But to reach that point, literally within shouting distance, you would have to ride all the way around Shinnecock Bay—probably a distance of ten miles.

By the way, you may find it entertaining to also walk out onto the beach facing the Atlantic Ocean. I did, and was astonished to see surfers in full wet suits hanging ten before the rollers. Malibu it ain't, but California, eat your heart out!

When you're ready, turn around and retrace your route a mile back to Ponquogue Bridge. It was at that moment, when I practically flew west, that I realized how strong the steady headwind had been on the ride east. Turn right across the Ponquogue Bridge, whose very new structure rises high over the water of the Shinnecock Bay. Look down to your right and you will see the remains of the old, original drawbridge, now serving duty on each shore as town piers. Just beyond it is Warner Island.

Once over the bridge, continue straight onto Lighthouse Road and follow the signs around past the Coast Guard station on your right.

Worth a stop is Tully's Seafood Market and Restaurant on your left. The restaurant is open only six months out of the year, and for dinner only, Fridays through Sundays in April, May, and September, and seven days a week during the summer. But the fish market is open year-round, and offers the most wonderful and somewhat unusual New England clam chowder. The chowder is not thickened; its broth is basically milk floating with butter, with the vegetables including peas and the clams so fresh they are sweet. Jim and I each had a generous cup, plus between us polished off an entire loaf of the freshly-baked, egg-dough, poppy-seed bread, riding away most satisfied.

Turn left onto Shinnecock Avenue. Less than half a mile later, at the next stop sign, turn right onto Ponquogue Avenue, where you can pedal in the wide painted shoulders. A mile later, you'll reach the railroad station of Hampton Bays for your journey back to New York City. Or return to the directions at the beginning of the ride to make your way back to your campsite or B&B.

MONTAUK POINT EXPLORER

Suffolk County, New York

Montauk is the summer retreat of the rich and not-so-rich. At more than 100 miles from New York City, it was once considered so far away that it really was a retreat. Now it is less than three hours away on the Long Island Rail Road, and is a favorite watering hole of many with beach houses or "summer shares" in a jointly rented house. Still, even now the distance is far enough to give you the feeling of truly getting away from echoing canyons of glass and steel. For the most relaxing results, plan this venture to be a minivacation of three or four days—particularly during the middle of the week when the place is the least crowded.

In addition to cycling, there's the beach. The ocean fishing into the surf from the beach at Montauk County Park is supposed to be excellent, so if that's your sport bring a collapsible rod and reel. Swimmers and sunbathers, bring your swimsuit, towel, sunscreen, and a long novel. By August the Atlantic Ocean is almost bathwater warm from the Gulf Stream current. Since it's a resort area, there are hundreds of overnight options ranging from seaside motels to bed-and-breakfast inns. And if you prefer camping, there are two parks on the way to Montauk Point that admit bike campers for free.

Since I am something of a loner and abhor mob scenes, I prefer to avoid the crush of summer crowds. But summer in this part of the world has nothing to do with the

Ride Ratings

Length: 29, 37 or 44 miles
Configuration: figure 8
Difficulty: flat to rolling; stiff headwind on eastbound leg; traffic is light to moderate
Surface: good pavement throughout; optional dirt ride

—Highlights: This ride can be combined with "Cedar Point Park Pilgrimage" for a total of up to 65 miles; it features the historic Montauk Lighthouse, local lobster and clam rolls, the beach, and camping at Hither Hills State Park or Montauk County Park.

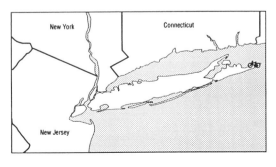

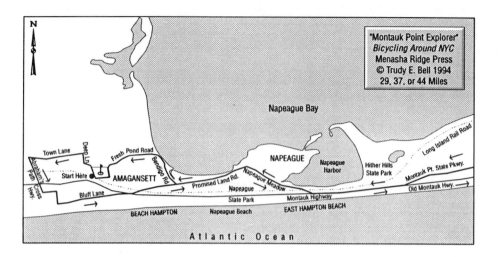

solstice and the equinox: it is culturally defined as that time between Memorial Day and Labor Day. Thus, a wonderful off-season time to plan a trip is the second or third weekend in September—the ocean is still warm, the weather mild (better for bicycling than August's humid heat), the hotels and motels still open—perhaps with slightly lower rates and greater availability, and the beaches nearly vacant. But don't make the mistake of doing (as I did) an off-season vacation in the spring. Unless you like raw, blustery days with fitful sun, late April is still too early for reliable cycling weather. The tip of Long Island is the last place winter leaves the tri-state area—but it is also the place where summer lingers into late September and early October.

The ride to Montauk Point is very popular with cyclists, particularly of the long-distance high-speed variety, and you will likely wave to many along the way. If you visit in May, you may even get to watch the lean, intrepid pedalers going for the annual Montauk Century (100 miles from New York City to Montauk Point).

The only drawback to this route is that much of it is unavoidably on the main Montauk Highway (New York State Route 27, Montauk County Route 80). I've designed this ride to parallel the highway by side roads as much as possible, but for long stretches the Montauk Highway is the only access. There is a silver lining: paved shoulders at least six feet wide, almost as good as separate lanes for cyclists. Also, the drivers are used to cyclists and tend to be considerate. Another trick for avoiding the moderately heavy traffic, at least for the first half of the trip, is to start your ride as early in the morning as possible. (Anyone game for sunrise over the Atlantic Ocean?)

The two longer versions of this ride begin and end in the resort community of Amagansett. The shortest version calls for you to board the Long Island Rail Road train in Montauk to return to either Amagansett or New York City; if you took the train out from the city and will be returning directly, there is no additional fare, as both Montauk and Amagansett are in the last fare zone. (*Note:* at certain times of the day between Memorial Day and Labor Day trains will not admit bikes. See the preface for information on obtaining a pass for your bicycle on the LIRR.)

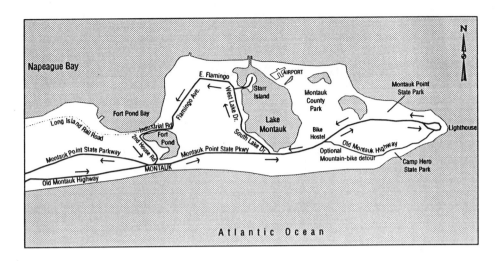

For a really long ride of 55 or 65 miles, strong riders can combine the trip to Montauk Point with the ride to Cedar Point Park, checking out two lighthouses: one at each end (see "Cedar Point Park Pilgrimage"). If you're planning a two-wheeled vacation of several days or a week, you can link both these rides with the ones to Shelter Island, Orient Point, and Mattituck, for a total round-trip distance of more than 150 miles (see "Shelter Island Vacation," "East to the Orient," and "Wine Country Wanderer").

The Montauk Point ride starts at the Amagansett station of the Long Island Rail Road (the "Cedar Point Park Pilgrimage" also starts from here). If you have driven out, you may park your car in the train station lot for the day, but overnight may get you a parking ticket; check with the local authorities. Since this railroad station is no more than a glorified wooden bus shelter, the ride starts with a small circle past some public restrooms and a store to pick up some snacks. But if you like seafood, save most of your appetite for some of the local delicacies nine or ten miles into the ride.

Turn left out of the east exit of the Amagansett railroad station, cross the railroad tracks, and make a sharp left onto Old Stone Highway (if you went to the south exit, you'll realize your mistake when you're faced with crossing the busy Montauk Highway; look left across the small station parking lot, and you'll see the east exit). As you ride, you may see some morning golfers on the green of the South Fork Country Club to your right.

After scarcely half a mile, turn left onto Sidehill Road. Follow it as it makes a sharp right, where it changes name to Deep Lane; cattails wave gently to your left, and an orchard is to your right. The road then makes an unexpectedly steep but short climb—enough to get your cardiovascular system going.

Turn left at the stop sign onto Town Lane. Here you're in absolute farm country, pedaling through cornfields. Enjoy the corn's rustling and its fresh fragrance. After a little more than a mile, turn left onto Abraham's Path. Here, ride slowly, for in a few hundred yards you'll turn left into a town park, where you'll find public restrooms. Fill your water bottles, for you'll be going through some arid territory before reaching the seafood stands seven miles ahead.

When exiting the park, turn left to stay on Abraham's Path. Ride over the railroad tracks and cross the busy Montauk Highway at the light. On the south-east corner of this intersection is the Amagansett General Store, where you may pick up fruit, raisins, or other snacks. Marvelously convenient, the store is open Sunday through Thursday from 6:30 A.M. until midnight, and 24 hours on Friday and Saturday.

Continue straight onto Cross Highway. Turn left at the "T" intersection onto Skimhampton Road, which will carry you onto Further Lane, which is lined with majestic trees. In less than a quarter of a mile, turn right at the next "T" intersection onto Indian Well Highway, and then left at the end onto Bluff Lane (the very appealing beach in front of you, alas, is only for town residents).

On Bluff Lane there are a remarkable number of fascinating natural sights and extravagant architectures to enjoy. The sandy land to your right is part of the Nature Conservancy's Double Dunes Preserve, so keep your eyes alert for their two windswept ridges. When you pass the Ocean Dunes Apartments, note the whale weather vane on the cupola.

In about three-quarters of a mile, there is the Town Marine Museum on your right, marked by an American flag and two anchors out front. Open seven days a week between 10 A.M. and 5 P.M., you can explore three floors of artifacts of the 19th century whaling industry, plus some sailing craft and tools of today's commercial fishermen. More or less across from the museum, on your left behind the first large hedge, note that in the yard of the shake house there is what looks for all the world to be a former windmill.

Continue straight on Bluff Lane, past the intersection where Atlantic Avenue plunges down to your right to the free public Atlantic Avenue beach. It is here that you really are riding along the edge of a bluff that commands an impressive view of the Atlantic Ocean. You'll pass some gray geometrical beach houses with domed skylights worthy of southern California rather than Long Island, and showing how the other 0.1 percent live; when I took this route in early July, there were also some gorgeous stands of daylilies and brilliant red roses twining around white fences.

Bluff Lane diagonally intersects the busy Montauk Highway. Cross the highway following the diagonal, watching carefully for the high-speed traffic, and continue straight onto Cranberry Hole Road. You'll stay on this level road (which the map says changes name to Promised Land Road, although there is no sign indicating that) for the next two and a half miles.

Part of Napeague State Park, the land here is essentially undeveloped; the trees get shorter and sparser until you are pedaling in the open sun with only scrub oak and scrub pine eking out an existence in the sandy soil. On a warm day, this unprotected part of the ride can be very hot, so don't push it. Take your time to enjoy the austere beauty of this miniature desert with its sand dunes off in the distance to your right.

After you've been riding about 10 minutes, you'll see a lone brick chimney several stories tall far off on private property to your left, which may have belonged once to an industrial furnace. You'll also pass an occasional beach home, and eventually the Multi Aquaculture Systems fish farm with its rusty warehouses; owned by the state of New York, the fish farm is not open to the public. By this time, the sand dunes are next to you on your right.

Eventually you'll reach an intersection where Napeague Meadow Road heads off to your right—a direction you also want to follow. (*Note:* if you continue straight here instead of turning, the road—now called Lazy Point Road—leads you on an optional 3-1/2-mile detour to visit the town of Napeague, which is distinguished by having a high proportion of boats to houses. There are several boat launching ramps on Lazy Point, including at least one for the public. But be forewarned: nowhere in this circuit of quiet back streets is there any public water, restroom, or a concession. When you're done, return to this intersection and take Napeague Meadow Road.)

Aptly enough, Napeague Meadow Road indeed goes through a large open meadow—or, more accurately, a salt marsh. Here you'll see a classic case of what's wrong with this part of the world: the marsh is quite beautiful in its marshy way, but its long vistas are marred by high-tension power lines and a guy-wired radio broadcasting tower topped with flashing red lights. Ah, Progress . . .

As you ride down Napeague Meadow Road, you'll be nearing what looks like a ship off your left. This is the Art Barge, the home of the Victor D'Amico Institute of Art. Its shell is indeed that of an old Navy barge beached on the shore of Napeague Harbor. There are no exhibits, and it is not open to the public: it is a school started in the late 1950s by D'Amico, a renowned director of education of the Museum of Modern Art. Today laymen, students, teachers, and professional artists can come for a few weeks' retreat and study with some of today's masters in media ranging from collage to clay to photography.

Just after the entrance to the D'Amico Institute, GET OFF AND WALK YOUR BIKE over the railroad tracks, which are diagonal to the road. Napeague Meadow Road ends at the busy Montauk Highway; carefully cross the highway, whose speed limit is a hefty 55 miles per hour, and head left on its broad, paved shoulder to continue east.

Within a quarter mile after joining the Montauk Highway, you at last have the opportunity to try a lobster roll at the stand called—ready for this?—The Lobster Roll. If you're a lobster fan, this is your one and only chance; I blew my opportunity, I discovered, when I held out for the Clam Bar another quarter mile ahead on the left, which does not serve lobster at all. Specialization. A clam roll, by the way, consists of deep-fried breaded clams on a hotdog bun, served with lemon and tartar sauce. Very fresh and sweet.

Now, you're on a neck of land with water visible on both sides: the Napeague harbor to your left and the Atlantic Ocean to your right. You're also at the beginning of what seems to be row of seaside hotels, with such names as Sun Haven, Sea Crest, Driftwood, and the Inn at Napeague. These are but the first of a host of places to stay. There are so many you might just be able to ride up and try for a room unannounced; on the other hand, this area is so popular in the summer that you may have better luck with a real reservation. *But note:* in the summer, many hotels and B&Bs out here insist that guests stay two nights on ordinary weekends and three nights on holiday weekends, complicating the plans of people who would prefer to move from one place to another.

The western boundary of Hither Hills State Park is quite evident because suddenly all buildings disappear, leaving the untouched dunes and scrub vegetation. Less than half a mile later, bear right at the "Y" intersection onto the Old Montauk Highway; ride carefully, because there is no shoulder. Three-quarters of a mile later, on your right, is the entrance to Hither Hills State Park campground.

Even if you don't intend to camp, a visit to the park is worth the detour. Hither Hills park has a general store, restrooms, hot showers, bathhouses, playing fields, a children's playground, and access through a line of dunes to a wide, beautiful, sandy beach. If you want to enjoy a lunch alfresco, the picnic grounds have water spigots and stone barbecue grills. Walk through them all and take your pick. I particularly recommend the second picnic ground you'll encounter when you walk from the entrance gate, because its high bluffs offer a fine view of the ocean and a little hollow secludes some eating spots from the salty breeze.

For camping, reservations can be made up to 90 days in advance for a minimum of two nights. But if you simply show up and there is space, you can stay for just one night—very easy to do during the week. I was there on a Monday early in July and to my surprise, in spite of the Independence Day holiday, the beach was virtually empty and a good number of the camp sites were free as well. The following April, my cycling companion Jim Arth and I had the place nearly to ourselves. Since there are no trees is this area, the camp sites are open, so some modesty is required. Hither Hills does not have special facilities or rates for bicycle camping; you'll just have to fit in with all the tents and RVs. Fortunately, there are not too many RVs, since the sites do not have electrical, water, and sewer hookups. For more information on dates and rates, call 1-800-456-CAMP.

When you're ready to hit the road again, turn right out of the park to continue east on Old Montauk Highway, which starts rising and falling over some rolling terrain. Once you leave the eastern edge of the park, you'll enter the town of Montauk Beach. Once again, you'll be passing one beach motel after another, with such names as Wave Crest, Panorama View, Gurney's Inn, Sunrise Guest House B&B, Surfside Inn, and Burcliffe by the Sea (which advertised cottages and fireplaces).

In front of the Wave Crest, there is a sign warning CAUTION: TURTLES so stop to look for some on the roadside. In April I didn't see turtles, but ample numbers of gulls wheeled and cried overhead, punctuating the rhythmic pounding of the steel gray Atlantic surf. In between the homes and hotels, you'll glimpse views of the ocean to the right, and in July you may smell the perfume of honeysuckle twining around the vegetation.

At the end of Old Montauk Highway, turn right at the yield sign to rejoin the main Montauk Highway (Route 27), staying once again on the wide, paved shoulder to ride through the downtown of Montauk. In a few hundred yards, you'll pass the Second House Museum on your right, which is in the oldest house in Montauk, built in 1746.

At Kirk Park on your left, take a few minutes to lock your bike and walk along the path to your left between 8-foot-high hedgerows of native marsh grasses. You'll reach a quiet, contemplative area with stone benches and a smiling green stone turtle for children; there is also a memorial tablet with a poem to Montauk Point. From the covered pier, you can stand with a fisherman or two and watch the windsurfers far out on Fort Pond.

Now you just continue east on the Montauk Highway all the way out to Montauk Point. The highway is characterized by long rises and long coasts. If you have a headwind, as I did both visits, just put 'er in low gear and have patience—all the more time to enjoy the scenery.

Half a mile after you rejoin the highway, you'll pass the Montauk Bike Shop, which offers rentals—an option if you do not feel like schlepping your bike out here by train. Also, if you're hungry, some of the shops in town are open even on a Sunday. After about a mile, you'll pass Rita's Stables on your left, which advertises horseback rides on the beach—something I highly recommend for lovers. While I have not gone horseback riding along the Montauk beaches, I did so one long-shadowed sunrise when my cruise ship was anchored off Ensendada in Baja California, and it was unbelievably romantic. Consider splurging to capture some of that spirit here.

Continuing another couple of miles east on your two-wheeled steed, you'll pass Montauk County Park on your left, another one of the Suffolk County parks that offers free camping to bike campers and beach camping for off-road vehicles. The main entrance is on East Lake Road, off to your left. There are restrooms, an Indian museum, and picnic areas. The bike camping areas are nestled apart in the brush, with wooden platforms for your sleeping bags and tents. After a rain you may prefer to pay a fee to stay in the standard campsites as the bicycle camping sites impressed me as having the potential of being a bit damp. For details about bike camping here, especially during the off season, call the Suffolk County Parks Department at (516) 567-1700.

Montauk County Park permits surfcasting for bluefish, weakfish, and striped bass, with no fee or registration required for reeling in dinner. You do, however, need a New York State fishing license to catch bass and perch in the park's freshwater Big Reed Pond; the season runs from the first Saturday in June to October 31. For more information, call (516) 668-5022.

After passing the park, the Montauk Highway begins a long steady climb, taking you past two horse ranches. Here you might want to stop for a moment to consider whether you want to continue on the main Montauk Highway all the way to Montauk Point, or opt for an off-road alternative that will take you the same destination.

If you want to stay on the reliable pavement, just follow your nose until you cannot travel any farther. At the crest, you have a view of the ocean, although it is rather blocked by vegetation. In a couple more miles, the Montauk Point State Park sign informs you you're almost at your destination, and you may see the lighthouse's light flashing in the distance. Right after entering the park's grounds, the highway's wide paved shoulder disappears. But as if to make up for that loss, the highway splits and the eastbound lane becomes a wide, one-way road. Within half a mile of entering the park, you'll be at the parking lot of the Montauk Point Lighthouse Museum. Skip down to the double asterisks (**) to continue your trip.

For more daring riders hankering for a little off-road adventure, look to your right as the Montauk Highway begins to climb just past the Montauk

County Park: you'll see a road in poor repair heading off past one of the horse ranches, and disappear into the trees beyond. The Hagstrom map of eastern Suffolk County indicates that this is a continuation of the Old Montauk Highway.

Ignore the DEAD END sign; it is a perfectly wonderful abandoned road, curvier than the map shows, winding through trees and past an occasional house, accompanied by 1940s-vintage telephone poles topped with ceramic insulators of a type seldom seen nowadays. After a mile and a quarter, the paved road abruptly ends at a gravel and dirt trail.

The trail is perfectly passable on a mountain bike, although Jim and I found that we preferred to walk or carry our skinny-tire road bikes over certain stony or muddy sections. The inconvenience was well worth it, for we felt as though we had suddenly walked back in time: when we emerged from the brush, we were confronted by a World War II-vintage red-and-white-checked radar station.

This long-rusted station belonged to the former Camp Hero, part of the Army's coastal defense system searching for U-boats in World War II. Camp Hero later became an Air Force base, and was ultimately decommissioned in 1980. As we walked our bikes among the abandoned bunkers, warehouses, heliport, and shop buildings, a four-foot exhaust fan began slowly turning in the wind, the unexpected grinding of its bearings causing us to jump as if spooked by a ghost.

What was most remarkable to both Jim and me, imbued with the cynicism of long-time denizens of New York City, was the excellent condition of these half-century-old ruins; there was no graffiti, no apparent vandalism, no stench of human urine or excrement. The decades-long history of Camp Hero is also apparent in its roads: some that by their decay were obviously 50 years old would suddenly meet ones that were equally obviously modern; others were in such ruin only a few chunks of remaining asphalt distinguished them from creek beds. All made fascinating riding, particularly since we were utterly alone—almost like the last people in the world.

There are so many roads with so many twists and turns, I cannot give you directions for getting yourself out to Montauk Point. All we did was head generally east, keeping the shoreline to our right and the flashing of the lighthouse ahead of us. Eventually we reemerged onto the portion of the Montauk Highway that is a one-way loop leading to the Montauk Point Lighthouse Museum. Just make a point of always staying on a cleared trail or road; it is also best if you're wearing long, light-colored pants and a long-sleeved shirt: this is prime country for deer ticks and their sometimes-incapacitating Lyme disease (see the introduction for more information).

(**) The Montauk Point Lighthouse Museum is open from 10:30 A.M. to 6 P.M. daily for a modest admission charge. After my 26-mile ride from Cedar Point Park, I bypassed the 137-step climb to the lighthouse's top, but am told it affords a fine view of Long Island's north fork and the shore of Connecticut.

The museum has a fascinating video on the workings of the Fresnel lenses that focus the light far out to sea, plus various historical exhibits and a gift shop. The lighthouse itself was authorized by President George Washington in 1795 and was completed two years later, and has been operated continuously since—making it the fourth oldest active lighthouse in the United States. The entrance to the museum is also the trailhead for a walking trail out along the bluffs above the ocean.

To continue your ride, turn right as you leave the lighthouse museum and folow the one-way road. In a hundred yards or so you'll come to the public cafeteria with bathrooms where you can refill your water bottles. The eating area also has large plate glass windows, so you can keep a watch on your bikes left outside. Don't make a big point of eating here, though, as the fare was—in Jim's words—typical tourist food at typical tourist prices, with even the seafood items being nothing special.

For your westbound return, leave the park by the same way you entered. The one-way road soon joins up with the other lane, and the wide paved shoulder resumes. In three miles, you'll again pass East Lake Drive and the entrance to Montauk County Park.

For the medium-length 38-mile ride, continue straight on the lane-wide paved houlder of the Montauk Highway for another seven miles and skip down to the quadruple asterisks (****), passing some landmarks familiar from your trip out.

For either the shortest 29-mile ride or the longest 44-mile ride, turn right at the Crow's Nest Restaurant and Inn onto Old West Lake Drive (Montauk County Route 70). To your right, between the quiet houses, you'll catch glimpses of Lake Montauk and you'll pass a smaller body of water on your left. After about a mile, continue right where your road joins West Lake Drive (Montauk County Route 77), riding on the wide painted shoulders. In another mile, you'll reach Snug Harbor on your right, with Star Island Road leading out to—surprise!—Star Island, home of two yacht clubs. If you're now craving an iced tea, you're in luck: both clubs are open to the public with restaurants and cocktail lounges. Star Island also has a U.S. Coast Guard Station, which features a yellow happy face painted on a fuel oil tank.

After exploring this little detour, continue north on West Lake Drive (Route 77), making the first left onto East Flamingo Avenue. After less than half a mile, turn left at the "T" intersection onto the busy Flamingo Avenue, continuing to ride on the wide painted shoulders. (Isn't it civilized of Long Islanders to offer that amenity to cyclists?) Begin a steady climb reaching the crest near a water tower shaped like a huge, gray, soft-ice-cream cone. Coast downhill for three-quarters of a mile.

For the shortest 29-mile ride, turn right into the Montauk station of the Long Island Rail Road. As this is the end of the rail line, you should have your pick of seats for the return back to New York City.

For the longest 44-mile ride, pass the railroad station, making the first right onto the unpromising sounding Industrial Drive, over the railroad tracks and past the power station—a section that turns out to be prettier than it sounds on paper. Make the first left onto Second House Road into suburbia. Turn right at the "T" intersection to rejoin the Montauk Highway (Route 27) heading west. (You may recognize the intersection with the Old Montauk Highway across the road.)

(****) Now, you'll stay on the Montauk Highway for the next five miles. In several miles the highway will crest to command a view of the entire Napeague

Bay. Half a mile later is an entrance to Hither Hills State Park to the left. On my return along this route in early July, by this time I was enjoying a tailwind and flying effortlessly at 16 to 18 miles per hour, making up for the considerable headwind that slowed me to 6 or 7 miles per hour on my way out. But be prepared; in one direction you will encounter a headwind—and if you sailed out here, allow twice the time to work your way back on the return.

Eventually you'll pass all the landmarks you noted on the way out, including the Clam Bar and the Lobster Roll, with the Art Barge ahead to your right. Shortly thereafter, turn right onto Napeague Meadow Road to continue retracing the morning's trip. Turn left at the "T" intersection onto what is marked as Lazy Point Road, but what the map calls Promised Land Road. Ride another mile and a half, past the chimney on the right. Eventually the road becomes Cranberry Hole Road.

Turn right at the "Y" intersection onto Bendigo Road, a quiet, shady lane that offers relief after the beating sun. Turn right at the "T" intersection onto Abrams Landing Road and take an immediate left onto Cross Highway, passing the Devon Yacht Club and its private beach. Take your time pedaling past the quiet beach homes—the amount of traffic you'll be encountering may be guessed from the fact that in one spot local kids have erected a basketball hoop over the road. Where the trees give way to another private beach with picnic tables, rest for a few minutes for a few sips of water and the view across the Napeague Bay—your last view of the ocean on this ride.

Then follow the road around to the left where it becomes Fresh Pond Road, which begins to roll a bit up and down. Less than a quarter of a mile off to your left, you may notice seven very old cabins tucked away almost invisibly into the woods: the unprepossessing Devon's Fancy. I walked onto the grounds and immediately fell in love. But forget about trying to rent one of them. According to a man relaxing with his coffee and morning paper, the waiting list is fully 10 years long. But in case you should have a decade to wait, Devon's Fancy is owned by George Polassis of Polassis House Antiques, located on the corner of Hedges and Marsh in Amagansett. Sigh . . .

Turn left out of Devon's Fancy to continue on Fresh Pond Road. In another mile the road climbs uphill, passing the golf course of the South Fork Country Club off to your right. Turn right at the "T" intersection onto Abraham's Landing Road, cross the railroad tracks, and head straight into the east entrance of the Amagansett train station.

APPENDIX I
The Care & Feeding of the Bicycle

Bicycles have an almost indefinite lifetime, if given proper care. Just go look at the bicycles locked at any station of the Metro at Washington, D.C.; commonly you will see ones from the 1950s and earlier still in service.

The three simplest things that will maximize a bicycle's life are: always store it indoors, always ride with fully inflated tires, and try to minimize the dirt that collects on the chain.

By indoors, I mean in a place free from dampness. Moisture is metal's worst enemy. Through tiny nicks in the paint, a steel frame will begin to pit and rust. Ditto for any moving part not completely lubricated. The chain will rust and seize, wearing down the teeth of the chainwheels and freewheels. Tiny brown spots of rust on the rims of the wheels will impede braking. The rubber of the tires begins to stiffen and crack. Mildew can form on the handlebar bag. It is truly a crime. I have seen cases where, by thoughtless placement—say, under a plastic sheet on an open porch—a novice cyclist has in one winter turned a $500-plus bicycle literally into junk: for once a bike needs hundreds of dollars of refurbishing, it may not even be worth reclaiming.

Most open porches are not dry enough, even if the bike is covered by a plastic sheet, as the sheet itself can trap condensation underneath. Enclosed summer porches, garages, or basements are better. Ideal are basements that have been waterproofed with the French drain system, or the warm storage rooms of large apartment buildings. Best of all is somewhere in your apartment or house itself. Make sure it's EASILY accessible, though: if you have to always climb up a ladder to get it down from hooks above the doorway, you simply won't use it.

The rubber of tires and inner tubes is slightly porous, and even after a week of sitting still will lose enough pressure to be detected by a gauge. After two or three weeks, even a novice's fingers can feel that the tires are noticeably softer. After several months of sitting, the tires may be completely flat.

The pneumatic tires are most bicycles' only shock absorbers. Proper inflation is vital for several reasons. First, it means less work for you while riding. If the tires are squishy, your weight on the bike will compress them further so a larger surface area of rubber contacts the road. That translates into greater rolling resistance, and more effort in pedaling, as if you were always dragging a brake.

Second, a too-soft tire under the pressure of riding is more likely to allow the inner tube to be pinched by the rim, creating a greater chance of a flat. And that's no fun.

Third, if you hit a pothole or bump hard enough, soft tires may let the impact be felt right on your front wheel's metal rim. The resultant ding in the rim, if bad enough, could give rise to a constant bump-bump-bump as you try to brake and the brake pads encounter the ding each revolution (which could lessen braking), and could lessen the secure hold of the rim on the tire—increasing the potential for a blowout. In a worst case, you might have to replace the whole front wheel—an expensive penalty for simply forgetting to inflate the tires.

Examine the tires on your own bike; chances are, either on a label or embossed in the sidewall itself is a suggested tire pressure or range of pressures. Either buy a bicycle-tire pressure gauge, or a floor pump with a built-in gauge. Check the pressure each week—say, before each Saturday ride, and pump the tires up to the recommended figure.

Don't, however, figure that if a little is good, more is better: *do not* exceed the recommended pressure. The friction of riding (particularly on a hot day) and braking heats the air inside the tires, increasing its pressure. If overinflated, the inner tube can literally explode (I had an overinflated front tire blow itself right off the rim while I was standing still consulting a map at the base of a long hill down which I had just braked fast after coasting.)

Speaking of explosions, exercise great care if you are tempted to inflate your bicycle tires with the air hose at a gas station. Do it only in tiny, tiny bursts. That air comes out very fast to fill the huge volume of an automobile tire. As a teenager, I didn't recognize the hazard; the inner tube exploded, and my ears rang for literally 10 minutes.

The chain is inevitably going to get dirty. There's no helping the fact that dirt will leap up and cling to the oil. But develop the habit, after each ride, of brushing off the worst of the dirt with a soft cotton rag (*not* paper towels—they shred and leave little bits of paper on the chain). If the chain is positively encrusted, especially with sand or sandy dirt, then you might want to clean it more thoroughly with rubbing alcohol or kerosene, and put a tiny drop of motor oil or sewing-machine oil (*not* vegetable-based 3-in-1 oil) into each link. Remember, if that grit is on the chain, it is also grinding against the chainwheels and the freewheel cogs, wearing them down. And those are expensive parts, so you want them to last 10,000 or 15,000 miles.

Chains, on the other hand, stretch, and have a useful life of only 1000 or 2000 miles. Some cyclists make a point of installing a new one each spring. Chains are relatively cheap, so that is good preventive maintenance. You can easily check if your chain has stretched to the point where it needs to be replaced. Adjust the gear levers to place the chain on the largest chainwheel. With your fingers, try to lift the chain off the chainwheel. If you can lift it more than an eighth of an inch, it's time for a replacement.

By the way, rubbing alcohol is one of the cheapest, safest, and best grease-cutters around, and it leaves no residue. Use it to remove oil and grime from your bike's wheel rims and frame, as well as from your hands. I prefer it to kerosene, which can be absorbed through the skin (be sure to wear rubber gloves), has a toxic vapor, and leaves an oily film. Work with adequate ventilation, as both are flammable.

THE "TWO-MINUTE BIKE CHECK"

Before each ride, the American Youth Hostels, some commercial tour groups, and other organizations running bicycle tours have the participants run through a quick series of checks to make sure their bicycles are ready to hit the road. It's a great habit to acquire before you ride each week, too—particularly the first ride in spring after winter's hibernation.

Once you memorize all the steps, the check really does take only about two minutes—for you will be routinely maintaining the bike and the adjustments will be minimal. (It's also a great way to assess the condition of a second-hand bike you may be think about buying.) If you discover a problem with your bike, the remedy follows in parentheses. If you are not willing or able to fix it yourself, take it to a bike shop.

Don't ignore a problem you discover. With bicycles the old cliché holds true: an ounce of prevention is worth a pound of cure. Particularly with wheels, the bottom bracket (where the pedals join the frame), and the headset (where the handlebar joins the frame), an expert five-minute tightening at a shop can prevent MAJOR dollars spent in repairs. In the descriptions below, a slash (/) means check first one and then the other, not both at once.

- WHEELS AND TIRES. Make sure both front and rear tires are inflated to the proper pressure. The proper pressure for any tire is usually embossed on the tire's sidewalls. Until you're experienced, check the pressure with a gauge rather than with your thumb. In most cases, at proper pressure the tire should feel pretty hard.

    Lift the front/back end of the bike and spin the wheel. When you sight directly down from the tire to hub, the wheel should appear to rotate in exactly one plane. If it appears to wobble, it may be out of true. (Tighten the appropriate spokes, or take it to a shop to have it trued.)

    With the bike resting on the ground, press against the top of the front/back rim perpendicular to the wheel, trying to push the top of the rim to the left or right. There should be no movement or clicks in the hub bearings. (If there is a slight movement, tighten the hub cones with a cone wrench, taking care not to overtighten.)

- BRAKES. With the bike stationary, squeeze the right/left brake levers as if you were braking hard. At its lowest point, there should be about an inch of clearance separating the lever from the handlebar grip. (If there is less than half an inch, tighten the rear/front brake cable.)

    Also, when the brake lever is squeezed, note the position of the pads pressing against the rim. Their entire braking surface should be against the metal of the rim, not partly on the rubber tire or partly in the air below the rim. (Adjust the position of the brake pads in the brakes.)

    While moving the bike forward, grip the right/left brake lever hard. The bike should stop securely, with no slipping of the brake pad. (Replace old worn pads.)

- QUICK RELEASES. If your wheels are held onto the frame with quick release skewers, check to make sure they are closed tightly. Tight means the skewer handles should require considerable effort to pull open or push closed. Position the handles to point toward the back of the bike, so they won't catch twigs and risk opening while you're riding. (If the skewers are too loose, screw in the conical end a little tighter and try again until it's secure.)

- HANDLEBAR AND HEADSET. Stand in front of the bicycle with the front wheel gripped between your knees. Try to twist the handlebar from side to side while holding the wheel still. It should not move. (If the handlebar is loose, tighten the bolt on top of the handlebar stem.)

  In the same position, try to lift the handlebar straight up out of the frame. There should be no slight movement or click. (If there is a slight but perceptible click, tighten the headset with a headset wrench, taking care not to overtighten.)

- PEDALS AND BOTTOM BRACKET. Spin the pedals on the ends of their crank arms. They should spin freely—unless they are of a design to stop in certain positions. (If they resist movement, they may need to be repacked with grease.)

  Grasp the pedal crank arms with your hands and try to move the cranks in and out perpendicular to the frame of the bike—that is, perpendicular to the plane in which the chainwheels spin. The pedal cranks should not move. (If you sense any slight movement or click, tighten the bottom bracket.)

- CHAIN DERAILLEURS. Check that all the attachment nuts and bolts are secure. Shift the rear derailleur into lowest gear—that is, onto largest cog in the back. Make sure the derailleur itself does not hit the spokes. While turning the pedals, shift through all the gears with both front and rear derailleurs, to make sure all are accessible without the chain jumping off either into the spokes or onto the axle. (If the chain jumps off, tighten the derailleur stop screws a quarter turn and try it again.)

- SEAT. Try to move the seat up and down in the seat tube, rotate it, push its nose up and down, or slide it backwards and forwards on its rails. The seat should remain firm. (If it moves, tighten the appropriate bolts. If the bolts won't tighten, replace the appropriate parts.)

- ACCESSORIES. Check to make sure that lights are working and reflectors are secure. Check that all bungee cords are tight, no straps are dangling in the spokes, the handlebar bag is zipped, the screws holding on racks and child seat are secure. As a final test, lift the bike a couple inches and drop it. If nothing falls off, you're ready to roll!

APPENDIX II
Resources for Bicycling in the Tri-State Area

Aside from this book, there are many other resources and opportunities for your bicycling enjoyment in and around New York City. Here is a representative sampling of those oriented toward touring (there are others with a bent toward racing that I have deliberately omitted).

Local and national bicycling organizations
Although this book is designed for the individual, couple, or family wanting to go on independent tours, the New York City area has much to offer for a group experience as well.

Perhaps the newest club is the *Five Borough Bike Club (5BBC)* of the *American Youth Hostels*. The annual membership fee will give you a bimonthly bulletin called *Bicycletter*, many issues of which have laid out a ride with really nice maps and a cue sheet. *Bicycletter* informs you of the host of day-long bike trips that the AYH 5BBC offers for FREE, and summer weekend trips for very modest cost.

Joining the parent organization, AYH, will also give you a youth hostel card, allowing you and older children to stay in hostels all around the country for a few dollars per night, plus cooking your own food and doing 15 minutes of cleanup work. Half a dozen of these hostels are also around the New York City area—not a bad way to consider spending a low-budget weekend. AYH also has an extensive program of bike trips specifically for teenagers. The AYH's national headquarters are 891 Amsterdam Avenue, New York, NY 10025-4403, or call (212) 932-2300.

The oldest bicycling club in New York City is the *New York Cycle Club (NYCC)*, having more than 1000 members. It holds monthly meetings, some of which occasionally feature programs on touring or family riding, and its hefty monthly *NYCC Bulletin* publishes articles and departments and a complete listing of free rides. The group tends to be oriented toward high-performance fitness riding and racing rather than touring, although it does run a series of C-rides. (Club riding is divided by terrain and distance; *NYCC Bulletin* gives you a way to determine your own level by how long it takes you to complete the 6-mile circuit of Central Park). For information, write NYCC, P.O. Box 199 Cooper Station, New York, NY 10276, (212) 242-3900.

Transportation Alternatives, Inc. (TA) is a bicycle advocacy organization founded in 1973 to support bicycling and other non-motorized transportation in the city. It has had remarkable success in obtaining access for cyclists on the George Washington Bridge and elsewhere, and it works to improve riding con-

---

ditions in the city's streets, parks, and bridges. Members receive discounts at certain participating bike shops in the city and receive an informative bimonthly newsletter *City Cyclist*, which is particularly helpful to bicycle commuters. TA also markets a few products. One is a wonderful T-shirt with a bicycle wheel on the front whose back reads ONE LESS CAR. The other is a superb Brooklyn Bike Map, printed on unrippable waterproof Tyvek. For information, write Transportation Alternatives, Inc., 494 Broadway, New York, NY 10012, or call (212) 941-4600.

Suited toward touring and family outings is the *Bicycle Touring Club of New Jersey (BTCNJ)*, which was founded in 1978 and now has more than 1500 members. The annual membership fee gives you the monthly newsletter *Masterlink*, which has a very friendly tone, some nice articles and departments and announcements of the monthly meeting, and opportunities to join club rides in northern New Jersey. The newsletter carries advertisements of interest to cyclists. Members also receive discounts at participating New Jersey bike shops. I'm a member. For information, write BTCNJ, P.O. Box 865, Montclair, NJ 07042-0865, or call (201) 284-0404.

There are several dozen other clubs of interest in the tri-state area—far too numerous to list separately. But updated directories of clubs around the country, including in the tri-state area, are published every year by two nationwide organizations. As these organizations have distinctly different missions, their club listings do not always totally overlap, and it is worth belonging to both (I'm a member of both).

Adventure Cycling Association (named Bikecentennial until its name change in 1994) is a nationwide bicycle touring organization in the U.S. Since its incorporation in 1974, it has developed and mapped a nationwide network of touring routes, and it offers low-cost bike-camping tours ranging from 5 to 90 days in length. In addition to its glossy magazine *Adventure Cyclist* (formerly *BikeReport*, the group annually publishes *The Cyclists' Yellow Pages*, a huge directory of every reference you'd need for planning a bicycle trip in the U.S. or abroad, including detailed information on books, routes, rides. It also lists bicycle clubs by state. The Adventure Cycling Association also sells merchandise and books of interest to touring cyclists. For information, write Adventure Cycling Association, P.O. Box 8308, Missoula, MT 59807 (headquarters are located at 150 E. Pine, Missoula, MT 59802), or call (406) 721-1776.

The League of American Bicyclists (formerly the League of American Wheelmen) is a nationwide bicycle advocacy organization, lobbying at the Federal and State level on bicycle-related issues and keenly concerned with safety on the road. With local bike clubs, the League sponsors regional bicycle rallies. Members receive its glossy magazine *Bicycle USA*, including its annually updated Almanac and TourFinder issues. The Almanac issue lists affiliated clubs by state, including those in the tri-state area. The TourFinder will help you find commercial tour organizations if you are interested in formal bicycle tours ranging from the tri-state area to overseas. For information, write the League of American Bicyclists, 190 West Ostend Street, Suite 120, Baltimore, MD 21230-3755, or call (410) 539-3399.

Commercial bicycle touring groups

There are many excellent bicycle touring companies all over the country, many of which are listed in the Adventure Cycling Association's *The Cyclists' Yellow Pages* and the spring TourFinder issue of the League of American Bicyclist's magazine, *Bicycle USA*. Two things should be noted: just because the headquarters of the group is outside the tri-state area does not mean that the group doesn't run tours nearby—maybe even day and weekend trips. Second, because women seem to sign up for formal tours more than men, a man might consider a tour a lovely low-key way to meet female cyclists—and at the very least, get a good bike ride, right?

American Youth Hostels runs weekend trips for a modest price and day trips for free. See information above.

The only major commercial bicycle touring company headquartered in the tri-state area is *Brooks Country Cycling and Hiking Tours*. Formerly named Country Cycling Tours, the group has been operating since 1976, and now offers more than 200 tours a year. They range from day trips of 25 to 65 miles starting only an hour's travel outside of New York City, to first class and deluxe cycling vacations in the U.S. and Europe. The modestly priced day trips are a perfect starter if you're a novice cyclist unsure about riding alone or venturing out of the city. The trips for a weekend or longer tend to be very pricey, although luxurious. Conveniently located on the city's upper west side near the American Museum of Natural History, you can ride your bike right to their offices and then have it loaded onto their van for the drive outside the city. In my early years of bicycle touring in the early 1980s, I traveled with this group quite often. For a catalogue, write to Brooks Country Cycling and Hiking, 140 West 83rd Street, New York, NY 10024, or call (212) 874-5151.

Bicycling for charities

Many charities have found that there are open-hearted cyclists willing to solicit pledges based on a certain number of miles ridden. Often there is a minimum pledge to be obtained as well as a registration fee, so call for information. These rides tend to be very well organized, with cue sheets and maps handed to each rider, and often donated food and other goodies. Most tend to cluster outside the city itself in the scenic areas of New Jersey and upstate New York.

The fliers announcing various fund-raising rides are often available at bike shops or are announced in bike club bulletins. Alternatively, you might call your favorite charity and ask if they sponsor such an event. My observation is, once you've been involved in one charity ride, announcements for many others come in your mailbox.

Right within New York City itself is one of the oldest charity rides, the *United Cerebral Palsy* Bike-a-Thon held every May since 1972. It consists of three simultaneous 35-mile rides making multiple circuits of Central Park in Manhattan, Prospect Park in Brooklyn, and Silver Lake Park in Staten Island. Having done this once in Central Park, I can say that the terrain is not flat and the rides can be an early-season challenge. Snacks and giveaways are included. For information, write to United Cerebral Palsy of New York City, Inc., Bike-a-thon Committee, 105 Madison Avenue, New York, NY 10157-0220.

Perhaps the biggest charity to raise money through annual bicycle tours is the *National Multiple Sclerosis Society*. The organization runs several distinctly different fund-raising rides in the tri-state area. Many are run year after year, although the details may vary each year.

The MS Fall Bike Tour is a fund-raising ride in October sponsored by the National Multiple Sclerosis Society through the five boroughs of New York City. Originally it was inspired by the American Youth Hostels' annual Five Borough Bike Tour, when in 1991 the traditional 5BBT was not held. With a course 34 miles long, it starts in Battery Park and takes you through all five boroughs of New York City. For more information and a registration form write to New York City Chapter, National Multiple Sclerosis Society, 30 West 26th Street, New York, New York 10010-2094.

G.O.D./MS-150 Bike Tour is an annual, two-day weekend ride of either 100 or 150 miles held in mid-May, which meanders through less-traveled roads and quaint communities of New Jersey, New York, and Pennsylvania. The route starts at Allamuchy Elementary School in New Jersey and follows the Delaware River through unspoiled farm country of Pennsylvania and New York. The tour includes fully catered meals, rest stops every 12-15 miles with snacks, with a massage from the Neuro-Muscular Skeletal Support Team at the end of the first day, and overnight in cabins at a camp in Milford, New Jersey. After dinner (usually the bicyclists' standard of spaghetti), you can mellow out to the sounds of a bluegrass band while toasting marshmallows around a festive bonfire. A barbecue awaits you at your return to the school, where you can shower and change in the gym.

I rode this in 1989 and had a wonderful time, and the route is truly beautiful—but the hilly territory in May can be a major challenge if you're not in terrific shape. If you're not up for 50 or 75 miles a day but would still like to be part of the fun, register instead for the Mennen MS Big Easy, a one-day 33-mile ride that meets up with the MS 150 cyclists on the second day and enjoys the same barbecue at Allamuchy Elementary School.

For more information about either ride, write to the National Multiple Sclerosis Society, Northern New Jersey Chapter, 60 South Fullerton Avenue, Montclair, NJ 07042-2681, or call (201) 783-6441.

Diet Pepsi MS-100 is a two-day fund-raising tour held each September since 1988. This one should be within the abilities of most people who have spent some good times on the bike during the summer. The basic 100-mile route takes you from Ramsey, New Jersey to Port Jervis, New York, with an optional "power loop" route for those who enjoy a real challenge and would like to ride 150 miles in two days. You'll follow country roads through apple orchards and farm lands, finishing the first day at cabins or in giant heated sleeping tents in picturesque Camp Sussex in Vernon Township. The ride ends with a chartered train ride back to Ramsey through the beautiful mountains of New York State. For more information, write to the National Multiple Sclerosis Society, Bergen-Passaic Chapter, P.O. Box 348, 730 River Road, New Milford, NJ 07646, or call (201) 967-TOUR.

Kraft General Foods Wheel & Rock to Woodstock is yet another annual, two-day 100- and 150-mile fund-raising ride held in mid-September for the

National Multiple Sclerosis Society. It differs from the camping MS rides in that the accommodations are more luxurious (although camping is available) and the food is kosher. The tour begins and ends at the Pines Resort Hotel near Monticello, New York, about two hours from Manhattan. Saturday's route will take you either 50 or 85 miles through Sullivan County, followed by an evening of comedy shows, music, and dancing. The second day's route ends with a barbecue picnic and live concert at Max Yasgur's Farm in Bethel. Woodstock fans from the 1960s can have their photos taken atop the monument on the very site where Jimi Hendrix, Crosby, Stills and Nash, and the Jefferson Airplane performed in 1969. You can shower and change at the Pines before returning home. The tour is challenging with the terrain moderately hilly. For information, write to the National Multiple Sclerosis Society, MS-150 Bike Tour, 11 Skyline Drive, Hawthorne, NY 10532, or call (914) 345-3500.

The Pedals of Hope Bike Tour of the *American Cancer Society* is a 30-mile loop that runs each May from Montclair State College in Montclair, New Jersey. For information, write American Cancer Society, 767 Northfield Avenue, West Orange, NJ 07052, or call (201) 736-7770.

The Saturday Bike & Hike-a-Thon of *Big Brothers/Big Sisters of Monmouth County, New Jersey* has been held annually each June since 1989. This one-day event has a 3-mile ride for children pedaling on their own, as well as routes of 10, 25, 40, 65, or 100 miles for adults. All the bike routes, plus the 5-mile hike, begin and end at the Brookdale Community College in Lincroft, New Jersey. Rest stops with food, bicycle support and maintenance, are provided. At the end you can join in a community celebration that features T-shirts, sports massage, prizes, mountain bike raffle, picnic, live music, and a bicycle freestyle demonstration. For information, write BB/BS of Monmouth County, 54 Broad Street, Suite 302, Red Bank, New Jersey 07701, or call (908) 530-9800.

The Bike Ride Plus of the *American Diabetes Association*, held in June, is one of the closest to midtown Manhattan. It takes riders through the towns of Springfield, Chatham, and Summit, the Great Swamp National Wildlife Refuge, and Nomahegan Park—doubtless covering some of the same ground as in the "Rahway River Ramble" and "Exploring the Great Swamp" rides in this book. The 5-, 20-, and 40-mile loops all begin and end at Union County College in Cranford, New Jersey; the 5-mile loop, ideal for children on their own wheels, stays within the park. At the end you'll be greeted by a post-bike-ride celebration and picnic. For information, write Bike Ride Plus, American Diabetes Association, Union/Essex Regional Chapter, 60 Walnut Avenue, Suite 100, Clark, NJ 07066, or call (908) 815-7838.

The *March of Dimes* Century Bike Tour cosponsored by the Sandoz Pharmaceuticals Corp. is a one-day event in early October through scenic Hunterdon County in New Jersey. A 25-mile loop is mostly on the flat-topped Hunterdon Plateau through woodlands and farmlands; a 50-mile loop is through the rolling Piedmont country; a century (100 miles) takes you up "cardiac hill" to the top of the Musconetcong Mountain. There's also a 1-mile "fun" ride for children. Lunch and dinner along with music and entertainment await you at the end. For information, write March of Dimes Century Bike Tour, March of Dimes North Jersey Chapter, 81 Two Bridges Road, Building 2, Fairfield, NJ 07004-1037 or call the tour hotline at (201) 882-0700.

The Annual *Red Cross* Challenge takes riders through the winding country roads of Orange County, New York and Passaic County, New Jersey, including Ringwood State Park and Skyland Botanical Gardens. Held in mid-October, you can enjoy the multicolored fall foliage on one of three loops: 15, 25, or 62.5 miles (the last being 100 kilometers, known in bicycling jargon as a metric century). The rides begin at Sterling Forest Ski Resort, where you will also return for a barbecue. For information, write Red Cross Bike Challenge, c/o Essex Chapter, 106 Washington Street, P.O. Box 838, East Orange, NJ 07019, or call (201) 676-0800.

The Fall Foliage Bike Tour Classic has been sponsored each October since 1989 by the *United Way* of Sussex County. Routes of 25, 50, or 100 miles will take you along the beautiful hill and valley roads of Sussex County, including the foothills of the Appalachian Mountains. Juices and healthful snacks are provided before, during, and after the tour along with a picnic lunch, a post-ride dinner, and rubdowns for road-weary participants. For information, write United Way of Sussex County, P.O. Box 231, Newton, NJ 07860, or call the Sussex County Bike Classic Hotline at (201) 579-3040.

The Cycle for Cancer Care sponsored by *Cancer Care*, Sharp Electronics, the Mennen Co., and the Bicycle Touring Club of New Jersey is an annual event each October that allows you to choose from a family ride and courses of 20, 25, 45, or a metric century. Riders are presented with a T-shirt, snacks, and a picnic at Waterloo Village, a reconstructed colonial village an hour west of Manhattan (Waterloo Village is featured in "Netcong Getaway" in this book). For information, write Cancer Care Inc., New Jersey Division, 241 Millburn Ave., Millburn, NJ 07041, or call (201) 379-7500.

If you want your tax-deductible pledge dollars to improve the lot of bicycling itself in New York City, consider the annual September fund-raising NYC Century Ride-a-Thon of *Transportation Alternatives*. You can choose from routes of 12, 35, 55, 75, or 100 miles linking Manhattan, Brooklyn, Queens, and the Bronx via New York City streets, bicycle paths, parks, and greenways (fully 30 miles of the century are on car-free paths). The proceeds go to support TA's campaigns to get the city to build more bicycle paths, expand secure bicycle parking, and gain legal bicycle access to certain routes and forms of public transportation now forbidden to bikes. For more information, write Transportation Alternatives, 92 Saint Marks Place, New York, New York 10009, or call (212) 475-4600.

There are also many one-shot, fund-raising bicycle tours that are held one year but not repeated after that. These are often mentioned in bicycle club bulletins and advertised by fliers distributed to bike shops, YMCAs, and other outlets. In addition, certain local not-for-profit organizations (such as the *Jaycees*) run fund-raising bicycle tours. Call the organization of your choice to see whether it happens to sponsor one.

Special bike routes

There are a number of special bicycle routes in the New York City area that, for some reason, have never all been written up in one place—and I have never seen a map of them all. They seem to survive more in the oral tradition of cyclists' conversation or in the club newsletters. Because some of them are closed certain times of the year, or may not be available every year, I have not included them on the trips in this book. But for a nearby change of pace, you may want to check them out.

In New York City, there are a number of paved bicycle paths. In Manhattan, one starts at East 23rd Street at the East River and takes you all the way around the tip of Manhattan to Battery Park. In Brooklyn, one runs the entire length of Ocean Parkway; another encircles the coast near the Bay Ridge section; and a third parallels Shore Parkway from Sheepshead Bay to Canarsie Beach (this one has a lot of traffic noise and is somewhat overgrown, and seems to be little used). I've ridden all of them at one time or another. In Queens, a bike path runs from Fort Totten near the Throgs Neck Bridge, alongside Little Neck Bay down to Northern Boulevard. There are plans afoot for building others.

Every weekend and holiday, the roads within Central Park in Manhattan and Prospect Park in Brooklyn are closed to automobiles and open to cyclists, roller-skaters, roller-bladers, joggers, skateboarders, pedestrians, and anyone else on nonmotorized wheels. Especially on a sunny afternoon in Central Park, the roads can be so congested you feel you are riding in a video game, and you must be alert for occasional racing cyclists that think they own the road and sometimes even do the circuit in a paceline. Prospect Park is less of a zoo. Early mornings always have the least traffic.

For many summers, the Bronx River Parkway has been closed to automobiles and open to cyclists from 10 A.M. to 2 P.M., from Scarsdale Road to the County Center (Tarrytown Road) in Westchester County. For updated information, call Freihofer Westchester County Bicycle Sundays at (914) 285-PARK.

The Henry Hudson Drive in New Jersey's Palisades Interstate Park offers seven beautiful miles of cliffs, waterfalls, lush foliage, views of the Hudson River, and few cars. The route north of the George Washington Bridge passes century-old vacation mansions of celebrities past and present, including Eddie Murphy and Gloria Swanson. The road is hilly, however, and the climb back up the Palisades can be a wheezer unless you zigzag your way up local streets. It is closed to automobiles before 10 A.M. on summer weekends, and is closed to cars altogether from late fall to early spring. Cyclists can ride it if they are wearing helmets.

INDEX